EBURY PRESS
THE COUSINS THACKERAY

Dhaval Kulkarni is a Mumbai-based journalist with over fifteen years of reporting experience across brands like the *Times of India*, *Hindustan Times*, the *Indian Express*, *New Indian Express* and *DNA*.

He writes on a broad range of subjects like governance and politics, caste, identity and social movements, environment and forests, health, infrastructure, heritage, culture and archaeology. He also reviews books.

THE COUSINS THACKERAY

UDDHAV, RAJ AND THE SHADOW OF THEIR SENAS

DHAVAL KULKARNI

EBURY PRESS

An imprint of Penguin Random House

EBURY PRESS

USA | Canada | UK | Ireland | Australia
New Zealand | India | South Africa | China

Ebury Press is part of the Penguin Random House group of companies whose addresses can be found at global.penguinrandomhouse.com

Published by Penguin Random House India Pvt. Ltd
7th Floor, Infinity Tower C, DLF Cyber City,
Gurgaon 122 002, Haryana, India

Penguin
Random House
India

First published in Ebury Press by Penguin Random House India 2019

Copyright © Dhaval Kulkarni 2019

All rights reserved

10 9 8 7 6 5 4 3 2 1

The views and opinions expressed in this book are the author's own and the facts are as reported by him, which have been verified to the extent possible, and the publishers are not in any way liable for the same. The objective of this book is not to hurt any sentiments or be biased in favour of, or against, any particular person, society, gender, creed, nation or religion.

ISBN 9780143448488

Typeset in Adobe Garamond Pro by Manipal Digital Systems, Manipal
Printed at Replika Press Pvt. Ltd, India

This book is sold subject to the condition that it shall not, by way of trade or otherwise, be lent, resold, hired out, or otherwise circulated without the publisher's prior consent in any form of binding or cover other than that in which it is published and without a similar condition including this condition being imposed on the subsequent purchaser.

www.penguin.co.in

MIX
Paper from
responsible sources
FSC® C016779

To

*the working class of Mumbai, which has built
this city with its sweat and blood.*

*My sister, Deepali Kulkarni-Kumta, who left us
too early and suddenly.
And my uncle, the late Ashok Atmaram Kulkarni—I wish
you were here to witness this moment.*

Contents

Preface ix

1. The History of the Thackeray Family and 'Prabodhankar' Thackeray 1
2. Quest for a Marathi Identity 17
3. The Tiger Comes to Life 31
4. Raj and Uddhav: The Early Years 42
5. Cracks in the Edifice 78
6. Raj's Estrangement and the Birth of MNS 123
7. The MNS Tastes First Blood: The Shiv Sena's Fortunes Decline 147
8. The Downfall of the MNS: The Shiv Sena Holds Its Own 183
9. The Hare and the Tortoise 205
10. The Snake That Ate Its Own Tail 236

Afterword: The Men behind the Image 251
Acknowledgements 259
Notes 263

Preface

If you can fill the unforgiving minute
With sixty seconds' worth of distance run,
Yours is the Earth and everything that's in it,
And—which is more—you'll be a Man, my son!

Rudyard Kipling, 'If'

Journalists have the rare privilege of watching history unfold.

As a reporter who has covered the Shiv Sena and Maharashtra Navnirman Sena (MNS) for over a decade, this book was born out of a desire to break the tyranny of 400-word news reports and place these political developments in the larger matrix of social, cultural and economic disruptions.

This book, the idea for which was germinating in my mind over the years, attempts to go beyond merely recording events by delving into the processes that shape them. For instance, why do these nativist movements, which claim to uphold the rights of the sons of the soil, strike a chord with a large section of the toiling masses?

That there was immense curiosity about both Uddhav and Raj Thackeray, even on foreign shores, was evident when the author visited Pakistan in 2011 as part of a media delegation. Then, the highest number of questions from members of the local media, civil society and people at large, were about these two estranged cousins and their uncle, Shiv Sena chief Bal Thackeray. This book is an attempt to satiate some of this curiosity by providing a deep-dive narrative into the political lives of Uddhav and Raj Thackeray, and their parties.

This is also an attempt to place before a larger, multilingual audience the life and times of that autodidact, 'Prabodhankar' Keshav Sitaram Thackeray. His strength of character stands in contrast to the politics played by these two parties who form the focal point of our narrative and under whose watch the Marathi *manoos* in Mumbai has retreated to the margins and beyond.

I have unsuccessfully tried to get both Uddhav and Raj Thackeray to open up about their version of events for this book.

As I juggled professional commitments and work on this book, with a tough deadline to match, these lines from Kipling's poem quoted at the beginning of this preface, often came to my mind. It is for the reader to judge if I have been successful in this effort.

1

The History of the Thackeray Family and 'Prabodhankar' Thackeray

> Though a battle's to fight ere the guerdon be gained,
> The reward of it all.
> I was ever a fighter, so—one fight more,
> The best and the last!
>
> Robert Browning, 'Prospice'[1]

The modest Kadam Mansion at 77-A, Ranade Road, Dadar West, Mumbai, has been demolished and a new structure takes shape at the site—an inevitable result of the old making way for the new. But the political legacy that was born in this building, located in a by-lane off the historic Shivaji Park precincts, continues to endure.

It was here that 'Prabodhankar' Keshav Sitaram Thackeray resided with his large brood, including his sons Bal and Shrikant. It was in this ground-floor flat that the Shiv Sena was born in 1966.

Prabodhankar's contribution to Maharashtra's social reform and anti-caste movements remains seminal. Born on 17 September 1885 at Panvel in Kulaba (today's Raigad district) near Mumbai, Prabodhankar launched the weekly *Prabodhan* (Enlightenment) in 1921. Though it ran for just five years, 'Prabodhankar' was permanently prefixed to his name.

In his autobiography, *Majhi Jeevangatha* (The Story of My Life), the Thackeray patriarch notes that his family, which belonged to the Chandraseniya Kayastha Prabhu (CKP) caste, originally hailed from Pali village in the small principality of Bhor.[2] The state was ruled by the Pantsachiv dynasty.

He recounts that the Thackeray family's ancestors added 'Dhodapkar' to their surname as one of them was the *killedar* (chief) of the Dhodap Fort near Nashik, but this was dropped by Prabodhankar's father.

Shaped like a lingam, the fort was ceded to the Marathas by the Nizam of Hyderabad in 1752 by the 'Treaty of Bhalki'.[3]

After the British besieged the fort, perhaps in the later period of the Peshwa rule, this Thackeray family ancestor fought bravely despite running out of provisions and was ultimately killed.[4]

Castes and their varying fortunes

Though Prabodhankar was a leading light of the *Bramhanetar* (non-Brahmin) movement, which sought to counter the overarching influence of Brahmins in Maharashtra, his autobiography notes a family fable. When Dhodap Fort was about to fall, his ancestor was saved by a Brahmin who mysteriously appeared before him, lauded his bravery and teleported him to his village at Pali![5] To commemorate this incident, the Thackeray family worshiped two silver images—one of a warrior, another of a Brahmin.

After his brothers insisted on dividing the family property at Pali, Prabodhankar's great-grandfather Krishnaji Madhav 'Appasaheb' relinquished his claim over it and left for Thane where he worked as a lawyer, making his reputation as an upright, helpful man.[6]

His son, Ramchandra aka Bhikoba Dhodapkar, a devotee of the Goddess, found employment in the courts and was transferred to the small causes court at Panvel where he lived until his death. His wife (Prabodhankar's grandmother) Sitabai, called 'Bay', worked as a pro bono midwife who did not discriminate on the basis of caste and religion in the line of duty. Bay was a woman ahead of her time and was disgusted by the practice of untouchability.

'. . . our Thackeray family was very poor. In three to four generations preceding me, there was no information of anyone owning even an inch of property. However, we had a hutment-like dwelling in Panvel village, where I was born,' says Prabodhankar, while describing himself as a self-made man.[7]

The year 1818 saw the fall of the Chitpavan Brahmin Peshwas, whose twilight years were marked by moral turpitude and caste-based excesses. The Peshwa reign was supplanted by the East India Company (1818) and later the British Crown (1858), and Brahmins eased themselves into the new order by virtue of their access to education and centres of power.

The CKPs are a small but literate and influential caste, with a high occupational status that equals the Brahmins. Ironically, while his son Bal Thackeray and grandsons Uddhav and Raj were to take a political position against north Indians, Prabodhankar traced the roots of CKPs to Bihar.

In his book, *Gramnyancha Sadyanta Itihas Arthat Nokarshahiche Banda* (A History of Village Disputes or Rebellion of the Bureaucracy), Prabodhankar writes that Mahapadma Nanda (third to fourth century BC), the ruler of Magadha in present-day Bihar, and first king of the Nanda Empire, was a greedy monarch who squeezed his subjects for money. This led to many CKP families migrating elsewhere, where they earned their living as warriors and scribes.[8]

In the seventeenth century, some of Chhatrapati Shivaji's bravest warriors were CKPs. Among them were his general, Netaji

Palkar, called *Pratishivaji* (another Shivaji) due to his valour, Baji Prabhu and Murar Baji Deshpande.

CKPs also served as ministers, scribes and diplomats in the Maratha court.

The war of succession between Shivaji Maharaj's daughter-in-law, Tarabai (wife of his younger son Rajaram), and his grandson, Shahu I (son of elder son Sambhaji), in early eighteenth century saw the emergence of a new power centre—Balaji Vishwanath Bhat from Srivardhan in the Konkan region who became Shahu's peshwa (prime minister). The reign of the peshwas saw the rise of the Chitpavan Brahmins and a corresponding decline of other castes like Deshastha Brahmins, Saraswat Brahmins and CKPs in the Maratha court.

During Keshav's formative years in Panvel, the grip of Brahminism on society was gradually weakened by a fledgling social reform movement.

In 1848, a young man from the 'mali' (gardener) caste in Pune, who was influenced by Thomas Paine's *Rights of Man*, and realized the demeaning brutality of the caste system after being insulted at a Brahmin friend's marriage ceremony, opened up education for the masses. Inspired by a school for girls launched by Christian missionaries, 'Mahatma' Jyotiba Govindrao Phule embarked on his life's mission for the emancipation of Bahujans (non-Brahmins) and women by becoming the first Indian to start a school for girls in Pune along with his wife, Savitribai.

Much before the Italian Marxist Antonio Gramsci and his theory of cultural hegemony, Mahatma Phule tried to break the culture and iconography of the upper castes and create and articulate an alternative value system for Bahujans through his Satyashodhak Samaj. He adopted the son of a Brahmin widow, born out of wedlock, and named him his heir. Phule launched the 'Satyashodhak Samaj' to champion the cause of the weaker sections and dismantle the caste system.

Like stalwarts of the Bramhanetar movement—Dr Babasaheb Ambedkar, Chhatrapati Shahu of Kolhapur, Dinkarrao Jawalkar, Keshavrao Jedhe and latter-day Muslim reformer Hamid Dalwai—Phule would motivate the young Keshav.

Prabodhankar and his family may have been far ahead of their times, when the mental construct of caste held sway in its most brutal, dehumanizing form.

Rebellion against injustice

Prabodhankar was eight or nine years old when the shadow of a Mahar (a Dalit) carrying a broom fell on him. His schoolmates claimed he had become impure. However, Bay, instead of bathing her grandson according to prescribed ritual, laughed to her heart's content and said since a Brahmin was pure and clean, Dada (Prabodhankar) would be purified if a Brahmin's shadow fell on him! She then made a Brahmin boy stand in a way that made his shadow fall on Dada (Keshav). She then gave the children a dressing down for believing in caste-based notions of purity before sending them away.

It may have been incidents like these that kindled the spark for unconventional thinking in young Keshav's mind, and eventually made him rebel against the social injustice.

In 1902, when Prabodhankar was seventeen, his father, Sitaram, who was also called 'Bala', and worked as a bailiff, died. His formative years were shaped by his mother, Kashi, also called 'Tai'. Prabodhankar credits his family's success to his disciplinarian mother. In his autobiography, his respect and admiration for her is evident.

He describes Tai as a self-respecting woman who hated egoistic behaviour and bragging and did not hesitate to speak her mind or use the rod to discipline her children. Tai inculcated a love for knowledge and the written word in Prabodhankar and nurtured his oratory by making him read the newspaper aloud every evening.

Prabodhankar dreamt of being a lawyer, but the family's precarious financial condition ensured he fell short of Rs 1.50 (a princely sum in those days) to pay the fees for the matriculation examinations.[9] But, he never let the lack of formal schooling stand in the way of his education, eventually evolving into a social reformer, orator, activist, writer, dramatist, screenplay writer and artist, even acting in films like *Acharya* and Pralhad Keshav Atre's seminal *Shyamchi Aai*. Keshav had two younger brothers, Yashwant (Bua, also called Bhau) and Damodar (Anna),[10] and two sisters. He married Rama Gupte of Amravati in 1910.[11]

In his autobiography, published in September 1973, weeks before his death, Prabodhankar says *bookbaji* (love for books) was an obsession he was unable to overcome.[12] From William Shakespeare to the Vedas, history and literature of the American Rational Publication Society, Prabodhankar's private collection had it all. He even travelled to Vadodara for the original Sanskrit version of Kautilya's *Arthashastra* and a book by German Indologist Rudolf von Roth, which were housed at the princely state's library.

Prabodhankar's rebellious streak became evident early in his life.

When his childhood playmate Manju (ten years old) was being married off to sixty-five-year-old Niloba Talojkar, he set the pandal on fire in protest.

To make ends meet, he looked for odd jobs like making rubber stamps, working as a photographer, a head clerk in the state public works department (PWD), publicity officer for the Warden Insurance Company and Wadia Movietone, and even painting signboards.[13, 14]

In those days, both Christian and Islamic missionaries preached their gospel aggressively in Mumbai. In his autobiography,

Prabodhankar writes that he joined hands with fellow CKP Gajananrao Vaidya to launch the Hindu Missionary Society in 1918 at Hirabaug in Mumbai's CP Tank area to counter this.

Vaidya performed the first public reconversion and thread ceremony of a Muslim youth, Wahiduddin, at the urging of his seventy-five-year-old father. Vaidya also conducted reconversions, including those of the 'Kolis' (fishermen) on the coastline of Mumbai and surrounding areas, who had accepted Christianity.

In 1921, Prabodhankar launched *Prabodhan*. He used the publication to attack orthodoxy and Brahminism and became the first public campaigner against dowry through his 'Swadhyayashram'. In his last public speech during the release of his autobiography, Prabodhankar noted, 'While there was much progress in the condition of women . . . they must progress even further. So much, that men must feel that women are taking their revenge on them.'[15]

Due to his poor financial condition, he shifted his residence constantly—to Panvel, Dadar, Karjat, Bhiwandi and Pune. During his stay at Sadashiv Peth in Pune, he regularly met reformers like Dinkarrao Jawalkar, Keshavrao Jedhe, Shridharpant Tilak (the reformist son of Lokmanya Bal Gangadhar Tilak) and P.N. Rajbhoj in that veritable citadel of orthodox Brahmins.

Prabodhankar, who penned around twenty-five books including the first work in Marathi on the art of public speaking, crossed swords frequently with Brahmin traditionalists like Bhaskar Balwant Bhopatkar. However, when Prabodhankar published a book, *Dagalbaz Shivaji* (Diplomat Shivaji), in 1926 to counter an Urdu book denigrating the warrior-king, Bhopatkar, who edited a Marathi newspaper called *Bhala* (spear), was quick to praise it.[16]

Other orthodox Brahmins were not so large-hearted and did not take kindly to his call for social reform. Shiv Sena chief Bal Thackeray, who was born in Pune on 23 January 1927, the sixth of ten children, would publicly recall that a dead donkey was thrown outside their house and a mock funeral procession of his father was carried out by orthodox Brahmins who felt offended by his writings.

Prabodhankar, who wrote plays and staged them through his Deccan Spark company, found himself in the cross hairs over his play, *Khara Brahman*, about the sixteenth-century poet-saint Eknath. Burning rags were thrown at their house in Pune and rumours were deliberately spread about his death in 1938.

'Shahir' Krishnarao Sabale, the famous balladeer of Maharashtra, recalls Prabodhankar throwing eggs at Lokmanya Tilak during a public meeting in Pune to protest his 'staunchly Brahminist views'.[17] 'The religion of the Hindus today is actually not a religion,' thundered Prabodhankar in his book, *Devlacha Dharma aani Dharmachi Devle* (The Religion of the Temple and the Temples of Religion). 'It is *Bhikshukshahi* [rule of the Brahmins], a nonsensical parable aimed at helping *Bhats* (Brahmins who perform religious rites) fill their coffers by cheating the innocent.'[18] The book, a bestseller even today, stands out for its caustic attack on Hinduism's ritualistic practices.

Questioning the role of temples in propagating and protecting the faith, the book is an angry shout against idol worship, calling idols 'just a stone. An inconsequential object like a doll in a child's play . . . The soul cannot attain salvation by worshipping such stones.'[19] Prabodhankar, who despite being a believer, opposed rituals and the priestly class, said that temples were fountainheads of caste discrimination ingrained in Hinduism and called for the wealth of shrines to be used for the Hindu society at large.[20]

There was more in store in *Jyotishyancha Magarmithit* (The Crocodile-like Grip of Fortune-Tellers): 'The true way of *purushartha* [manliness] lies in effort rather than falling into the trap of horoscope readers and becoming inert . . .'[21]

Prabodhankar wrote voluminously, even contributing to the weekly *Agrani* launched in 1944, and edited by the hard-line

Hindu Mahasabha member Nathuram Godse. Prabodhankar had a condition—he would express what he felt was correct.

In his autobiography, *Jasa Ghadla Tasa* (As It Happened) Prabodhankar's son and Raj's father, Shrikant, said the editor sent a letter demanding that he use the term 'Mister' instead of 'Mahatma' when writing about Gandhi. Dada (as Prabodhankar was called) refused to allow even a single word that he wrote to be altered and stopped sending his work to the magazine thereafter.[22]

However, this doyen of the non-Brahmin movement, who lived at Dadar, ensured that after the assassination of Gandhi by Godse in 1948, an incensed mob that tried to attack Brahmins was pacified.[23]

Non-Brahmin movement

In 1925, the Rashtriya Swayamsevak Sangh (RSS) was formed at Nagpur by Dr Keshav Baliram Hedgewar, a Telugu Brahmin. Inspired by V.D. Savarkar and Dr B.S. Moonje, a Hindu Mahasabha leader, Hedgewar 'believed that the deep social divisions among the Hindus of India were responsible for . . . a thousand years of foreign domination on the subcontinent'.[24]

While the organization is often accused of presenting a 'Brahmanical model of Hindu fundamentalism',[25] the Shiv Sena is seen as having a base among various castes in Maharashtra and the model is 'one of broad-basing the caste system but with an emphasis on Hindu, Sanskritic and regional ideals'.[26] Those who have studied Prabodhankar's life attribute this to his 'Bahujanized' view of Hindutva.[27]

In private conversations, BJP and RSS veterans grudgingly admit that the Shiv Sena, which is a parallel force competing for the same ideological target group in Maharashtra, is a natural hindrance to their expansion in the state due to its wider social base.

Few Maharashtrians who worship the Goddess during Navratri may be aware of Prabodhankar's role in launching the public celebration of the festival as a rebellion against the 'Brahmin-dominated' Ganesh Utsav that precedes it.

The Ganesh festival was celebrated at Dadar through donations collected from people of all castes, though the festivities and organizing committee were dominated by Brahmins.[28]

In 1926, Prabodhankar and social reformers Rao Bahadur Sitaram Keshav Bole and Dr Babasaheb Ambedkar opposed the monopoly of the Brahmins and demanded that non-Brahmins and erstwhile untouchables be involved in the festival. A group of around 600 people, including Bole and Prabodhankar barged, into the *pandal* (tent) pitched at the foot of Tilak Bridge in Dadar before the idol was consecrated. Prabodhankar threatened that if the erstwhile untouchable Hindus were not allowed to worship the idol by 3 p.m., he would destroy it.

Finally, a compromise was reached. Dalit activist Ganpat Mahadeo Jadhav aka Madkebua, Ambedkar's close associate, was allowed to give flowers to the Brahmin priest as offerings to the idol. However, obscurantist caste Hindus were rattled by this revolt and announced the festival would not be celebrated again. This led to allegations that Prabodhankar was responsible for the celebrations being stopped.

Prabodhankar, Bole and their associates then started celebrating Navratri as a festival of the masses with Prabodhankar holding up Goddess Bhawani of Tuljapur, worshipped by Shivaji Maharaj, as Maharashtra's presiding deity. Though Navratri was celebrated during Shivaji Maharaj's times, Ganesh worship took precedence during the reign of the Brahmin peshwas. Lokmanya Bal Gangadhar Tilak had later revived the Ganesh worship tradition through public celebrations.

In 1926, this non-Brahmin group started the 'Lokhitawadi Sangh' which launched the 'Shiv Bhawani Navratri Mahotsav' at

Dadar to revive the tradition and unify the Bahujan Samaj,[29] and the festivities spread across Maharashtra. It is said that the figure of the goddess was drawn by Prabodhankar and the snarling tiger, which was to become an integral part of the Shiv Sena's imagery later, was also sketched by him.

Though Prabodhankar shifted from Dadar to Karjat because of ill health in 1929, Navratri celebrations carried on in Khandke Building where the Thackerays once lived. This is located near the Shiv Sena Bhavan—the Shiv Sena's headquarters.

Ironically, the Shiv Sena used the Ganesh Utsav (festival) more than the Navratri utsav to spread its influence, notes journalist Sachin Parab, who has chronicled the life and work of the Thackeray patriarch. Since other castes had been included in the Ganesh Utsav by then, the need for a separate Navratri celebration to counter it had died down.[30]

Despite his association with the reformist 'Rajarshi' Chhatrapati Shahu of Kolhapur, who called him *vaand* (a rustic word meaning wayward), Prabodhankar did not hesitate to lash out at him in the very second issue of *Prabodhan* (1 November 1921) for arresting a group of Maratha students in October for entering the sanctum sanctorum of the Ambabai temple at Kolhapur.[31]

Bal Thackeray's younger sister Sanjeevani Karandikar said her father was not against Brahmins per se, but opposed caste-based discrimination. 'When I married a Brahmin [Janardhan Karandikar] in January 1958, it created a flutter. But, Dada [Prabodhankar] told people he was not against Brahmins [as a social group] but Brahminism [a caste-based social position].'[32]

No history or chronicle of modern-day Maharashtra can be complete without mentioning 'Karmaveer' Bhaurao Patil (1887–1959). Born to a Maharashtrian Jain family in Kolhapur, Patil, a member of Phule's Satyashodhak Samaj, started the Rayat Shikshan Sanstha in 1919 to educate non-Brahmins. The institution, which runs over 700 schools, colleges hostels, and residential schools, pioneered the 'earn and learn' concept[33] for underprivileged students.

Patil, who considered Prabodhankar his guru, took him along to meet Mahatma Gandhi at Seth Vithaldas Damodar Thackersey's palatial bungalow in Pune to seek financial aid for the struggling Rayat from the Harijan Sevak Sangh's funds. Then, Prabodhankar was staying in Pune. When Gandhi seemed to dither, Prabodhankar did not mince his words, accusing the Mahatma of staying in a luxurious house that could put the Taj Mahal to shame. An annual grant of Rs 1000 for Patil's Shahu Chhatrapati Harijan Boarding was approved by the executive committee of the Sangh within a fortnight.[34]

The Shiv Sena's birth had its roots in a campaign launched by Prabodhankar through his periodical in 1922. Prabodhankar, who was then staying at Miranda Chawl in Dadar, noted that the large-scale influx of 'Madrasi' (south Indian) youth to Mumbai as cheap labour led to the fall of average wages in government, semi-government and private firms. Senior stenotypists then used to earn between Rs 125 and Rs 120 per month, while it was between Rs 60 and Rs 75 for juniors. The advent of south Indians brought it down to just Rs 50 to Rs 25, causing distress to local job seekers.[35]

After two articles in *Prabodhan*, the 'Madrasis' in Dadar and Matunga joined hands to unsuccessfully charge him with promoting enmity between groups on the grounds of religion, race, place of birth or language.

At the same time, educationist S.R. Tavde had returned from America with a diploma in higher education and applied to the Government of Madras for a job. But his attempt was stonewalled on minor grounds. Prabodhankar met the chief secretary of Bombay state which resulted in an order being issued stating that local candidates would have first preference in recruitments in any department.[36] This incident may have laid the seeds of the Shiv Sena's birth in 1966.

'Jai Maharashtra', the slogan of both the Shiv Sena and the Maharashtra Navnirman Sena (MNS), was also thought up by him.[37]

Despite the breadth and depth of his knowledge, Prabodhankar insisted that all writing had to be accessible to the common man. Pandharinath Sawant, who later became executive editor of *Marmik*, the first cartoon weekly in Marathi launched by the Thackerays, notes how he was upbraided for writing a tough-to-understand piece in the weekly.[38]

Strict, disciplined, quick-tempered

In his personal life, Prabodhankar was a strict disciplinarian and quick-tempered, known for using *Thakri bhasha* (aggressive, caustic language that is a characteristic of the Thackerays).

Though his wife, Rama, was in-charge of the children's education, Prabodhankar himself taught them Marathi and English. As his son Shrikant, eighth of Prabodhankar's ten children, admitted later, his mother lived amid 'live embers'.[39] Prabodhankar insisted on a clean plate, and the food had to be served in a particular manner. If there was even a slight change, he would fling the plate in her face, he told senior journalist Dnyanesh Maharao.[40]

Prabodhankar changed many jobs and professions, which may have put the household under immense financial and mental stress. This included playing cameos in films, like the role of an orthodox Brahmin in *Mahatma Phule* produced by P.K. Atre, and writing screenplays for Marathi and Hindi movies.

Shrikant recalls some painful incidents. In 1941, the Thackerays lived at Dadar. While Ramabai had been hospitalized (she died in February 1944), Prabodhankar had lost his eyesight and sat glued to his bed. Bal and Shrikant were just thirteen and ten years old and the youngest son, Ramesh, was a baby.[41]

The family was facing a financial crisis and there was not a morsel of food at home. The house was raided as they had defaulted on rent worth Rs 80. Prabodhankar's friend, Shah, paid off the rent collectors and sent a sack of grain to help them.[42]

According to another anecdote, Chhatrapati Shahu Maharaj of Kolhapur often bragged he could 'make donkeys out of people by luring them with money' and had his own ways of testing the character of men, often in their most trying times.[43]

In 1921, Prabodhankar, who had been ailing for three months with typhoid and pneumonia, was facing financial difficulties. His friend Shripatrao Shinde, who edited *Vijayi Maratha*, and others including an advocate representing the Kolhapur durbar visited him at his Miranda chawl residence in Dadar, and handed a letter from Shahu Maharaj asking for a booklet to be written based on the Puranas.

Prabodhankar, who believed that the Puranas were 'useless riff-raff', refused. The advocate then produced a cheque for Rs 5000 and called it *prasad* (gift in this case) from the Chhatrapati, which should not be turned down.[44]

However, despite his precarious condition, Prabodhankar was not one to be browbeaten. 'Why just a Chhatrapati, even if Lord Brahma gives such a *prasad*, I will spit on it. Take it away . . . If Maharaj wastes money on such activities, then tell him that my respect for him has diminished,' he thundered.[45]

After recovering from his illness, when Prabodhankar met Shahu Maharaj at his Mumbai residence, Panhala Lodge, in Khetwadi, his diwan, Sabnis, thanked him for saving his honour. When the nonplussed Prabodhankar questioned him, Sabnis said that he had told the royal that Thackeray could not be lured with money. However, Shahu Maharaj had insisted that Prabodhankar would easily succumb considering his illness and financial state and had sent the trio to test him.

After Shinde and others communicated Prabodhankar's refusal, Maharaj declared in English, 'He is the only man we have come across who cannot be bought or bribed.'[46]

Cartooning for a living

Senior journalist Dinoo Randive, a schoolmate of the Thackeray siblings at Dadar's Orient High School, noted that Bal and Shrikant stood out because of their felicity for drawing and music respectively.[47]

Randive, who like the Thackerays resided at Dadar, said Bal's drawings, usually of deities like Radha and Krishna, would appear in the school's handwritten magazine. When the Quit India movement was under way, Randive launched a handwritten magazine for which Bal wrote headings in his beautiful handwriting.

Though this may come as a surprise to those who have seen Bal Thackeray in his later avatar as a fire-spewing demagogue, Randive notes that back in the day, he spoke very little.[48] In 1939, when Bal was around thirteen, his father had seen him eagerly watching a cartoon drawn by Banbury in the *Times of India* and asked him to make sketches, which he corrected. 'My first guru in cartooning was my father,' Bal said, adding that he considered political cartoonist Sir David Alexander Cecil Low and artist Dinanath Dalal as his other icons.[49] Low would leave a lasting influence on Bal and later, on his nephew, Raj.

Bal, who loved Walt Disney's cartoons and watched the animation film *Bambi* (1942) around twenty-five times, was apprenticed at the Haldankar art school and started working at the Pathare-Pathare studio. He also designed showcards and paper publicity for movies like *Nargis*, *Mera Suhag* and *Mohan*.[50] When

Bal was on the verge of joining the Sir J.J. School of Art, the artist and film-maker Baburao Painter had 'advised him to shun the rigours of academic curriculum and, instead, join a painter's studio'.[51]

In 1945, Bal joined the *Free Press Journal* (*FPJ*). Another legend in cartooning, R.K. Laxman, also worked with the newspaper. When K. Shankar Pillai of the reputed *Shankar's Weekly*, was chosen to accompany Jawaharlal Nehru on his tour to Russia, he approached Bal to draw cartoons for the magazine during his absence.[52]

Dinoo Randive remembers Bal's cartoons in *FPJ*, especially those which appeared on Sundays and were a humorous take on events of the week. 'He attained name as a cartoonist very rapidly,' he notes.[53]

Thackeray's disagreements with his south Indian bosses, namely managing editor A.B. Nair, and editor Hariharan, culminated in him quitting *FPJ* in 1959. Incidentally, the south Indians, pejoratively called *Yandu Gundu*s due to their thick accent, were the first targets of the Shiv Sena's ire upon its launch in 1966.

After quitting *FPJ*, Thackeray was the only Maharashtrian in a team of six partners that launched an English periodical called *News Day*. He quit the publication after disagreements with his south Indian colleagues on issues including his opposition to the powerful Congressman S.K. Patil.[54]

Bal, with younger brother Shrikant, then launched a cartoon weekly *Marmik* in 1960. Like Atre's daily *Maratha*, which fought for a Samyukta (united) Maharashtra, *Marmik* would catalyse the birth of the Shiv Sena six years later.

2

Quest for a Marathi Identity

'The manners of the Marathas are simple and honest. They are honest and reserved. If anyone is kind to them, he may be sure of their gratitude. But if anyone injures them, they will take their revenge and risk their life to wipe off their dishonour. If anyone in distress appeals to them, they will leave aside all thoughts of self in their anxiety to help. Even if they have insult to avenge, they will never fail to warn their enemy. In battles, if they pursue their fugitives, they always spare all who surrender.'

Xuan Zang, seventh-century Chinese pilgrim[1]

With its evocation of iconography and imagery, the politics and sociology of Maharashtra are intricately linked to history. Chhatrapati Shivaji Maharaj's (1627/30–80) rebellion against the Mughal Empire under Aurangzeb shook its foundations and eventually led to its disintegration. Under the reign of the peshwas (1713–1818), the Maratha confederacy ruled most of India.

Like the Marathi author, humorist and journalist 'Acharya' Pralhad Keshav Atre famously claimed, '. . . only Maharashtra has history, the rest have just geography. . . .'[2] It is this imagery that nativist parties like the Shiv Sena and the MNS lay claim to in order to evoke 'Marathi pride' for mass mobilization.

There are many views about the etymology and antiquity of the term 'Maharashtra'.

According to scholars like Mahamahopadhyaya Datto Vaman Potdar, the term is around 2000 years old. There are references to 'Trik Maharashtra' (three countries of Maharashtra) in the seventh-century Aihole inscription by Ravikirti, the court poet of King Pulakeshin II, at the erstwhile Chalukya capital in Karnataka. The thirteenth-century poet-saint Dnyaneshwar mentions the *Maharashtra Mandal* in his *Dnyaneshwari*. The *Sutrapath* of Mahanubhav saint 'Sarvadnya' Chakradhar Swami (thirteenth century) notes that Maharashtra comprises the region in which Marathi is spoken and lists its boundaries.[3]

Mahatma Phule described Maharashtra as a region originally populated by Mahars (a Dalit caste many of whose members converted to Buddhism with Dr Babasaheb Ambedkar in 1956). J.T. Molesworth too said Maharashtra may mean 'the country of the Mahars', a view with an echo in the works of scholars like Rajaram Ramkrishna 'Rajaramshastri' Bhagwat and John Wilson.[4] Indologist R.G. Bhandarkar traces the origin to a community known as *Rashtrika* or *Rathika* who called themselves Maharathi or Maharatta, and S.V. Ketkar's view holds that it arose from a combination of 'Mahars', who were the first inhabitants, and 'Ratta'.[5]

Archaeological excavations have discovered evidences of Palaeolithic, Mesolithic and Chalcolithic era fossils and tools in Maharashtra.

Maharashtra has been populated through the Savalda (2500–2000 BC), Daymabad (2200–1000 BC), Late Harappan/Sindhu (2200–2000 BC), Malwa (1700–1400 BC) and Jorwe cultures (1500–1200 BC and 1200–900 BC). The Chalcolithic late Jorwe culture declined due to reasons like recurring droughts and the advent of people from the Megalithic cultures from today's south India with iron weapons and horses.[6]

A favourable environment led to Maharashtra being repopulated and ruled by the Ashmaka Mahajanapada, which was among the sixteen Mahajanapadas between the sixth and fourth centuries BC,[7] and dynasties like the Maurya, Satavahana, Vakataka and Chalukya.

The Seuna Yadavas, who ruled parts of present-day Maharashtra, Karnataka and Madhya Pradesh from Devgiri in Aurangabad, were defeated and their dominions annexed by Alauddin Khilji between the last decade of the thirteenth century and early fourteenth century. The Tughlaks, Bahamanis, the five Deccan Sultanates and the Sultanates of Gujarat and Khandesh also controlled parts of Maharashtra till the sixteenth century.

In the early seventeenth century, Shahaji Raje Bhosale, a Nizamshahi general, crowned a boy prince of the dynasty as ruler with himself as the regent. But faced with the might of the Mughals, Shahaji took up service with Adilshah and was sent to Karnataka. Shahaji sent his wife Jijabai and younger son Shivaji (1627/30–80) to manage his *jagir*s (fiefs) of Pune and Supe.

Shivaji Maharaj, who founded the Maratha Empire by taking on the Mughals and Adilshah, has a talismanic appeal over the masses for his benevolent rule, love for his subjects, tolerance for other faiths and respect for women, including those captured in war. It was his iconography, legacy and memories of his fierce resistance to rulers much more powerful than him, like the Mughals, that was used by the Shiv Sena and also the MNS for political mobilization. '*Jai Bhawani, Jai Shivaji* (Hail Bhawani, Hail Shivaji)' remains the popular slogan for their cadre.

However, historians and activists like the late Govind Pansare, leader of the Communist Party of India (CPI), who was shot dead by unidentified assailants in 2015, rejected the narrative of using Shivaji Maharaj for communal polarization. They stress on his rule being secular and his army including sizeable numbers of Muslims.[8]

The legend of Shivaji Maharaj holds such sway over Maharashtra that every shade of political thought in the state, ideological left to the Hindu right-wing and liberal movements like farmer leader Sharad Joshi's 'Shetkari Sanghatana' have tried to lay claim to his legacy and its pull on the common Maharashtrian.

As Prabodhankar noted: 'Shivaji Maharaj's image and deeds are in our hearts like the life-force itself.'[9]

Maharashtra's sensibilities have also been shaped by the Bhakti sect, with poet-saints like Namdeo, Dnyaneshwar and Tukaram, who attacked notions of caste purity. It is also the cradle of the social reform, rationalist and anti-caste movement led by Mahatma Jyotiba Phule and Savitribai Phule, Dr Babasaheb Ambedkar, Chhatrapati Shahu of Kolhapur (who started caste-based reservations in 1902) and R.D. Karve (the pioneer of family planning and sex education in India).

Though there is a controversy over whether he was Shivaji Maharaj's guru, Saint Ramdas, who was his contemporary, urges: '*Maratha Tituka Melwawa, Maharashtra Dharma Vadhwawa* (Unite the people of Maharashtra and forge Maharashtra dharma).' This 'Maharashtra dharma' can be interpreted as a strong sense of identity and self-respect about being a Marathi speaker with its social, historic and cultural underpinnings.

With his opposition to caste-based discrimination and insistence on an inclusive version of Hinduism, Prabodhankar was part of this larger social reform movement in Maharashtra, a foot soldier of 'Maharashtra dharma'.

Linguistic provinces

'If a province has to educate itself and do its daily work through the medium of its own language, it must necessarily be a linguistic area. If it happens to be a polyglot area difficulties will continually arise and the media of instruction and work will be two or even more languages. Hence, it becomes most desirable for provinces to be regrouped on a linguistic basis. Language as a rule corresponds with a special variety of culture, of traditions, and literature. In a linguistic area all these factors will help in the general progress of the province.'[10]

During the pre-Independence years, the Congress was committed to the creation of linguistic provinces in independent India. It also formed separate circles for Andhra (1917) and Sindh (1918).[11]

Provincial Congress Committees (PCCs) were formed by linguistic areas after the 1920 Congress session at Nagpur. In *India After Gandhi*, Ramachandra Guha notes that though Jawaharlal Nehru was supportive of India's linguistic diversity in 1937, he was beginning to have 'other thoughts' a decade later.[12]

The reasons were evident. The country had been divided on the basis of religion and further fissiparous tendencies, this time on the grounds of language, were dangerous. He favoured existing administrative units which were multilingual and multicultural to 'provide an exemplary training in harmonious living'.[13]

Nehru articulated his concerns in the Constituent Assembly three months after Independence and garnered the support of C. Rajagopalachari and Sardar Vallabhbhai Patel. The Assembly appointed a committee of jurists and civil servants, which recognized the appeal of the demand. It however said that linguistic provinces could not be supported considering the need for India to evolve as a nation in the 'prevailing unsettled conditions'.[14]

This 'caused dismay among large sections of the Assembly'.[15] A fresh committee was appointed with Nehru, Patel and former Congress president Pattabhi Sitaramayya as members, which revoked the Congress's position on linguistic provinces. However, movements seeking to unite Kannada, Marathi and Gujarati speakers were renewed along with a demand for a Sikh state in Punjab.[16]

However, the 'most vigorous movement' was that of the Telugu speakers of Andhra, notes Guha. Telugu-speaking people of the Madras Presidency argued they were being discriminated against by Tamils. On 19 October 1952, Potti Sriramalu, a Gandhian, launched a fast unto death to demand the creation of Andhra Pradesh. On 15 December, he passed away, plunging Andhra into chaos. Government offices were attacked, trains were halted and protestors killed in police firing, forcing Nehru to capitulate.[17]

Finally, the new state of Andhra was inaugurated at Kurnool on 1 October 1953.[18] This was the first linguistic state in Independent India, leading to similar demands by other linguistic groups.

Forced into action, the Government of India appointed a States Reorganization Commission (SRC) to recommend broad principles to solve the linguistic problem. In 1954–55, the Commission visited 104 towns and cities, interviewed over 9000 people and received 152,250 written submissions. One of these was from the Bombay Citizens Committee, which included prominent industrialists such as J.R.D. Tata, and the city's top lawyers, scholars and doctors.[19]

The Committee wanted Bombay to be kept out of the state of Maharashtra citing reasons like the presence of people across linguistic denominations, its importance in India's economic life, physical isolation from the Marathi-speaking heartland and Marathi speakers comprising just 43 per cent of the population.[20]

Mumbai's history

'Mumbai Nagari badi banka, jashee Ravanachee dusari Lanka'
(Mumbai, a city that rivals in its splendor, Ravana's Lanka made of gold)

'Shahir' (bard) Patthe Bapurao

From 1672 onwards, the East India Company, which held suzerainty over Mumbai, started bringing in occupational communities like farmers, gardeners, weavers, cooks, cobblers, tailors, barbers and butchers.[21]

Mumbai was fast changing its character from 1529, when it was like an isolated backwater with just around 400 houses of Kolis (fishermen), Bhandaris and others.[22]

The population of Mumbai, which stood at around 1.80 lakh in 1813, jumped to 5.50 lakh in 1864.[23] The East India Company had given concessions for trade and many Gujarati traders started firms in partnership with Europeans.[24] The Parsis, whose Sasanian ancestors in Iran were defeated by Arab conquerors at the Battle of Nihavand in AD 641, had fled the country for Indian shores, arriving at the Gujarat coast.[25]

Around 1638, the Parsis were 'engaged in mercantile pursuits' as 'bankers, shopkeepers and were following various other trades'.[26] The Parsis served the British as brokers and coiners.

Dorabjee Nanabhoy Patel was the first Parsi to migrate to Mumbai from Surat in 1640, followed by another Parsi named Ranjee between 1640 and 1663.[27] By the beginning of the nineteenth century, Parsis, Gujarati banias and Bohris had a monopoly over trade in Mumbai. The hold of Parsis over Mumbai's trade was gradually eroded by Khoja Muslims.[28]

The Maharashtrians, who had few indigenous mercantile castes, lagged in commerce. Gyan Prakash writes in his book, *Mumbai Fables*, that under the British, Mumbai developed its reputation as a city of commerce serviced by merchants belonging to different communities. The East India Company shifted its headquarters from Surat to Mumbai in 1686 to escape the Maratha attacks.[29]

After the victory of the British over the Marathas in 1818 and growth in the trade of opium to China from Mumbai, the city flourished.[30]

Senior journalist Darryl D'Monte writes that a Parsi businessman, Cowasjee Nanabhoy Davar, started the first cotton spinning mill, Bombay Spinning and Weaving Company, in 1856, and it began operations two years later.[31] Soon, other mills were launched by the Baghdadi Jew Elias David Sassoon, the Tatas and Thackersey Mooljee. By the end of the century, Mumbai had over eighty textile mills.[32]

These mills were staffed by workers from Maharashtra and immigrants from the United Provinces, including Muslims. Those seeking work migrated to Mumbai during the cotton boom of the 1860s and suffered from poor living conditions and long working hours.[33]

By 1921, says Shashi Bhushan Upadhyay in 'Cotton Mill Workers in Bombay, 1875 to 1918: Conditions of Work and Life', 35.53 per cent workers came from Ratnagiri, followed by 9.42 per cent from the United Provinces, 6.63 per cent from Satara, 6.18 per cent from Poona, 4.47 per cent from Kolaba and 2.99 per cent from Ahmednagar. A 1940 survey by the Bombay Mill Owners Association quoted by Upadhyay says Marathas, including Kunbis, formed around 51.8 per cent of all male workers, followed by Hindu migrants from the United Provinces (called 'bhaiyas' in local slang) 13.8 per cent, Harijans (11.9 per cent) and Muslims (5.2 per cent).

These Maharashtrian-dominated mill districts, called 'Girangaon', comprising areas like Lalbag, Parel and Byculla, had their own avant-garde, working-class culture.

This included *shahir*s (balladeers/bards) like Amar Shaikh, Atmaram Patil and Shaikh Jainu Chand, poets like Narayan Surve and actors like Bhagwandada Palav, gymnasiums, wrestling pits and cultural troupes. It was here that the Communist Party of India first struck roots in Mumbai. And the leftist polymath, Shripad Amrut Dange, had unlettered workers from the Konkan coast and the Ghats under his thrall through his sparkling speeches inspired by the works of Karl Marx, verses from the Vedas and the *Meghadutam* of Gupta-era poet Kalidasa that he knew by heart.

The growth of the textile mills, development of the port, engineering industry and railways (the first passenger railway ran from Boribunder to Tannah [Thane] on 16 April 1853), made Mumbai the most prominent mercantile centre of the colonial era.

In 1951, Marathi speakers comprised 43.6 per cent of Mumbai's population, down from 50.2 per cent in 1881. The number declined further to 42.8 per cent in 1961.[34] In 1881, those speaking Gujarati (including Kutchi) were 28 per cent, followed by Urdu speakers (12 per cent) and English speakers (1 per cent).[35]

Maharashtra has few indigenous mercantile castes and this was reflected in the Marathi-speaking population in the city. The Maharashtrians of Mumbai then consisted of a relatively small literate elite (Brahmins and Prabhus [Kayasthas] by caste), together with a vast majority of mill workers, labourers, domestic servants, artisans and cultivators.[36]

Samyukta Maharashtra movement

In *India After Gandhi*, Ramachandra Guha notes that 'behind the veneer of cosmopolitanism', the Gujaratis, who feared losing Mumbai to Maharashtrians, dominated the 'Save Bombay' movement. The Gujarati elite, including Parsis, were not happy with the idea of having Marathi-speaking politicians and ministers if Mumbai became Maharashtra's capital.[37]

The Samyukta Maharashtra movement, which called for the formation of a state of Maharashtra, with Mumbai as the capital, was led by a rainbow coalition of leaders that included S.A. Dange, Acharya Atre, freedom fighter 'Senapati' P.M. Bapat, journalist V.R. Kothari, Congressman Shankarrao Deo, Keshavrao Jedhe, the economist D.R. Gadgil, socialists like S.M. Joshi and shahirs like Amar Shaikh and Prabodhankar. Dr Babasaheb Ambedkar also supported Samyukta Maharashtra.

The Samyukta Maharashtra agitation remains the most widespread mass movement in the state post-Independence. The Samyukta Maharashtra Parishad submitted a document to the SRC mounting a theoretical defence of the principle of linguistic states, which it said would deepen federalism by bringing together speakers of the same language into one consolidated, cohesive unit.[38]

Marathi speakers were spread across three political units—Hyderabad, Bombay state, and the Central Provinces—and it made a strong pitch for the creation of Maharashtra with Mumbai as its capital.[39] The Parishad argued that Mumbai had long been inhabited by Marathi speakers and the region around it was dominated by their brethren. Economically, Mumbai depended heavily on the Marathi hinterland and its modes of transportation all lay through Maharashtra. The city had more people speaking Marathi than any other language.[40]

Speaking at a meeting organized by the Maharashtra Seva Sangh on 20 February 1954, Prabodhankar stressed how the battle for Mumbai was between 'the poor, looted Maratha [Marathi speakers] versus capitalists, moneylenders and traders who looted them'.[41] The Brahmanetar leader, Keshavrao Jedhe, who presided over the meeting, promised that the language and culture of non-Marathi speakers would be protected and called on them to join the struggle.[42]

In his statement to the Linguistic Provinces Commission in 1948, Dr Babasaheb Ambedkar stressed Maharashtra would be a viable province. He noted that the Gujaratis were not the natives of Mumbai. They did not come to Mumbai voluntarily but had been brought by officers of the East India Company to serve as commercial *adhatia*s (go-betweens). They did not come to trade on the basis of free and equal competition but were privileged with certain exclusive trading rights given to them by the East India Company.[43]

'Once it is established that Bombay belonged to Maharashtra the claim of Maharashtra to include Bombay cannot be defeated by the argument that the trade and industry of Bombay is owned by the Gujaratis. The claim of mortgagor to his land cannot be defeated by the mortgagee on the ground that the mortgagee has built up permanent structures on the land. The Gujaratis, assuming they have built up the trade and industry of Bombay, are in no better position than a mortgagee is,' he says.[44]

In October 1955, the SRC recommended a separate state of Vidarbha comprising Marathi-speaking districts, but Bombay state would remain a bilingual province of Gujarati and Marathi speakers. The SRC respected the arguments of the Samyukta Maharashtra movement but claimed they could not disregard fears of other communities.[45]

The communists led the charge on Samyukta Maharashtra and said they were committed to linguistic states and pointed to the Soviet Union as 'an exemplary multi-national federation'.[46]

Communist leader Lalji Pendse writes in his book, *Maharashtrache Mahamanthan* (The Churn for Maharashtra), that the Samyukta Maharashtra Parishad opposed the SRC's recommendations. In a resolution passed on 23 October 1955, it reiterated the demand for the creation of the state of Maharashtra with Mumbai as the capital.[47]

On 21 November 1955, the discontent spilled over on the streets of Mumbai with four lakh workers in textile mills, the port, Bombay Municipal Corporation (BMC) and engineering workshops going on strike. Mobs headed to the Oval Maidan in south Mumbai for a *morcha* (protest march). The police resisted leading to fifteen people being killed and 300 injured—the first martyrs in the struggle for Maharashtra's statehood.[48]

On 16 January 1956, the Centre announced three new states based on languages, including Maharashtra, Gujarat and bilingual Bombay, to be administered from Delhi. Gyan Prakash writes that anticipating opposition, left leaders, including Dange, were arrested. The workers called a strike, and violence gripped the city.[49]

The protests gave the slogan that would dominate the Samyukta Maharashtra movement for the next five years: '*Mumbaisaha Samyukta Maharashtra Zhalach Pahije* (Samyukta Maharashtra must be formed including Mumbai)'.[50]

A grand alliance of opposition parties formed the Samyukta Maharashtra Samiti (SMS) in February 1956 to oppose the decision. Eventually, the Central government announced a bilingual state consisting of all Marathi- and Gujarati-speaking areas, including the city of Mumbai. However, the Maha Gujarat Parishad objected to this.[51]

This time, the predominantly Marathi textile mill workers of Mumbai led the charge, with women participating in sizeable numbers. Sahadeo Jagare, a jobber at Sewri's Swan Mills, said these protestors feared a centrally ruled Mumbai would affect working-class interests.[52]

In the 1957 elections, public ire against the Congress was palpable, though it held on to power. Of the 133 seats in Maharashtra, it got just thirty-two against the Samiti's 101, down from 119 of 141 in 1952. However, the Congress came to power in the bilingual state due to its better performance in Gujarat, Vidarbha and Marathwada.[53]

In the battle for Samyukta Maharashtra, Prabodhankar's son, Bal, then a twenty-eight-year-old fledging cartoonist, found himself on the wrong side of the law in 1954. He had drawn a cartoon of then chief minister of Bombay state, Morarji Desai, hated for his rejection of Marathi aspirations, on the front page of a magazine called *Mumbai*. In it, Desai was depicted as a *narabhakshak* (cannibal) standing on a heap of human skulls, representing state repression of the Samyukta Maharashtra movement.[54] A case was registered, forcing Bal to go 'underground' (he stayed overnight at his sister's house nearby, coming home for lunch and dinner!) However, he was not arrested.[55]

Bal attended public meetings during the Samyukta Maharashtra movement. After the SRC report was submitted in October 1955, Bal, who was then working with *FPJ*, contributed cartoons under pen names like 'Maratha', 'Mavla' and 'Bahirji' on a pro bono basis to around seven to eight Marathi weeklies because his service rules prevented him from working elsewhere. He also drew for the *Samyukta Maharashtra Patrika* launched by Dinoo Randive.[56]

Senior journalist Randive recalls that even if the cartoons did not carry his byline, the lines and the nub made it clear that it was Bal Thackeray's work.[57] 'He would not organize public meetings and morchas, but his cartoonist's pen used to work. Then, his pen had acquired a different edge. A weapon becomes blunt if used over a period of time. But Balasaheb's palette was different, it became more potent,' writes Randive.[58]

One of the Shiv Sena's biographers, senior journalist Prakash Akolkar, notes in *Jai Maharashtra: Ha Shiv Sena Navacha Itihas Aahe* (Jai Maharashtra: This Is History Called the Shiv Sena), that faced with the prospect of losing the support of Marathi speakers, the Congress leadership consented to the formation of Samyukta Maharashtra with Mumbai as its capital.[59]

In 1959, the Congress Working Committee (CWC) passed a resolution recommending the formation of Maharashtra, including Mumbai. Its purpose achieved, the SMS was disbanded. The state of Maharashtra was finally born on 1 May 1960.[60]

At the time, the then undivided CPI held sway over the working class, especially the textile mill workers, who looked upon Dange as their hero. Dange said that Mumbai as an administrative entity separate from Maharashtra would be dominated by communists. This led to the date for the formation of Maharashtra being shifted from 1 April to 1 May (Labour Day).[61]

Though Marathi-speaking areas like Karwar, Belgaum, Nippani and Dang had been eventually kept out of it, the state of Maharashtra, with Mumbai as its capital, was born after a struggle that claimed 106 lives.

3

The Tiger Comes to Life

It is people like me
builders of your grand edifice
Who add to your glory
day after day, O City . . .
We toil thus
So many of us
And die exhausted
like a burnt-out candle.

Narayan Surve, 'Mumbai'[1]

Though Marathi speakers had secured their own state, they felt their identity was threatened in their own capital. They also felt left out of the process of development while other communities seemed to prosper.

Political analyst and assistant professor in the department of civics and politics at the University of Mumbai, Dr Deepak Pawar, notes that after Maharashtra was formed, the Samyukta Maharashtra Samiti, which was the first, broad-based, non-Congress alliance in India, gradually fell apart due to the discord among its constituents. This left the Marathi speakers in Mumbai without a political platform to articulate their concerns.[2]

In *Nativism in a Metropolis: The Shiv Sena in Bombay*, sociologist Dipankar Gupta writes that Maharashtrians felt migrants were wrongfully taking advantage of Mumbai's bounty. This was because non-Maharashtrians dominated commerce and were generally more affluent than Maharashtrians. They were also better represented than Maharashtrians in well-paid jobs due to their education and expertise.[3]

Though the Samyukta Maharashtra Samiti was successful in securing Mumbai as the capital of Maharashtra, this did not result in the domination by Maharashtrians of the cultural or economic life of the city wrote Gupta. 'Bombay still bears a pronounced non-Maharashtrian character. To add to this, the fact that the Maharashtrians comprise 43 per cent of the total population, and are, therefore, though a dominant-minority, not a majority community in the capital of their own state, may have added to their feelings of insecurity and deprivation.'[4]

Though Mumbai was the capital of Maharashtra, non-Maharashtrians dominated the public space.

Roots of anger

Even after Maharashtra was formed, economic issues like lack of employment continued to fester. The Samyukta Maharashtra movement had kindled aspirations in the minds of Marathi speakers, especially the youth, but its leaders had not taken necessary steps to fulfil them. The Shiv Sena stepped into this void.[5]

Dinoo Randive recalls that in 1961 then chief minister Y.B. Chavan said that Mumbai was the capital of Maharashtra but was dominated by others and hence, it was necessary to give Mumbai a Marathi imprint.[6] Balkrishna Nar, a textile mill union activist, said the Marathis were bullied by hawkers and *paraprantiya*s (outsiders) on the streets. They were dominated by the organized Madrasis and Gujaratis. The Shiv Sena expressly countered this.[7]

'The Marathi manoos, the true son of the soil, felt he was getting a raw deal,' said senior Nationalist Congress Party (NCP) leader Chhagan Bhujbal, who joined the Shiv Sena in 1966.[8] 'There were times when working-class Maharashtrians like *mathadi*s [head-load workers] who wore caps had them rudely thrown off their heads by people from other communities, who derisively called them *ghati*s. Slogans like *Mhane Mumbai tumchi, bhandi ghasa aamchi* [Mumbai is yours, now wash our utensils] were commonly used to jeer at Maharashtrians,' he added.[9]

In 1963, north Indians had assaulted Maharashtrians in Jogeshwari. The Communist Party's muscle man, Krishna Desai, and Marathi youngsters from Girangaon retaliated in kind.'[10]

Vaibhav Purandare states in his book, *The Sena Story*, that Maharashtrians, who had gained political strength, were questioning their continued economic backwardness and seeking an improvement in financial prospects.[11]

'Shahir' Krishnarao Sable said an organization named 'Maharashtra Hitavardhini' had been launched in Girangaon to counter the increasing marginalization of Maharashtrians. Sable was the member of the organization which had Congress leader, Barrister Ramrao Adik, as its president.[12]

As scholar-editor, the late Dr Aroon Tikekar, noted that even those who disliked or hated violence of any kind were convinced that the Marathi manoos was getting a raw deal. Local Marathis felt uneasy about the loss of their hold on Mumbai, which despite the contributions of non-Marathi communities like Parsis and Gujaratis, had a distinct Marathi stamp, especially in sociocultural and political activities for over a century.[13]

In *The Emergence of Regionalism in Mumbai: The History of the Shiv Sena*, Sudha Gogate argues that the Shiv Sena was not the only movement of its kind in India. The decades of the 1960s and '70s saw anti-Bengali outbreaks in Assam, riots in Telangana against 'Gair Mulkis' (outsiders) and Chaluvalligars (protestors) of Karnataka were hostile towards outsiders.[14]

'All these movements seemed to have one characteristic in common, an attitude of hostility to outsiders, though the definition of an outsider changed from time to time. The Shiv Sena, perhaps because of its dramatic rise and its location in India's foremost metropolitan city, attracted the greatest attention from academic as well as non-academic quarters,' said Gogate, while adding that these regionalist movements were a 'complex, multi-dimensional phenomenon'.[15]

Gogate refers to a 1970 study of migrants to Mumbai by the Tata Institute of Social Sciences (TISS). It inferred that the lower-middle-class Marathi citizen of Mumbai was comparatively less happy and less adjusted to the city than the lower-class north Indian or south Indian migrant. The study put forth the hypothesis of relative deprivation as a possible explanation.[16]

Purandare added that the Shiv Sena's formation was preceded by phases of economic development and economic competition between Maharashtrians and non-Maharashtrians.[17]

The literacy rates in Mumbai grew from 16.3 per cent in 1872 to 23.8 per cent in 1931, 40.8 per cent in 1941, 49.3 per cent in 1951 and 58.6 per cent in 1961.[18] The period leading to the Shiv Sena's formation had seen the economy faring well. Between 1962 and 1967, the number of office jobs went up by 28 per cent as against an 8 per cent increase in blue-collar industrial sector jobs. Though the Shiv Sena's founding in 1966 followed periods of economic growth, this relatively bright employment scenario may not have corresponded with the Maharashtrian perception of job prospects.[19]

Enrolment in the University of Bombay also rose from 24,000 in the early 1950s to around 90,000 in the early 1970s. While competition intensified, Maharashtrians held a fewer top-ranking and white-collar jobs than other communities in Mumbai, compared to their percentage in the population.[20]

A survey in the early 1950s by a University of Bombay professor, D.K. Lakdawala, in 'Work, Wages and Well-Being in an Indian Metropolis,' showed Maharashtrians lagged behind other communities in terms of occupational status and education. The study highlighted the percentage of Maharashtrians earning a middle- to upper-middle-class salary of Rs 500 to Rs 1000 per month, which was 4 per cent and lower than south Indians (7.9 per cent) and Gujaratis (10.2 per cent).[21]

Later studies also concluded that Maharashtrians were under-represented in higher-status administrative, professional and clerical jobs. This under-representation was higher in the newer industries and businesses like chemicals, pharmaceuticals, insurance and other service industries. Here, Marathis were employed largely in the lower-income brackets for manual labour.[22]

It was in this void that the Shiv Sena stepped in as a redeemer, an alter ego for the Maharashtrians.

'Even many Congress leaders felt that the Shiv Sena was doing something where their own party had failed. Congress leaders from rural Maharashtra who came to Mumbai, felt lost and naturally, their sympathies lay with the Shiv Sena,' explained Chhagan Bhujbal.[23]

'The economic competition between Maharashtrians and "outsiders" in Bombay is not a canard set afloat by Sena propaganda to delude Maharashtrian voters. Maharashtrians are economically behind several other communities in Bombay,' noted Mary Fainsod Katzenstein.[24] This led to the Shiv Sena mobilizing Maharashtrian middle-class support in its initial days.

A magazine, a movement

The Shiv Sena may well be the first political party in India to be born out of a cartoonist's expression. As Bal Thackeray admitted in a 2009 interview, after quitting *FPJ* in 1959, he had little opportunity for work.[25] Eventually, after consulting his father, he decided to launch *Marmik* and strike out on his own.

The Thackeray brothers had initially planned to launch a weekly in English called 'Cartoonist', but Prabodhankar thought it should be in Marathi. Though names like 'Tirandaz' (archer) and 'Anjan' (eye-opener), were considered, the name 'Marmik' (witty), was suggested by Prabodhankar.[26]

In the first issue of *Marmik*, the Thackeray brothers claimed they were starting the weekly 'to get money for their livelihood'.[27] While the Marathi literary scene had magazines like *Stri*, *Kirloskar*, *Mauj* and *Jyotsna*, *Marmik* stood out due to its style of writing and cartoons.[28]

Shrikant, called Shirya, or Shiri, by his elder brother, wrote features and film reviews for *Marmik*, under the pseudonym 'Shuddha Nishad'. After the Shiv Sena launched its mouthpiece *Saamna* in January 1989, Shrikant began writing a column on films titled 'Chanderi Dunia' (celluloid world).

Film critic Dilip Thakur, who was close to Shrikant, notes how his film reviews were a draw for *Marmik* readers, beginning with the headline.[29] 'Balasaheb would draw the cover page cartoon for *Marmik* and Pappa's [Thakur's term for Shrikant] review would appear on the last page. So, people would say, the *Marmik* cover is to be seen and then it is to be read from the last page. His opinions would be scathing. Sometimes, his criticism would begin right from the title. For instance, when *Shaan* was released in 1980 the title of his review said: '*Rahile nahi kasle bhaan, kadhla shaan, keli ghaan* [They lost sense, made a film like *Shaan*],' said Thakur.[30]

In 1963, some Maharashtrians approached Bal Thackeray complaining about discrimination in job opportunities. Soon after, Shrikant Gadkari, a friend, met him and showed him the telephone directory with numbers of non-Maharashtrians who occupied top positions in various companies.[31]

Chhagan Bhujbal, then a student of engineering at the Veermata Jijabai Technical Institute (VJTI), recalled how *Marmik* started publishing these lists under the column 'Vacha aani thanda basa' (read and stay silent), which was soon renamed 'Vacha aani utha' (read and rise).[32]

Marmik also carried names of Maharashtrian workers who had been retrenched by industrial units in Mumbai and reported about Marathi students being deprived of opportunities despite being qualified.[33]

'The column carried names of non-Maharashtrians in senior positions. It also pointed out that while the officers were non-Marathis, Maharashtrians occupied menial posts like those of peons and office boys. I was then secretary of the college student union. My fellow students complained that it was getting tough to find jobs and urged me to meet Bal Thackeray,' said Chhagan Bhujbal.[34]

Bhujbal joined the Shiv Sena in 1966 and was present at Shivaji Park at its first rally. He later became one of its first *shakha pramukh*s (branch head).

Marmik, with its cartoons, satire and columns that espoused the cause of the Marathi manoos, had struck a chord. This led to young people flocking to Thackeray's Ranade Road house, which also served as the *Marmik* office, complaining about discrimination.

Articles in *Marmik* pointed to the influx of migrants from other states to Mumbai and voiced apprehensions about Maharashtrians being ousted from the city. It also criticized south Indians for recruiting and promoting their own by using connections and influence in an office or industry.[35]

'. . . *Marmik* really began to work on my mind. Every week, the magazine spoke about the injustices done in Bombay and Maharashtra to the sons of the soil. And I found I was terribly attracted to the emotional personality of Bal Thackeray and his father, as expressed in the magazine,' said Diwakar Raote, who would later go on to become a senior Shiv Sena leader.[36]

Raote was among the eighteen people present at Kadam Mansion when the Shiv Sena was formally launched in Prabodhankar's presence on 19 June 1966.

Mary Katzenstein explains that the Sena's preoccupation with south Indians 'must be explained at least partially in cultural terms' as their numbers were, contrary to common belief, somewhat less in the white-collar occupations compared to Gujaratis.[37] The south Indian's formed just 9 per cent of Mumbai's population, which was less than half of Gujaratis.[38] But, when compared to the Maharashtrians, the south Indians stood out because of their languages, dress, food and culture than Gujaratis. This made them more conspicuous, contributed to the belief that they outnumbered other communities in white-collar occupations and also made them likely targets for nativism.[39] However, the Shiv Sena would soon change its targets from the south Indians to Muslims, Buddhist Dalits and north Indians.

Prabodhankar catalysed the idea of a political party being formed to give this campaign an organized form. It was the Thackeray family patriarch who gave the organization its name—Shiv Sena (Army of Shivaji Maharaj).

'Shivaji's Army'

On 5 June 1966, *Marmik* announced the launch of membership for an organization called the Shiv Sena to 'counter the onslaught of Yandu-Gundus on the rights of the Marathi manoos'.[40]

At 9.30 a.m. on 19 June 1966, a Thackeray family friend, Sahadev Naik, broke a coconut in front of Chhatrapati Shivaji Maharaj's bust.

'And intoning Chhatrapati Shivaji Maharaj Ki Jai, we started the Shiv Sena,' said Thackeray.[41]

Marmik claimed that when the registration of the Sena's membership was launched, around 2000 youngsters had listed their names within an hour. The next day, it reached 10,000 and shot up to 20,000 and 30,000 within a month and three months respectively. The sales of the weekly, which served as an important means of communication with its members, also rose from 18,532 in 1965 to 25,475 in 1966 and 37,638 in 1969, indicating a surge in the Sena's popularity.[42]

In its July issue, *Marmik* carried an oath that Shiv Sainiks had to take. This included the Marathi manoos helping each other, not selling property to outsiders, Marathi shopkeepers buying their goods from Marathi wholesale traders, Maharashtrian-run establishments employing sons of the soil and boycotting Udupi hotels and shops owned by non-Maharashtrians.[43]

The pledge had a striking point: 'Young Marathi-speaking boys should develop excellent communication skills in the English language, and learn English steno typing as well.'[44] This was probably aimed at ensuring the employability of Marathi youth in newer industries.

Four months after the launch of the new organization, *Marmik* readers were told that the Shiv Sena's first public meeting would be held at Shivaji Park at Dadar on 30 October 1966, with Bal Thackeray, the editor of *Marmik*, signing off as a 'humble Maharashtra Sevak'.[45]

Though the Shiv Sena's initial constituency would cover the white-collared Marathi middle class, Bal Thackeray visited the working-class Girangaon belt before the public meeting, drumming up support in various gymnasiums and cultural groups. A day before the Shivaji Park rally, he also addressed a meeting at Parel's Ganesh gully grounds.[46] Boys from Parel and Lalbag would serve as Thackeray's personal bodyguards and the Sena's storm troopers. The Parel constituency gave the Shiv Sena its first member of legislative assembly (MLA) in 1970.

Though the communists dominated Girangaon, Bandu Shingre, an aggressive Shiv Sainik from the area, who quit the party to form his 'Prati Shiv Sena' in the 1970s, said there was seething anger in people like him at the CPI's capitulation to China when the country invaded India in 1962.[47]

Bal Thackeray admitted that before the public meeting, a well-wisher, Prof. D.V. Deshpande, had asked why he had chosen the huge Shivaji Park ground as the venue. An apprehensive Deshpande suggested that the King George School ground, which was around a tenth of the size, might be a better choice. Bal Thackeray however refused. 'No, the arrow has already left the bow. I can't backtrack,' he said.[48]

According to Vijay Gaokar, a former Shiv Sena corporator from Girangaon, Thackeray was indeed considering holding the meeting at the King George School grounds, but the Sena's supporters from the mill belt insisted that it happen in Shivaji Park. The mill workers from Konkan turned up to make the rally a huge success.[49] Around four to five lakh people thronged the grounds, a figure far beyond all initial expectation. Prabodhankar admiringly said that the crowd proved that 'Maratha blood has not yet become impure, and Maharashtrians are ready to combat injustice'.[50] 'Maharashtra is not a land of weaklings. It is a tiger's offspring. History knows the outcome of playing mischief with it,' he warned.[51] Congress leader Ramrao Adik, the intellectual Prof. S.A. Ranade who contributed to *Marmik*, and advocate Balwant Mantri, also spoke on the occasion.

Bal Thackeray, the 'Shiv Sena pramukh', demanded that only those proficient in Marathi get jobs in Maharashtra.[52] He countered charges that the Marathi manoos was parochial and added that if this were the case, Mumbai would not have been a cosmopolitan city. He pointed to M. Bhaktavatsalam, the chief minister of Tamil Nadu, saying that only those who were well versed in Tamil would get jobs in that state. Moreover,

K. Kamaraj, the Congress boss, had also spoken out against the use of Hindi. Thackeray warned Kamaraj against 'teaching nationalism to Maharashtra'.[53]

Senior journalist Kumar Ketkar, now a Congress Rajya Sabha member of Parliament (MP), notes that Bal Thackeray's legacy was providing a sense of 'collective identity and communal pride to the Marathi manoos, who was feeling marginalized in a rapidly globalizing city of Mumbai'.[54]

4

Raj and Uddhav: The Early Years

A multitude of people and yet a solitude.

Charles Dickens, *A Tale of Two Cities*

There is an anecdote discussed among those who have known Raj Thackeray since his youth. A student in the first year of the Bachelor of Fine Arts (Applied Art) at the reputed Sir J.J. Institute of Applied Art in Mumbai was being ragged by a group of seniors. Once, the boys pushed him around. The boy kept silent, but his uncle, who doted on him, got wind of the incident. Incensed, he had the 'guilty' boys brought to his bungalow in suburban Bandra where they were 'punished' and warned in his nephew's presence. This incident is indicative of the relationship that Raj Thackeray shared with his uncle, Shiv Sena chief Bal Thackeray.[1]

In June 1948, Bal Thackeray, then twenty-one, married Sarla Vaidya (sixteen), later rechristened 'Meenatai' and called 'Ma' in the household. In 1964, Shrikant married Meenatai's younger sister Kunda aka Madhuwanti in an arranged match. Thus, Uddhav and Raj are first cousins twice over.

Uddhav was born on 27 July 1960, after two brothers, Bindumadhav aka Binda (1952), and Jaidev (1955).[2] Less than a month after Uddhav's birth, his father and uncle would launch

Marmik on 13 August, on P.K. Atre's birthday. Though the boys were christened by their grandfather, it was Shrikant who nicknamed Jaidev and Uddhav as 'Tibba' and 'Dinga' to rhyme with Binda (who was also called Bhai[3]). Bal and Meena also had a daughter who was born premature and passed away soon after.[4] The Thackeray children had a special name for Bal—Pilga, minted by the young Bindumadhav.[5]

Born on 14 June 1968, Raj was named 'Swararaj' by his musician father. However, after he took to cartooning, he was asked by his uncle to shorten it to Raj. His passport still retains his birth name.[6]

Though Raj was close to Bal, family friends say it was Raj's elder sister, Jaywanti, who was the apple of her uncle's eye as the only daughter of her generation in the Thackeray family.[7]

The year 1968, when Raj was born, was crucial for the Shiv Sena.

The Sena, which had earlier claimed to be a non-political force, contested the elections to the BMC for the first time in an alliance with the Praja Socialist Party (PSP). The two parties won forty-two and eleven seats respectively of the eighty-three and thirty-two segments that they contested from, but the Congress retained power with sixty-five of 127 seats. The Shiv Sena would continue to strike such alliances and understandings with the Republican Party of India (RPI), various factions of the Congress and even the Muslim League, before forging a lasting alliance with the Bharatiya Janata Party (BJP) in 1989.

This 'saffron alliance', or 'yuti' as it is referred to, continued for twenty-five years, before a resurgent BJP pulled the plug before the 2014 assembly elections after a tussle over seat-sharing.

Shrikant, with his love for music had chosen names based in Hindustani classical music for his wife and children (Madhuwanti, Jaywanti and Swararaj). Jaywanti started calling Uddhav 'Dadu', a play on Dada (elder brother), which was picked up by Raj as well.[8]

Jaywanti, or 'Tai' (elder sister), as she is called, completed her BA from Ruparel College and is married to Abhay Deshpande.[9]

The other Thackeray

Though he lived largely in the shadow of Bal, who was attached to him and was three years older, Shrikant was an accomplished music director, having inherited their father's love for music and art.

In his autobiography, Shrikant says that when he was one-and-a-half years old, he suffered from epileptic fits. The Thackeray family then lived in Dadar's Miranda chawl. Prabodhankar, who had a drama troupe, asked one of his violin players to play the *alaap* (opening part) of Raga Bhairav. The infant Shrikant, who was lying on his mother's lap after a bout of epilepsy, suddenly came to his senses much to the doctor's surprise. Prabodhankar, who would later teach his son to play the sitar, predicted he would become a musician.[10]

Shrikant was later taught by C.V. Pantvaidya to play the violin. As a young musician, Baburao Mohile, father of composer Anil Mohile, suggested that Shrikant play the violin before the legendary classical vocalist, Bade Ghulam Ali Khan, began his performance at Dadar's Dhuru Hall. Khan saheb arrived at the venue when Shrikant was playing and sat through his performance. Afterwards, Khan saheb said, '*Arre bachche, bahut surele bajate ho, aur sunao* (Child, you play very melodiously, play more).' After Shrikant finished playing a raga, Khan saheb came to the stage and made him (Shrikant) perform with him![11]

Shrikant began his career in music with Columbia, which was HMV's sister concern, and later as a violin player on All India Radio (AIR), accompanying classical vocalists like Ustad Faiyaz Khan and Madan Mohan, who was a singer before becoming a music director.[12] In 1971, he started a company named 'Prerana

Chitra' with Prabhakar Niklankar to produce Marathi movies.[13] Shrikant and Niklankar worked on a film called *Shoora mi Vandile* (I Salute the Brave), which was released in January 1976 and met with moderate success.[14]

Shrikant was the first to make Mohammad Rafi sing a Marathi song, 'Tuzhe roop sakhe gulzar', composed in the style of a qawwali in 1971. Rafi recorded a Koli geet (folk music of the fishermen community in Maharashtra) for him later.[15] Shrikant recorded around ten to twelve songs with Rafi.[16] Shrikant also cut ghazals with Shobha Gurtu and composed the score for the popular devotional song in Marathi—'*Shodhisi manava, rauli mandiri* (O humans, you search for God in temples, when he resides inside you . . .) . . .'—sung by Rafi.

Raj recalls Rafi, clad in a *lungi* and kurta, striding into their house early in the morning, asking his mother about the lunch menu before settling down, harmonium in hand, with Shrikant to practise his tunes.[17]

Shrikant was also a cartoonist. When the Times Group launched its Marathi daily, *Maharashtra Times*, in the 1960s, he was hired as a cartoonist and produced pocket cartoons. When he left, the newspaper decided against hiring a new hand, choosing to instead borrow R.K. Laxman cartoons from the *Times of India*.[18] Like Laxman's 'Common Man' and his brother Bal's 'Kakaji', Shrikant popularized a cartoon character called 'Banyabapu'.

Shrikant's acquaintances say he was a 'brilliant music director who never used his brother's influence for personal benefit'.[19]

Pandharinath Sawant, an old-time Thackeray family associate, who was the executive editor of *Marmik* from 1990 to February 2019, said when the Shiv Sena began gaining influence in Mumbai and Bollywood, some music directors approached Shrikant to compose the score for their films.[20]

'However, Shrikantji refused to work for them. He told them off, saying they were not approaching him for his talent, but to curry favours with his elder brother,' said Sawant. He noted that Shrikant's life moved around music and *Marmik*. 'The Shiv Sena would have lacked a strong medium for its publicity had he not handled *Marmik* efficiently,' he added. Shrikant, who had no inclination towards politics would, unlike his brother would often draw non-political cartoons.[21]

Singer Uttara Kelkar, who was coached by Shrikant, notes she was struck at his command over Urdu, interest in homeopathy and minute observation that helped him as a cartoonist. Kelkar, who also noted Shrikant's habit of keeping away from the crowds, said Shrikant preferred to remain immersed in music with little to do with the materialistic world. 'I would tell him, Shrikantji, keep your principles in check, you will get many more recordings. But after all, he was a Thackeray who would never accept defeat. He used to say, I will do a little work, but of my choice,' she added.[22]

Shrikant's younger sister Sanjeevani Karandikar said her brother Shrikant was 'loving and calm but could be moody at times as he kept thinking about music and was composing tunes in his mind'.[23]

Though political ambition would drive a wedge between Uddhav and Raj later, Shrikant had no inclination towards politics. 'Shrikant's most sterling quality was his ability to keep away from power. As the Shiv Sena's clout grew across Maharashtra, he refused to be drawn into the party's internecine politics. Party veterans say that the kid brother could have secured for himself a cushy position in the Sena without much effort. That Shrikant didn't do so is an eloquent testimony to his character,' mentioned a photo-biography of Bal Thackeray published by Raj in 2005.[24]

Shrikant stayed 'regally aloof' to the trappings of power even after the Shiv Sena came to power in Maharashtra in 1995, though loyal Shiv Sena workers often turned to him for moral support.[25]

'Balasaheb and Shrikantji were like Ram and Lakshman,' says an associate of the Thackeray clan, adding that Shrikant was a *manasvi* (intense) sort of person, who would not hesitate to speak his mind and call a spade a spade'.[26]

Dilip Thakur says that while people kept their distance from Shrikant, he liked traits like punctuality, speaking the truth, honesty and commitment. He also mentions that Shrikant's plain-speak made people misunderstand him.[27]

Despite the warmth between the two brothers and his distance from active politics, was Shrikant at the receiving end of politics within the Shiv Sena?

From 1960, when *Marmik* was launched to 1966, the Thackeray brothers worked in tandem.

However, after the Shiv Sena was launched, Shrikant shouldered *Marmik*'s responsibility. In 1985, this was abruptly taken away from him and *Marmik* was brought under the control of the party organization as it looked to expand across Maharashtra. A separate office for *Marmik* was started at Shiv Sena Bhawan in Dadar.[28]

Thakur wrote that Shrikant found it tough to digest this shock on *Marmik*'s twenty-fifth anniversary and tried to suppress his feelings behind a pair of sunglasses during the function at Mumbai's Shanmukhananda Hall. Shrikant took some time to overcome this setback. He added that Shrikant's intense personality manifested itself as Thakur heard his frank opinions about the Sena's internal politics for the first time.

Uncles and nephews

Bal Thackeray had tremendous affection for Raj. Though Raj was a student of Balmohan Vidyamandir at Dadar, which is where his family lived, he often stayed with his uncle at Matoshree (the Thackeray family residence at Kalanagar in Bandra East). During school days, Raj would travel from Bandra to attend classes where his mother would send him lunch in the afternoon. He would go home to Dadar on the weekends.[29]

Raj gradually imbibed his uncle's mannerisms. These traits would gradually manifest themselves as he joined politics. Conversely, Uddhav was close to Shrikant and would spend time with him.

In his autobiography, Shrikant revealed that Uddhav was critically ill when he was a year old, with his parents giving up hope of his survival. A shattered Bal Thackeray even broke the *devhara* (wooden structure housing idols and photos of deities) in their home. However, Shrikant took Uddhav to the hospital and nursed him. Thereafter, they became close. They also shared a common hobby—photography.[30]

Shrikant had special affection for Uddhav even later in his life and would cherish gifts given by him on his birthday like musical instruments or books about films.[31]

Before Bal Thackeray and his family shifted to 'Matoshree' in September 1966 and Shrikant and his family to 'Krishnakunj' around 2000, the extended Thackeray clan stayed under the same roof at their modest ground-floor apartment in Kadam Mansion (it was also called Joshi building).

In 1969, Bal Thackeray was incarcerated at the colonial-era Yerwada Jail for around three months with aides Manohar Joshi and Dattaji Salvi after riots broke out in Mumbai over the boundary dispute with Karnataka.

Raj, who was a few months old then, was close to his uncle. On 9 April, Shrikant, accompanied by their families, visited his brother at prison. 'I picked up *Fatya* [a nickname for Shrikant's son], but he had forgotten me. *Fatya*, who used to jump on me . . . and go berserk once he heard my voice, was turning away. I felt bad. But he will attain that level of affection again,' Thackeray wrote in his journal.[32]

At home, Prabodhankar, the pater familias, ensured strict discipline. The grandchildren had to return home before dark and say their evening prayers, followed by an *arati* (worship ritual).[33]

The children completed their schooling in the nearby Balmohan Vidyamandir.

Uddhav was an obedient child who rarely bothered his parents. He always woke up on his own for school. Speaking to senior journalist and editor Dnyanesh Maharao, Shrikant recalled how Uddhav only expected a cup of tea to be served by his mother, who woke up after he called out to her. Sometimes, when she did not wake up, Uddhav would leave for school without his morning tea. 'I have never seen him shake his mother to wake up and prepare tea. He is not only calm but very understanding. Rarely do we come across the youngest child of a family who is so understanding,' added Shrikant.[34]

As the Sena supremo's children, Uddhav said that they did not get any special treatment at school. As a father, Bal would dote on his children, never slapping them even for those dreaded red marks on their report cards.[35] Speaking to compère Sudhir Gadgil before the launch of the biopic *Thackeray*, Uddhav said the easiest way to skip school was to cling to his father, who would then tell their mother: '*Udya baghu!* (Let it be, we will send him to school tomorrow!)'[36]

Bal Thackeray's eldest son, Binda, who held a diploma in printing technology, ventured into the film industry and the restaurant business. He started the Drums Beat restaurant at Tardeo and a hotel at Kandivali. He also produced music cassettes under the 'Bindatone' banner and launched a production unit called 'Samudra video'. He cut an album by Nadeem-Shravan and produced *Agnisakshi* starring Nana Patekar and Manisha Koirala. Binda, who lived separately from the Thackeray family at Bandra, passed away in a car accident at Lonavala on 20 April 1996, months after his mother's sudden demise.[37]

Jaidev was later estranged from his father and family and had challenged his will in the Bombay High Court before finally withdrawing the suit.[38]

Raj was a mischievous child, given to mimicking people, tomfoolery and pranks, which led his grandfather to lovingly call him 'Bhampadya' (buffoon). His uncle called him 'Tinu' in his childhood and often illustrated his feats in the cartoon column 'Jatra' in *Marmik*.[39]

'While Uddhav was shy, Raj, was streetwise, flamboyant and like quicksilver even in his childhood,' said a long-time Dadar resident, who has seen the cousins from close quarters. He claimed that a young Raj would often be seen trying to impress girls in the first flush of his youth.[40] Another Dadar resident recalled Raj playing gully cricket as a youngster.

Kirti Pathak, Uddhav and Raj's paternal cousin (Sanjeevani Karandikar's daughter), recalled how there would scarcely be a day when Raj would not play pranks or practical jokes in his childhood. A taxi driver who would park his vehicle near their Dadar residence, and have a snooze, once had the scare of his life when Raj lit a cracker near his head during Diwali, recalled Pathak.[41]

'Raj was two years younger than me and we did a lot of *masti* together. Raj was very mischievous, and his mother would get complaints against him almost daily. He was the apple of everyone's eye as the youngest in the family. His childhood ability to mimic people manifests itself in political rallies even today,' said Pathak. He would also eat green chillies and relish the green chilly pickle made by Sanjeevani Karandikar.[42]

In contrast, Uddhav, or 'Dingudada' as Pathak and her sister Swati called him, was the typical 'good boy'. Pathak says her mother Sanjeevani had nicknamed him 'Shravanbal' (an ideal son, called so after the character of Shravan in the Ramayana who serves his aged parents). Uddhav would eat with his left hand, and Pathak would often try and ape this mannerism.[43] Sanjeevani recalled Uddhav as 'a child with a different temperament', who would not be involved in any mischief unlike children of his age.[44]

Uddhav, who was shy around girls, would never lose his temper or demand anything from his parents. 'He was very quiet since childhood. This may sound like an exaggeration, but he never shouted at anyone or lost his temper. He has tremendous control over his emotions, which may have helped him as a wildlife photographer,' said Kirti Pathak, adding that Uddhav would also not like sounds of crackers being burst.[45]

Shrikant Sarmalkar, who was part of Bal Thackeray's informal security detail, said while Uddhav would stay out of trouble, Raj got into fights in his childhood. 'Once, when he was staying at Matoshree, Raj went to the nearby MIG colony and fought with some boys after someone pushed him when he was eating pani puri. He asked for my help but said I must not tell Pilga [Bal Thackeray] about his exploits,' said Sarmalkar, who later became a Shiv Sena MLA.[46]

However, two of Raj's schoolmates said he was a shy child in school.[47] 'In school, both Uddhav and Raj were shy students. Raj may be a crowd-pulling orator today, but I doubt if he took part in any elocution competitions in school or even spoke in the class,' said one of their schoolmates, adding that the cousins had taken great efforts to evolve as politicians later in their lives.

Chhagan Bhujbal, who was then a senior Shiv Sena leader, remembers how he indulged Uddhav and Raj in their childhood. 'Uddhav was calm. Raj was naughty and would keep running around,' he said. Bhujbal recalled how he had to install a grill over his well at Nashik because Raj would peep into it during visits to the farm.[48]

Raj imbibed his father and uncle's love for cartooning and the arts, and was gradually influenced by European painters, with a special love for works in pastels and soft shades. Though his father and elder cousin Uddhav were photographers, Raj did not take to the camera, preferring the palette instead.[49] Raj's father tried to bring him into the world of music by making him learn the tabla and later the guitar, albeit unsuccessfully. His heart clearly lay in cartooning.[50]

Raj, a cricket aficionado and an 'expert at underarm bowling' in street cricket, was sent to cricket coach Anna Vaidya to learn the game. Once, during net practice, a full toss hit him so hard that his leg was swollen. Bal Thackeray then said, 'It's fine that the ball hit your leg. What if it had hurt your hand? My dear, don't you want to become an artist? Please don't land yourself in a situation where you will neither be a cricketer nor an artist!' Raj gave up cricket as a result.[51]

Bal tried to get Uddhav into cartooning, but failed, although he drew cartoons for *Marmik* from 1979 to 1980.[52] But he had an eager disciple in Raj.

Bal would often sketch and ask his nephew to do the artwork or draw a rough sketch and ask him to do the final one. Bal would also ask Raj to copy David Low's cartoons before he started working independently. Raj, who dreamt of getting into J.J. School of Art since standard seven, had his first cartoon published in *Marmik* when he was in standard ten.[53] Though his father was also a cartoonist, Raj would attribute the influence on his brush strokes to his uncle. 'He would watch me draw, guide me, and if necessary, pull my ears. Balasaheb was an immaculate teacher. After my cartoons were published, he would always call me for feedback. He inculcated in me the culture that one should not draw cartoons on other's physical disabilities,' said Raj. He also noted that his uncle was a better cartoonist compared to the legendary R.K. Laxman due to the finesse of his lines.[54]

'A cartoonist needs a *halkat* [naughty] nazar,' the Shiv Sena chief would say. His nephew had imbibed his uncle's love for the lines, lampoonery and keen sense of observation, which helped him notice, sketch and accentuate physical characteristics of people, a must for any caricaturist. Raj used to draw cartoons in

Marmik and freelanced for *Loksatta*, the Marathi morninger from the Indian Express Group, for two years between 1986 to 1988.

After Raj's estrangement from the Shiv Sena, his uncle, while speaking to senior journalist Nikhil Wagle noted that 'if Raj did not get into this [politics], he would have become a good cartoonist'. He added that Uddhav had a good hand for cartooning though he later turned to photography.[55]

After passing out of school in 1983, Raj, who described himself as a 'below-average' school student, secured admission to J.J. Institute for the applied arts course. 'Then, there were times when he would mark his attendance and then go to watch a movie or come to Ruparel College at Dadar to meet friends,' noted an old-time associate.[56]

Raj would also spend time with friends at the *katta* (informal gathering place) outside Kirti College at Dadar. A journalist from the vernacular media, who was then a Bharatiya Vidyarthi Sena (BVS)—the student wing of the Shiv Sena—worker, recalled Raj as being '*dhamaal* company' (fun to be with), due to his ability to mimic people and hold a conversation.[57]

Kirti Pathak, who also studied at Ruparel College, which was Raj's stomping ground, said both Uddhav and Raj used to go to college by either bus or train and never put on any airs. Raj's typical attire would also consist of jeans, a khadi kurta and shabnam bag.[58]

'I still remember Raj, with his hairstyle modelled around Amitabh Bachchan, wearing a T-shirt and bell-bottom trousers. He used to hang out with his friend Jay Kowli [who is now the Secretary General of the Boxing Federation of India] and play cricket. Kowli was Raj and Uddhav's mutual friend. Uddhav, on the other hand, was very low-profile and would keep his identity as the Sena supremo's son under wraps. He could be seen at a *vada pav* stall near Prabhadevi with his friends, was very shy and not very eager to keep company with a larger circle,' recalled a senior journalist, who was then associated with the BVS.[59]

It was in Ruparel and through a common circle including Shirish Parkar (who later became one of the nine general secretaries of the MNS after its launch) that Raj met Sharmila, daughter of Marathi theatre personality, Mohan Wagh, whom he later married in 1990. In 1988, Uddhav tied the knot with Rashmi Patankar of Dombivli. Jaywanti, who was Rashmi's friend, had suggested her as a prospective bride for 'Dadu'.[60] The marriage was solemnized at Dadar's Raja Shivaji School.

A family friend of the Patankars said before the marriage, Uddhav used to travel to Dombivli (located in the extended suburbs of Mumbai) by suburban railway to meet Rashmi.[61]

Both Jaywanti and later Raj were married at the Vanita Samaj Hall at Dadar. Though Raj attacked superstar Amitabh Bachchan later as part of his nativist politics, he was a fan since childhood. Amitabh also attended his wedding reception.[62]

'Many celebrities attended Raj and Sharmila's wedding. When invitees came to know that Amitabh Bachchan was scheduled to arrive with his family, our relatives and friends waited for him. There was a huge crowd in the hall and people were unwilling to disperse. An irritated Raj said that while it was his marriage, people were waiting for Amitabh,' said Kirti Pathak.[63]

Raj dropped out of college in the fourth year and launched an advertising agency, Chanakya, with friend and college-mate Anand, son of Congress leader Nanabhau Embadwar, along with Shashank Tanksal from Dhule and Vijay Raut from Amravati. The agency's office was located in Shiv Sena Bhawan.[64]

Anand Embadwar said Raj dropped out in the fourth year of the five-year degree course as he felt there was nothing substantial for him to learn there. 'His interest lay in cartooning, which was not taught in the institute. His guru in cartooning was Balasaheb Thackeray. Raj saheb would draw cartoons of the dean and teachers in the bathroom and on other walls. Once, one of our professors praised him for his art but added that the place where he was drawing it was wrong as these cartoons needed to be on paper rather than the walls,' he explained.[65]

Embadwar said Chanakya was Raj's brainchild.

'We used to work on campaigns for companies like Rashtriya Chemicals and Fertilizers (RCF) and also took subcontracts from advertising agencies. There was a demand for Raj saheb's caricatures from abroad,' said Embadwar, who is an MNS office-bearer. Chanakya was run for around three years since 1987, before Raj's political priorities took precedence.[66]

Later, some of Raj's friends, including Embadwar and Raut, launched Vishwa Animation, to get into the animation industry and Raj was involved in an advisory role.[67]

Youth politics

In 1988, the age for voting was reduced from twenty-one to eighteen years, leading to more youngsters joining the Shiv Sena, whose chief was acquiring a halo as a hard-line Hindu leader.

At the time, student politics in Maharashtra often took a violent turn. Though many current leaders in Maharashtra are products of this varsity politics, this was a time when parties would often bribe, threaten or even kidnap students to secure their support in elections to colleges, the university student council or senate.

In 1989, Owen D'Souza, a National Students Union of India (NSUI) worker, and first-year student of law at the Jitendra Chauhan College of Law at Mithibai College campus in Vile Parle, was on the way to file his nomination when he was killed outside the college. He was stabbed sixty-four times and his fingers were chopped off. The perpetrators were never brought to justice. This led the state government to proscribe campus elections in 1994. The ban was formally lifted in 2018.[68]

Raj, who had friends within the BVS, would accompany them during campaigning from 1985 onwards. BVS old-timers recall how Raj had managed to strike a chord with students in Pune during the varsity polls campaign as a common worker and not as 'Balasaheb's nephew'.[69]

Embadwar added that before becoming the BVS president, Raj had visited Amravati to scout for some business opportunities when the local university elections were under way. 'He met students across party lines, and the BVS, which was poorly placed, won the elections for the first time,' he said.[70]

Moreover, during his days at J.J., Raj had made his presence felt. Though the institute had a substantial Maharashtrian numbers, the prevailing culture was elitist and these students felt overawed. 'This was broken by Raj saheb, who ensured that some lectures were also conducted in Marathi. Marathi students gradually edged out others in college politics,' explained Embadwar.[71]

The BVS did not figure very prominently in the Shiv Sena's pecking order. Senior leaders of the student wing thought that appointing Raj as the BVS president might help attract the youth on the strength of the Thackeray surname and also ensure the front got its due within the organization.

A senior Shiv Sena leader who cut his teeth in the BVS recalls, 'In 1988, we were competing with the Congress party's NSUI and Sanjay Chitre was the BVS president. Since we worked on shoestring budgets, we had to go to Balasaheb for funds and Sanjay used to coordinate this. Raj and Rajan Shirodkar [close friend and business associate later] were in our group. We thought that if Raj became the BVS chief, it would ensure better coordination and access to Balasaheb. Eventually, Rajan Shirodkar, Shirish Parkar, Dilip Karande and others met Balasaheb and urged that Raj be given a formal role.'[72]

There was another reason for this. Bal Thackeray had two huge Great Danes who were let loose at Matoshree. The BVS leaders were scared of these canines and would try to shift the responsibility of approaching their party chief![73]

Raj, now twenty, who had his first brush with politics when he accompanied his uncle to rallies as a child, was anointed as BVS chief in 1988.

Another BVS veteran said they had initially planned to appoint Raj as the general secretary of the wing, but the proposal may have been shot down by his uncle. 'How was a Thackeray supposed to play second fiddle to anyone else? Raj was appointed as BVS chief and Sanjay Chitre was accommodated as a *pramukh sanghatak* [chief organizer],' he added.[74]

At the time, Raj was far from the fiery orator that he would later become and would be overwhelmed by stage fright. 'For around two years, he would feign stomach ache or other ailments to keep away from the mike, which was natural considering his age,' his friend said, adding that even so, there was an aura around his surname.[75]

In 1990, Raj finally spoke in public on the issue of educational institutions hiking fees after a morcha from Azad Maidan to Mantralaya. His uncle later patted him on the back for his maiden speech and gave him suggestions to improve his oration.[76]

In the 1980s, Dilip Hate, or 'Bhai' as he was called, a former BVS hand and an accused in the murder of CPI MLA Krishna Desai, quit the students body to form his own All India Students Organization (AISO). The new front was gradually emerging as a challenger to the BVS in colleges in and around Dadar and was often aided by the NSUI when it came to taking on the Sena's boys. Raj's appointment as the BVS president helped the organization re-establish itself.[77]

Journalist Kapil Patil, who is now a member of the Maharashtra legislative council (MLC), remembers how Raj, Unmesh Joshi (senior Shiv Sena leader Manohar Joshi's son), and Shirodkar used to visit him in the offices of *Sakal* and *Navshakti* and talk about what they were doing.

'However, Raj could not capture the prestigious University of Mumbai student council. I was working for Chhatra Bharati [the Socialist students union], which got two or three seats. We used to align with the NSUI on ideological grounds after the elections,' said Patil, adding that Raj however worked hard to take BVS to the youth across Maharashtra.[78]

Raj, while admitting to a similarity between their voices, denied he was imitating his uncle. While speaking to senior journalist Dnyanesh Maharao, he recalled how Meenatai once mistook her nephew's voice on the intercom as that of her husband![79] 'Raj grew up with saheb (Bal Thackeray) and *vahini* (sister-in-law/Meenatai). Hence, it was natural that he would pick up Balasaheb's mannerisms. It is wrong to say he copied these traits,' said Pandharinath Sawant, the Thackeray family associate.[80]

Though it is believed that Uddhav entered politics much later than Raj, Shiv Sena and MNS insiders said he began working behind the scenes at almost the same time as his younger cousin but took a more active role post-1995.

On 11 April 1990, Uddhav attended his first public function at the Shiv Sena shakha in Mumbai's eastern suburb of Mulund which was organized by Shishir Shinde, who later became a Sena MLC. Uddhav inaugurated water taps in slums as his formal initiation into politics.[81]

After the launch of the Shiv Sena mouthpiece *Saamna* in 1989, Shinde, who was nominated for the BMC elections in 1992, at Uddhav's behest, said that Uddhav and Raj would sit in its Prabhadevi office. 'Uddhavji started working in the party administration in 1990. He also played a major role with Subhash Desai in *Saamna*'s launch,' said Shinde, who was then close to Uddhav, even bringing his wedding suit from a tailor at Dadar.[82]

Uddhav gradually started helping his father run the party.

In the early 1990s, Uddhav was seen as being low-profile and not given to political machinations. 'He was quiet and soft-spoken, but had a good sense of humour, which would make people notice him,' said a senior journalist, who has covered the Shiv Sena for over three decades and is close to the Thackeray family.[83]

In 1991, Shinde shot into public attention after he and a group of Sainiks broke into Wankhede Stadium in Mumbai and vandalized the pitch to prevent an India–Pakistan cricket match from being played there. The Shiv Sena is opposed to the Pakistani cricket team playing on Indian soil due to the country's role in fostering terror activities. 'Before going to Wankhede, I called up Uddhavji and told him about my plan. He gave me the green signal but asked me to be careful,' said Shinde, who was then considered Bal Thackeray's blue-eyed boy.[84]

In December 1993, Raj organized a morcha of the unemployed before the Maharashtra legislature building during its winter session in the state's second capital at Nagpur. Sudhakarrao Naik was the chief minister. A then close associate and personal friend of Raj Thackeray claimed it was the rousing response of the youth to this campaign that may have sparked off the competition and internecine war between the two cousins.[85]

'Raj toured Maharashtra extensively to generate support for the morcha. Senior journalist, the late Narayan Athavale [elected as a Shiv Sena Lok Sabha MP in 1996] wrote his *nivedan* [memorandum]. It was evident that the Nagpur morcha would be huge. A night before the morcha, Raj got a call from Matoshree asking him to ensure that Uddhav too got to speak at the public meeting. Raj, who was staying in Hotel Centre Point, was disturbed as he felt Uddhav wanted a share of his credit,' the former associate said.[86]

The next day, when Uddhav was sitting on a makeshift dais on a truck, Manohar Joshi (who became the Shiv Sena's first chief minister of Maharashtra) announced that Uddhav would make a speech. Raj addressed the around 50,000-strong morcha and was accompanied by Shiv Sena leaders as he met Chief Minister Sudhakarrao Naik to present a memorandum. However, Uddhav, who had made his first public speech, claimed this was spontaneous.[87]

'Even then, Raj was the more dashing of the two and this manifested itself in events like the 1990 attack on the Akhil Bharatiya Vidyarthi Parishad (ABVP) office at Matunga due to rivalry in student politics. In contrast, Uddhav was mild and lurked in the shadows,' said a journalist who had observed the rise of the Thackeray cousins.[88]

Cracks surface

As was evident, Raj's rise within the Sena was not without heartburn, especially among the old guard. Like most transitions, this would lead to some shake-up within the party.

Insiders claim that Raj, who was aggressive, and even brash, would often overrule party veterans who had seen him since his childhood.

Raj would often sit at a popular Chinese restaurant at Shivaji Park with his friends and political associates. 'Uddhav's group felt that instead of this top-down approach the organization should be built ground-up and the monopoly of some leaders needed to be challenged. This is also where sparks flew,' said the BVS worker-turned journalist quoted earlier.[89]

'Raj was blunt. The party's old guard was uneasy at his rising political graph. They gradually started pitching Uddhav as a counterweight. Though Uddhav formally entered politics later with his career trajectory picking up post-1996, the seeds for his launch were sown during this period. However, there was consternation at the rise of the cousins as the Shiv Sena was attacking the Congress for perpetuating a cult of dynasty,' said an associate of Raj Thackeray since his BVS days.[90] The veteran Shiv Sena beat reporter and Thackeray family associate recalled that after Raj and later Uddhav became active in the Shiv Sena, some senior leaders had voiced their apprehensions in a party meeting, only to be blasted by the Sena supremo.[91]

While the Shiv Sena leadership, which had been associated with the party since its launch, was greying, Raj attracted young blood. These two generations had their distinct way of doing things and hence, friction was obvious, especially in a party like the Shiv Sena where the rank and file are known for aggression. Some in the Shiv Sena's old guard also felt Raj's rise would lead to a decline in their stature.[92]

In 1990, Shishir Shinde, then a Sena *vibhag pramukh* (division chief with an area covering one Lok Sabha constituency in Mumbai), had urged Bal Thackeray that Uddhav be nominated for the state assembly from Mulund instead of the BJP's Wamanrao Parab. Similar demands were made by Shiv Sainiks from Parel by Bal Thackeray's own admission.[93] Shinde later identified himself as a Raj loyalist and was elected to the state legislative assembly as an MNS MLA in 2009. After falling out with Raj in 2017, Shinde returned to the Shiv Sena the following year.

Asked about who would inherit his legacy, Thackeray in an interview in 1992 said that 'there was no urgency to do so as it was not decided when he [Thackeray] would die'.[94] Speaking to Maharao, Thackeray dismissed speculation in the media about a succession battle between his son and nephew.[95]

While denying he had 'imposed' them on the Shiv Sena, Thackeray said 'Dadu' and 'Raja's' organizational work had lessened his load.[96]

It was one of Thackeray's associates, Madhav Deshpande, who gave vent to this simmering discontent.

In March 1984, the Congress government had managed to push through a bill that gave it the right to supersede elected representatives in the cash-rich BMC and appoint an administrator, then municipal commissioner, D.M. Sukhtankar.

The civic body came under the administrator's control from 1 April 1984, breaking a 107-year-old tradition. In the legislature, the bill was opposed by politicians across party lines like Hashu Advani (BJP), F.M. Pinto (Janata Dal) and Manohar Joshi of the Shiv Sena. Despite tumultuous scenes, it was pushed through. The BMC general body too saw uproar.[97]

In 1985, the Shiv Sena, which was smarting after its electoral reverses during and after the Emergency, when it supported Indira Gandhi, received a shot in the arm. Maharashtra chief minister Vasantdada Patil had a running battle with Bombay Pradesh Congress Committee (BPCC) strongman Murli Deora. After Sena veteran Pramod Navalkar made an allegation in the Maharashtra legislative council about the Centre's alleged plan to bring Mumbai under Central rule by severing it from Maharashtra, Patil gave the Shiv Sena a political opportunity that would ensure it seized power in the civic body. 'There is a chance that some are planning to carve Mumbai out of Maharashtra . . . But, if such attempts are made, we must stay alert and oppose it,' he said.[98] Vaibhav Purandare mentions how extensive reports appeared in the regional and national newspapers about the Central government's 'plan' to make Mumbai centrally administered. One of the reasons for this was its importance as India's richest city.[99] Patil's statement set the cat among the pigeons. Veteran socialist leader and a stalwart of the Samyukta Maharashtra movement, S.M. Joshi, said since the chief minister himself had made such a statement 'some such plan could really be afoot'.[100] It was obvious that the chief minister's statement had sent ripples among Marathi speakers in Mumbai, who feared being marginalized, and the Shiv Sena was quick to latch on to them.

Launching the Shiv Sena's election campaign for the April 1985 BMC elections at Nehru Nagar in Kurla, Bal Thackeray lashed out at 'plans' to break Mumbai—the jewel in Maharashtra's crown—from the state. 'Mumbai belongs to Maharashtrians . . . The Shiv Sena will teach a lesson to those conspiring to break Mumbai from Maharashtra,' he thundered.[101]

The issue dominated media space. Socialist veteran Madhu Dandavate warned that moves to alienate Mumbai from Maharashtra would be met with mass protests. Unlike other parties which also accommodated non-Marathis as candidates, the Shiv Sena, which fought the elections alone, after attempts at an alliance with the Opposition Progressive Democratic Front fell through, fielded only Maharashtrians.[102]

Uddhav, who had completed his bachelor's in applied arts from J.J. Institute and started an advertising agency with two friends called Chaurang, joined the Shiv Sena's BMC poll campaign. Artist Ravi Paranjape's illustrations were also used in the campaign.[103] When the results of the BMC elections were declared, it was clear that the beneficiary of this linguistic polarization was the Shiv Sena, which swept seventy-four of the 170 seats, with the Congress (I) at a distant thirty-seven, followed by the BJP (thirteen) and Janata Dal (ten). A newspaper even credited Patil for the Sena's success! Speaking in a victory rally, a jubilant Thackeray said no one would dare to break Mumbai from Maharashtra. He promised to devise a way to stop the influx of outsiders to Mumbai.[104]

After the 1985 BMC polls, the Shiv Sena's Chhagan Bhujbal was elected the fifth mayor of Mumbai.

There is an interesting postscript to the Shiv Sena victory in the civic body and then chief minister Vasantdada Patil's role in it.

G.R. Khairnar, the BMC official, who later earned the moniker of Mumbai's 'Demolition Man', by taking on the underworld and destroying their illegal constructions, had angered Vasantdada Patil by demolishing unauthorized parts of a hotel owned by his stepson Chandrakant in Mumbai in May 1985.

Khairnar said he was summoned to Bal Thackeray's residence. Thackeray told Khairnar that he had been called by Patil to his official bungalow the previous day and asked to teach Khairnar 'a lesson'.

'I told Balasaheb this was a criminal offence. But Balasaheb told me that he had to sustain the Shiv Sena and needed Patil's help for it,' said Khairnar, who had run-ins with Thackeray and the Shiv Sena later.[105]

The Sena marches on

By 1991, much water had flowed under the bridge.

Bhujbal, who belonged to the agrarian and other backward classes (OBC) Mali community, was uneasy at being sidelined in favour of Manohar Joshi, a Brahmin. In the run up to the 1990 state assembly elections, Bhujbal, who had retained his rustic touch despite spending his formative years in Mumbai, had led the Shiv Sena's charge in rural Maharashtra.

After the Shiv Sena wrested control of the BMC, it held a statewide conclave at Mahad in Raigad where it resolved to expand across Maharashtra. Bhujbal's vociferous, aggressive speeches delivered in a theatrical style played a role in this.

Bhujbal's parents had come to Mumbai from Nashik and set up a wholesale vegetable business at Byculla market. Orphaned at the age of five, the 1947-born Bhujbal grew up in Mazgaon, studying in the municipal school near Padamsee Wadi and managing the vegetable business.[106] A diploma holder in engineering, Bhujbal was attracted to the Shiv Sena and took charge of its shakha in the Mazgaon area, contesting and losing the 1968 BMC polls. He was later elected to the BMC in 1973.

Veteran journalists who covered the Maharashtra legislative assembly recall how the firebrand Bhujbal, the lone Shiv Sena legislator in the house between 1985 and 1990, would leave his mark. By taking an aggressive stance in the house and on the streets on issues like Hindu–Muslim conflagrations and Maharashtra's border disputes with Karnataka, Bhujbal was aligned with the Shiv Sena's changing profile to a hard-line, pro-Hindutva party.

Even today, the pride on Bhujbal's face is palpable as he recalls how he and actor Dada Kondke, known for his bawdy films with double entendre dialogues and songs, were responsible for taking the Shiv Sena to the rural masses post-1985. 'There were times when Shiv Sena leaders from Mumbai would visit rural areas and claim that Bhujbal and Kondke would address rallies even when we were not present, just to ensure crowds turned up,' he said.[107]

Incidentally, while the MNS would later raise the issue of theatres not screening Marathi films, it was similar 'direct action' that led to Kondke coming close to the Shiv Sena. Kondke's movie, *Songadya*, was released in 1970, and despite its success, the management of a cinema hall in Mumbai took it down to screen the Hindi movie *Tere Mere Sapne*. Kondke approached Bal Thackeray who ensured 'Sena style' action was taken. *Songadya* was back on the screens. This led to Kondke becoming good friends with the Thackerays.[108]

In 1990, the Shiv Sena, riding on the back of its alliance with the BJP and with a large section of Sharad Pawar's cadre and second-rung leadership from his Congress (S) migrating to it after he decided to merge his party with the Congress, secured a huge political opening in the Maharashtra assembly. It put up a stellar show, notching up fifty-two seats, followed by the BJP at forty-two in the 288-member house. Though the Congress held on to power, this election, according to political scientist Suhas Palshikar, marked the decline of the party in Maharashtra, a state which was known for its traditional dominance.[109]

Shiv Sena insiders recall how Raj and Uddhav played a role in the campaign, with Uddhav mostly staying behind the curtains. The Shiv Sena's second-rung leadership was gradually being established. Apart from Raj and Uddhav, leaders like Narayan Rane, the late Vitthal Chavan, Gajanan Kirtikar and others rose within the ranks in this period.[110]

With Jayant Jadhav, whom Bal Thackeray considered as his son (and who was killed in 1996, allegedly by members of the Arun Gawli gang), Uddhav worked on an audio-visual campaign, which was shown in villages using 'videoraths'.[111]

It was but natural that Bhujbal would have considered himself a natural claimant for the post of leader of Opposition. However, Thackeray threw his weight behind Joshi, who had registered his first victory in the state assembly from Dadar. Later, Thackeray would recall that Bhujbal had arranged for *gulal* (coloured powder used during celebrations) and firecrackers anticipating his own appointment, only to be disappointed after losing to Joshi.[112]

A defection and a crisis

Gradually, the Bhujbal–Thackeray rift was growing. After then prime minister V.P. Singh announced the implementation of the Mandal Commission report that provided quotas to OBCs, Thackeray opposed the move, which was ironic as the OBCs form a bedrock of the party's support base. However, Bhujbal had beaten Thackeray to it by supporting Singh's decision, only to be chastised by his boss.[113]

Singh, who had toured Maharashtra in the period, invited Bhujbal to join his Janata Dal. Bhujbal also skipped a joint rally called by the Shiv Sena and BJP to welcome the Somnath–Ayodhya rath yatra when it reached Mumbai. In March 1991, Bhujbal, whose patience seemed to be running out, accused Joshi of having failed as an Opposition leader and sought his replacement. Thackeray summoned the warring duo for a reconciliation.[114]

These tensions came to a head during the winter session of the state legislative assembly at Nagpur in December 1991. Bhujbal dropped a bombshell by defecting to the Congress with his seventeen MLAs (some of whom returned to the Shiv Sena later). Bhujbal, an MLA from Mazgaon in Mumbai, was appointed as revenue minister. There was another whammy in store for the Shiv Sena—its ally, the BJP, snatched the leader of Opposition post from Joshi for Gopinath Munde.

'The iron entered my soul when I was denied the position of the leader of the Opposition. To mollify me, I was made mayor again, but by then I had understood that I had a place as long as I stuck to what was handed out to me; I should not think of wanting a post which would be above my standing. It is funny how God teaches you a lesson, I had entered the fray to fight against a class barrier, I was excluded on grounds of caste,' said Bhujbal.[115]

Those were the days when the Shiv Sena lived up to its name and acted like an aggressive private militia. The surprise defection led to incensed Shiv Sainiks taking to the streets against Bhujbal who had to move under police escort. Boards denouncing Bhujbal were put up outside Shiv Sena shakhas. Former Mumbai mayor and veteran Shiv Sainik, Mahadeo Deole, once recalled how they would storm the venues of Bhujbal's rallies and public engagements to disrupt them.[116]

Vageesh Saraswat, then a journalist working with the Hindi daily *Dopahar* on the political beat, remembers how Raj's cartoons depicting Bhujbal as 'Lakhoba Lokhande', the protagonist-cum-confidence trickster in Acharya Atre's famous play, *To Mee Nhavech*, (I am not him), were put up as posters across the city.[117]

In the 1992 BMC elections, the Shiv Sena kept its alliance with the BJP in 'abeyance'—the two parties had tied-up in 1989 after an unsuccessful attempt in the 1984 Lok Sabha polls—and decided to contest 200 of 222 seats on its own. It also dropped thirty sitting corporators, of which some had established contacts with Bhujbal.[118]

However, the Congress (I) trumped the Shiv Sena by winning 112 seats as compared to the latter's seventy. The BJP won thirteen seats. Chandrakant Handore of the Congress was elected Mumbai's mayor.[119]

After the Shiv Sena was trounced in the 1992 BMC polls, Shiv Sena functionary Madhav Deshpande, who Purandare noted was the party observer during the 1968 BMC elections, and by 1992 was a 'nobody',[120] held a press conference. In it, he alleged that Thackeray had held the Shiv Sena hostage to his personality and alleged that his pro-Hindutva stance smacked of opportunism. He also charged Uddhav and Raj with 'interfering' in the Shiv Sena's affairs and questioned their contribution to the organization. He claimed there was resentment in the Shiv Sena leadership over this.[121]

Deshpande, who had accused Thackeray of cutting leaders to size by pitting some against others, was planning to hold a public meeting of 'loyalist' Shiv Sainiks.[122]

Thackeray, who found his leadership under attack after an electoral debacle, used some shock treatment on the party faithful.

On 18 July 1992, *Saamna* which had Bal Thackeray as the editor, carried a cryptic two-line announcement on its front page: '*Akhercha Jai Maharashtra* (The Final Goodbye)'. It said: 'Balasaheb Thackeray, along with his family members, says a final Jai Maharashtra to the Shiv Sena.' This led to throngs of Shiv Sena leaders and Sainiks making a beeline for Matoshree where they were told that the party supremo was firm on his decision.[123] The next day, Thackeray wrote an editorial in the newspaper explaining his stance. While referring to his 'struggles' as the Shiv Sena completed twenty-seven years, Thackeray wrote: 'There are some dogs who are running amok. They have no idea about what we have suffered all these years. They are barking at this non-existent dynastic rule.'[124]

Without naming Deshpande, the editorial lashed out at the 'male buffalo'[125] from Ghatkopar. Questioning Deshpande's contribution to the party, Thackeray said the idea of anointing son or nephew as the party's whole-and-sole had never occurred to him. The Sena supremo claimed he put his foot down on Uddhav's nomination to the assembly from Mulund or Parel, and BVS office-bearers elected Raj as their chief despite his opposition. Attacking Raj and Uddhav was a pretext to target him. Thackeray then delivered the clincher: 'We are saying farewell . . . No one should try and meet me, my son or nephew about the Shiv Sena. We have chosen our own paths.' The editorial said the entire Thackeray family was leaving the Shiv Sena.[126]

In a public meeting on July 20 at Shiv Sena Bhawan at Dadar in pouring rain, Thackeray announced he was going back on his word after being 'persuaded' by hysterical Sainiks, some of whom had threatened to set themselves ablaze.[127] Shiv Sena leaders and elected representatives were heckled and not allowed on stage by the mob. Some leaders like Manohar Joshi were even roughed up.[128]

Like in 1978, when he announced his resignation at the Shivaji Park grounds after the setback in the BMC elections but withdrew it after being similarly 'requested' by frenzied Sainiks, Thackeray emerged stronger from the crisis. He also underlined something obvious—for most Sainiks, there was little distinction between him and the organization. Dissent, if any, would be countered with an iron fist. He would remain at the apex of the Shiv Sena's hierarchy, drawing his influence and power from his talismanic appeal over the party faithful.

Raj Thackeray noted that while Sharad Pawar and A.R. Antulay's nephews, Ajit and Mushtaque, had entered politics and become a minister and an MLC respectively, fingers were being raised at his political foray.[129]

Path to power

Bhujbal, with whom Raj later crossed swords, was obliquely responsible for his rise within the Shiv Sena.

'After Bhujbal's exit, the Shiv Sena had few central, Mumbai-based leaders capable of touring rural Maharashtra and striking a chord with voters. Leaders like Manohar Joshi, Sudhir Joshi and Pramod Navalkar were from the white-collared class and did not have Bhujbal's rousing oratory. It was here that Raj, with his mannerisms modelled on his uncle, came into the picture,' noted a journalist familiar with the Shiv Sena and Raj at the time.[130]

Uddhav too continued to work for the party in the shadows. Though he lacked his cousin's charisma, he held an undeniable hold over Shiv Sainiks as their party supremo's son.

In 1994, Uddhav played a pivotal role in organizing a party conclave at Nashik during the Kumbh Mela. Uddhav, Subhash Desai, Shishir Shinde and legislator Babanrao Gholap ensured that this was done in just thirteen days.[131]

Sanjay Nirupam, who was then editor of the Shiv Sena's newly launched Hindi eveninger *Dopahar ka Saamna*, and was gradually emerging as the party's poster boy for north Indians, recalled how journalists at the convention spoke in murmurs about the *vivad* (rift) between the cousins.[132]

Nirupam remembers how Uddhav used to be petrified of speaking at public meetings. 'I had organized rallies for him at locations like Andheri and Asalpha. He used to be wary of addressing the people or the media.'[133]

Shishir Shinde said he had asked for Uddhav to be fielded from Mulund in the 1995 polls. 'I said Uddhavji should come only to submit his nomination form and then collect his certificate as the victor. We will handle the rest.'[134]

In the 1995 campaign, Bal Thackeray addressed around 100 public meetings, while Raj attended over 150. Uddhav spoke at about eighty. The party cadre would ask for Raj wherever 'Balasaheb' could not go. 'There is another irony here—just as Bhujbal's exit was responsible for Raj's growth in the Sena—he had to quit it like Bhujbal himself after feeling boxed in and marginalized,' said the journalist quoted earlier.

While Raj was being pitched as Bal Thackeray's political successor, Uddhav was gradually working on himself. Those familiar with the elder Thackeray cousin noted that despite his underrated style, Uddhav was a persistent learner.

One of Raj's friends had an interesting anecdote to narrate. 'Around 1997, Raj felt like learning badminton and we would play at Dadar. May be because age was on our side, we picked up fast. Soon, Uddhav also joined us. Once, while playing, Uddhav fell down and we laughed. He did not say anything then, but stopped coming to play from the next day onwards. He however enrolled for classes at Bandra's MIG Club and soon attained a commendable mastery over the game,' he added.[135]

Former Shiv Sena MLA Bhaskar Jadhav said some in the party were rooting for Uddhav as they felt Raj and his coterie were too brash. 'For instance, at the Shiv Sena's convention in 2000 at Amravati, the ego projections of Raj and his men rubbed people, including senior leaders and elected representatives, the wrong way. On the contrary, Uddhav came across as calm and soft-spoken, and reminded us of Maasaheb (Meenatai), who was like a mother to us.'[136]

Jadhav rebelled after being denied the Sena nomination from his Chiplun assembly constituency in Ratnagiri district in 2004 in favour of Uddhav loyalist Prabhakar Shinde. He later joined the Nationalist Congress Party (NCP) and became a minister of state and the party's Maharashtra president.[137]

While Uddhav prepared an audio-visual campaign through video tapes like 'Ajinkya', Raj fine-tuned the party's campaign strategy including that for audio-visual media. The Shiv Sena's use of songs lampooning the Sharad Pawar–led Congress regime with songs like '*Baramati, Baramati kiti mothi tyanchi sheti* (The man from Baramati, i.e., Pawar, has huge landholdings)' turned out to be popular.[138] So did another one: '*PM tera CM diwana, Dawood ko dale daana*'—a take on allegations that Pawar was in cahoots with underworld don Dawood Ibrahim.[139]

'Raj came out with a "Shiv Sena Top 10" song compilation that became popular. These were remixes of old Hindi film songs with a take on the political scenario. Balasaheb wanted us to harness the audio-visual media's impact, and Uddhav led the ideation of a video called *Avhan aani Aavahan* (The challenge and the appeal) which explained the Shiv Sena's ideology and our plans for Maharashtra if we were elected,' said a member of the ideation team.[140]

The younger generation, which was the natural electoral catchment of the Shiv Sena, tried to locate Bal Thackeray in his nephew's persona.

In the assembly elections, Raj ensured that many of his loyalists, including Arjun Khotkar (a Shiv Sena minister in the Maharashtra government), were nominated by the party.

The Shiv Sena–BJP's charge paid off. The Shiv Sena managed to win seventy-three seats followed by the BJP's sixty-five, while the Congress could manage only eighty seats. The saffron alliance secured the support of independents, most of whom were Congressmen who contested sans the party symbol because of the infighting between factions led by Sharad Pawar and Sudhakarrao Naik and formed the first non-Congress government in Maharashtra.

Manohar Joshi was sworn in as chief minister before a crowd of lakhs in a public ceremony at Shivaji Park. This was the first government headed by parties which did not have their ideological moorings in the Congress.

'There were four factors responsible for the victory of the Shiv Sena and BJP in 1995. This included Balasaheb's image and persona, BJP leader Gopinath Munde's charges against Sharad

Pawar, 1992–93 communal riots in Mumbai and Raj's statewide tours and the BVS campaign,' said an MNS functionary associated with Raj since his BVS years.[141]

One of Raj's friends claimed his leader had 'helped Shiv Sainiks' during the 1992–93 Mumbai riots, especially in the conflagration that took place after the March 1993 bomb blasts but refused to elaborate further. 'Then, the circumstances were such that even a calm man like Uddhav was incensed. During a visit to Matoshree, I recall an angry Uddhav saying something had to be done,' he added.[142]

'Before the results, Uddhavji, Manohar and Sudhir Joshi and I myself toured Maharashtra to solicit the support of independent candidates, who we thought could be elected, and secure their commitments,' said Shishir Shinde. 'I stayed with Uddhavji in a room at Hotel Centre Point in Nagpur. We managed to bring independents like Anil Deshmukh and Harshavardhan Patil on board.'[143]

'After the Shiv Sena–BJP government came to power, both Uddhav and Raj acquired clout. They would sit in the *Saamna* office, where Uddhavji's cabin was sober yet impressive, while that of Raj saheb had interiors that jelled with his personality,' remembered Shinde.[144]

Kiran Wadhivkar, a secretary of the Shiv Sena, who quit the party with Narayan Rane in 2005, recalled that both Raj and Uddhav were frequent visitors to Shivalaya, the party office near the state secretariat at Nariman Point.[145]

Raj was gradually emerging as a power centre and influencing appointments within the party and government. But there was a section within the Shiv Sena that wanted his wings clipped. Sena ministers who wanted to be on his right side were quick to put up his photographs along with those of the party chief in their cabins. 'But they were asked by the powers that be to remove Raj's photos,' said one of Raj's former business partners.[146]

Raj's company, Matoshree Realtors (later rechristened as Matoshree Infrastructure Private Limited after being converted from a partnership firm to a private limited company[147] and headed by Rajan Shirodkar), forayed into the construction industry in 1991 as civil contractors for a large turnkey project.[148] After the Shiv Sena–BJP government came to power, the firm ventured into slum rehabilitation schemes, which were among the regime's most ambitious yet controversial projects.

'Matoshree started developing a scheme at Dadar. Dadar was seen as Manohar Joshi's area, and Joshi sir perhaps did not take too kindly to it. Gradually, there was an attempt from within the party, especially by the old guard which felt threatened at his rise, to ensure anything Raj did would acquire a hue of controversy,' noted one of Raj's associates.[149]

Another associate of Raj's, who has stayed with him through thick and thin, noted that Joshi seemed to be uncomfortable at Raj's growing influence.[150]

Uddhav's gradual rise within the party was meant to counter Raj's influence. However, in an interview to *Saamna*, Uddhav claimed that his decision to join politics was meant to 'only help his father', that he had no political ambition and was not eager to accept any responsibility within the party.[151]

A senior journalist recalls how a senior Shiv Sena leader, now a minister in the Devendra Fadnavis government, talked down to Raj. 'We were in the *Saamna* office at Prabhadevi with Raj when the leader entered. The Shiv Sena had launched a membership drive and Raj told him to visit Konkan to oversee its progress. The Sena leader was livid and questioned Raj's authority to give him orders.'[152]

The journalist, who has tracked Raj's career since his early days, claimed some Shiv Sena ministers had clear instructions—in no condition were they supposed to complete works sought by either Raj or his men unless they were given explicit orders by the party leadership.[153]

A former Shiv Sena leader denies this charge. 'Though Raj met Balasaheb frequently, Uddhav and Smita [the wife of Bal Thackeray's second son, Jaidev] had better access to Balasaheb as they stayed close to him, be it at Matoshree or at Dadar, where he shifted when Matoshree was being reconstructed during the Sena–BJP regime. While Smita would see that her instructions were relayed via Balasaheb, Uddhav would often tell ministers or Shiv Sena leaders in Balasaheb's presence about things he wanted done. This implied Balasaheb's concurrence.'[154]

Rising discontent

'During this period, Raj's disillusionment was becoming apparent. But he had little scope outside the party or within,' added the journalist. When Shiv Sena veteran, Dattaji Salvi, who led the Bharatiya Kamgar Sena (BKS)—the Shiv Sena's labour wing—was sidelined, there was a whisper campaign alleging that this had been done at Raj's behest. Salvi stepped down as BKS president in 1994 at the age of seventy-five and was replaced by Ramakant More.[155]

Launched in August 1968, BKS had played a major role in the Shiv Sena's attempt to undercut the influence of communists in Mumbai's labour movement, allegedly at the behest of the Congress. Even as the Sena fought pitched battles with the left for dominance of the textile and other unions in Mumbai, Bal Thackeray's proximity to Chief Minister Vasantrao Naik earned it the moniker 'Vasant Sena'. The Shiv Sena's critics alleged it broke strikes at the behest of industrialists, beginning with one in T. Maneklal & Company in 1969, after which it became a force to reckon with in the industrial world.[156]

Salvi, who was from the Konkan region, was a textile mill worker, and affiliated to the Congress party's Indian National Trade Union Congress (INTUC). He joined the Shiv Sena after hearing Bal Thackeray speak in 1966 at Amar Hind Mandal in Dadar. A Maratha with a booming voice to match his well-built body, Salvi was roped in by Thackeray to broad-base the Sena's leadership, which was dominated by upper castes like CKPs, Brahmins and Saraswats. Old-timers recall how Salvi's voice could be heard on the ground floor of the old Sena Bhawan when he spoke in his third-floor office.

Elected to the BMC as a Shiv Sena corporator in 1968 by defeating veteran activist-socialist Prakash Mohadikar from Dadar, Salvi led BKS and was called 'Commander' by the cadre for his aggressive and theatrical style of public speaking. Despite his association with the Shiv Sena, Salvi was also influenced by Marxist theoretician M.N. Roy.

Before and after the Shiv Sena came to power, there were attempts to sideline leaders like Salvi and Wamanrao Mahadik, who was elected as the first Shiv Sena MLA in 1970 from Parel. His supporters and journalists who have witnessed the period upfront claim that these developments were blamed on Raj by his detractors within the Shiv Sena.

In the 1996 Lok Sabha elections, Raj ensured that business magnate Parvez Damania was fielded by the Shiv Sena from the traditional Congress bastion of Ahmednagar. Damania lost by around 50,000 votes against Maruti Deoram (Dada Patil) Shelke of the Congress from the seat in the sugar belt of western Maharashtra. Nirupam said that Raj had managed to accommodate men of his choice in the Sena's list of candidates.

Gradually, discontent regarding Raj's 'high-handedness' was growing even as Uddhav's popularity was on the rise. The duo was part of the Shiv Sena's delegation that discussed seat sharing with the BJP for the 1996 Lok Sabha polls along with Chief Minister Joshi and senior leader Subhash Desai.

In 1996, Congress leader Suresh Kalmadi resigned his Rajya Sabha seat after being elected to the Lok Sabha from Pune. The

Shiv Sena, being the senior partner in the ruling saffron alliance, staked claim to it. Within the Sena, there were two claimants, said Nirupam—Parvez Damania, who was being propped up by Raj and Kanhaiyalal Gidwani, who was Chief Minister Joshi's choice. However, Uddhav pushed for Bihar-born Nirupam to be elected to the Upper House of Parliament and prevailed.[157]

A March 1996 profile by *Outlook* described Raj as 'the man who could be the next Bal Thackeray' and added that the cadre saw the 'abrasive' Raj, then twenty-eight, as 'the Sena supremo's mirror-image', down to his bullet-shaped cufflinks.[158] The profile makes a mention of controversies in which Raj was being embroiled, his 'five-star' approach to politics and the fear of dynastic succession. 'But now, when Raj and Uddhav have got together, another doubt has surfaced—whether they will be able to work together or will drift apart,' reported Lekha Rattanani.[159]

Despite the hiccups, Raj was still seen as being on the route to be anointed as his uncle's political heir. But it all came crashing down when Ramesh Kini, a resident of Laxmi Niwas building at Matunga in Mumbai, was found dead at Alka Talkies in Pune on 23 July 1996 during the night show of the John Travolta starrer *Broken Arrow*.

5

Cracks in the Edifice

The best laid schemes o' Mice an' Men,
Gang aft agley.
An' lea'e us nought but grief an' pain,
For promis'd joy!
(The best-laid plans of mice and men often go awry).

Robert Burns, *To a Mouse, Collected Poems of Robert Burns*

Chhagan Bhujbal, who faced a shock defeat at the hands of the Shiv Sena's Bala Nandgaonkar from Mazgaon in 1995, had been accommodated by the Congress in the state legislative council. Bhujbal, who had a score to settle with both the Shiv Sena and the Thackerays, was appointed as leader of Opposition.

'I was chosen by Pawar saheb [Sharad Pawar] to lead the Opposition in the Upper House as the Congress, which was traditionally the ruling party, had no experience of sitting in the Opposition or taking on an aggressive stance,' recalled Bhujbal.[1] 'One of my workers told me about the Ramesh Kini case. His widow, Sheela, revealed how her husband was called to Sena Bhawan and threatened to vacate the flat.'[2]

Bhujbal held a press conference later in July at his official residence and introduced Sheela Kini. Sheela alleged that on

23 July 1996, the day his body was found at Alka Talkies, her husband had left home claiming he was going to the *Saamna* office. Sheela, who had sought help from Bhujbal, accused Raj of being involved in her husband's death and questioned a suicide note in her husband's pocket and a 'hasty' post-mortem which deduced ischemic heart disease as the cause of Ramesh's death.[3]

It was alleged that Kini's landlords, Laxmichand and Suman Shah, were pressurizing the family to vacate the flat for a paltry amount as they wanted to redevelop the structure and were flaunting their influence with the Shiv Sena and Raj to browbeat him into submission.

The Kinis resided in the building under the *paagdi* system, an informal arrangement popular in old areas of Mumbai, where the tenant who takes the property on rent becomes part owner.[4]

The case had elements of a Bollywood potboiler—property, allegations of kidnapping and homicide, charges of conspiracy involving political bigwigs and above all, a frail woman intent on taking on the might of the system. What added to the mystery was that Kini, a freelance photographer, had found himself in Pune on a day when railway traffic between the two cities had been affected by torrential rains.

'Kini was a man of modest means, why would he go to Pune just to watch a movie when he could have done that in Mumbai? Before leaving home, he had promised his wife he would be back soon,' questioned Bhujbal.[5]

Apart from his suicide note, which said that the reasons for his extreme step were known to his advocate, telephone numbers of his lawyer and his brother-in-law and a vial containing sodium cyanide were found on his body. At 9.30 a.m. on the same day, Kini had handed over two letters in a closed cover to his lawyer. In one of them, Kini stated that he was threatened and mentally tortured by his landlords, forcing him to leave his flat.[6]

The autopsies conducted at the state-run Sassoon Hospital at Pune on 23 July and later at Mumbai threw up discrepancies.[7] The post-mortem at Pune had not recorded if the sodium cyanide found with Kini had been detected in the corpse and mentioned the cause of death as ischemic heart disease. The second autopsy conducted in Mumbai reserved the cause of death pending a forensic report. An expert committee opined that alcohol intoxication with unknown poisoning, fatal cardiac arrhythmias due to alcohol intoxication and ischemic heart disease could be the probable causes of death. It further opined that there was no evidence suggestive of physical injury leading to death.[8]

In court, Sheela's lawyer said the detection of alcohol was 'intriguing' as Ramesh was a teetotaller.[9] Sheela also claimed that her husband had never watched an English movie in his life.[10]

History of violence

The Shiv Sena's political history and its espousal of a creed of violence made it vulnerable to such charges.

On 5 June 1970, Krishna Desai, the CPI MLA from Parel, who had launched the 'Red Guard' to counter the Shiv Sena's growing muscle in Girangaon, was stabbed to death, allegedly by Sainiks. The police arrested nineteen youth, believed to be Sainiks, for the murder which had shaken up the city, and three of them were acquitted.[11] In October that year, the Shiv Sena won its maiden seat in the state assembly during the by-polls from Parel, where its Wamanrao Parab defeated Desai's widow, Sarojini.

Though Bal Thackeray claimed that the Sena was not related to the murder,[12] according to Dipankar Gupta, around three weeks after Desai's death, the Sena chief congratulated the Sainiks responsible for it at a rally in Robert Moncy High School in Mumbai and declared they must not miss a single opportunity to massacre communists.[13] Earlier in September 1967, Thackeray had declared in *Marmik* that his objective was the 'emasculation of the Communists', and three months later, Shiv Sainiks attacked the CPI's office at Dalvi building in Parel.[14]

The Shiv Sena had similarly used muscle to break the hold of the communist-dominated unions through the BKS, which did 'not believe in class struggle but in co-operation between the workers and the management'.[15] The Sena also clashed violently with Dr Datta Samant and Dina Bama Patil's union in the Godrej factory at Vikhroli (1972), where a police sub-inspector and two havaldars (constables) were lynched to death.[16]

The Shiv Sena's ire would not spare one of its own who broke ranks. In March 1989, the Sena's nominee Prakash Paranjape lost the mayoral elections in Thane to Manohar Salvi of the Congress by just one vote. It was alleged that cross-voting in the mayoral and deputy mayoral polls by at least two Shiv Sena corporators had carried the day for the Congress. Bal Thackeray called for the 'traitors' to be taught a lesson and 'Dharmaveer' Anand Dighe, the Shiv Sena's powerful chief in Thane, issued statements saying the punishment for traitors was death.[17]

On 21 April, Shridhar Khopkar, a party corporator, was murdered in broad daylight in Thane.

Ramdeo Tyagi, then police commissioner of Thane, alleged that the Shiv Sena was responsible for Khopkar's murder.[18] Dighe, who passed away in 2001 in a road accident, was among those arrested for the murder and charged under the stringent Terrorist and Disruptive Activities (Prevention) Act, 1987. The Shiv Sena's role in the 1992–93 riots, where Justice B.N. Srikrishna concluded Thackeray was 'like a veteran General' who 'commanded . . . Shiv Sainiks to retaliate by organized attacks on the Muslims', is well documented.[19]

In January 2019, Nilesh Rane, the elder son of Shiv Sena dissident and its former chief minister, Narayan Rane, alleged that Bal Thackeray was responsible for Dighe's death, with his 'murder' being made to resemble 'death during treatment' after the road accident.[20]

Before he fell out with underworld don, Arun Gawli, Bal Thackeray had proudly claimed him to be a Hindu counterweight to another don, Dawood Ibrahim, a Muslim.[21]

'The second-generation of Shiv Sainiks had gradually forged a link with Mumbai's dreaded mafia. They could not be protected without their links to those at the top,' explained a senior journalist and editor, who is a trenchant critic of the Shiv Sena. He added that this combination of politics and muscle made the party easy prey to allegations like those in the Kini case.

Fallout of the Kini case

The legislature saw tumultuous scenes with demands for Raj's arrest.[22]

Both Bhujbal and his counterpart in the Maharashtra legislative assembly, Madhukarrao Pichad, sought a Central Bureau of Investigation (CBI) probe into Kini's death for a free-and-fair investigation.

Raj claimed innocence but admitted to having close ties with Laxmichand Shah and his son Suman, owners of the building in which Kini lived.[23] Stating he had never met Kini,[24] Raj alleged the charges were a conspiracy by Bhujbal and Sharad Pawar.[25] In the assembly in August, Joshi gave a clean chit to Raj,[26] which incensed the Shiv Sena's detractors.

'After the Kini case broke, Raj held a press conference at Churchgate. He did not disown Suman Shah or deny his friendship with him. This helped me make up my mind to stay with Raj as he was not a fair-weather friend,' said a then MLA of the Shiv Sena, who shifted to the MNS later.[27]

Saamna blamed Sheela for her husband's death and Bal Thackeray angrily questioned if Kini was a 'Mahatma Gandhi'.[28]

Never one to mince his words and habituated to calling a spade a shovel, Thackeray also attacked social activist, Pushpa Bhave, who had taken up Sheela's cause, as a *bhavin* (prostitute) in an uncharitable pun on her surname.

During their investigations, the police arrested a BVS worker, Ashutosh Rane, who was close to the Thackeray family, Raj in particular. The police brought Rane to court with a burqa on his face in a manner usually reserved for hardened criminals.[29]

Pushpa Bhave, who lived just a building away from the Kinis, is a strong voice of dissent, being associated with the Samyukta Maharashtra movement, Dalit Panthers and unorganized sector workers. 'Sheela Tai was very lonely during those days,' recalled Bhave.[30]

'There were many forces acting behind the scenes,' said Bhave, adding that Kini's brain, which had been preserved with his viscera for forensic examination, had mysteriously gone missing. 'Perhaps, they decided to dispose it off as Kini may have been hit on the head before his death,' she claimed.

The journalist turned politician, Kapil Patil, who had been running his own Marathi eveninger, *Aaj Dinank*, since 1993, plunged into the coverage of the Kini case.

Patil claimed that his editorial position, wherein he questioned the disappearance of Ramesh Kini's brain, and another where he asked if Maharashtrians would be compelled to commit suicide in the Shiv Sena's regime, upset the Sena chief. 'He asked one of the newspaper's financers, Shiv Sena Rajya Sabha MP Mukesh Patel, to either make me change my stance, or close it down. I chose the latter option,' said Patil, in a conversation at his office located in the Shiv Sena's heartland of Parel in central Mumbai.[31]

Patil shut down his newspaper in October 1996, on the very day Patel had been warned by the Shiv Sena supremo. 'Fifteen days later, I launched a new Marathi eveninger called *Saanj Dinank*, with an advertising campaign that saw posters the size of a newspaper plastered across Mumbai,' he said. 'These posters carried slogans like "Who killed Ramesh Kini?", "Who killed *Aaj Dinank*?" When the paper was launched, it sold 50,000 copies, with the circulation touching 70,000. However, I was squeezed gradually in terms of newsprint availability and logistics and soon, *Saanj Dinank* too bit the dust.'[32]

Vaibhav Purandare noted that the Kini case was the first real crisis that the Shiv Sena and the fledging saffron alliance government faced. This was also the strongest case ever to have been made against the Thackeray clan and the way it was handled undermined the state government.[33]

The Shiv Sena could have taken the wind out of the Opposition's sails by handing the case to the CBI. However, Purandare says the Sena leadership pressurized its government, which reluctantly refused to involve the CBI. While Chief Minister Joshi maintained a 'studied silence', the Shiv Sena and Raj defended themselves aggressively.[34]

Even today, some within the Shiv Sena and MNS claim that the Kini case was mishandled by their own government by design, rather than by default. They allege that attempts were made to implicate Raj for the 'indiscretions' of his associates.

'Bal Thackeray proudly called himself the remote control of the Shiv Sena–BJP government. Despite Manohar Joshi being chief minister, the real power lay elsewhere. Then, why didn't the government immediately announce a probe to bring about a detente with the Opposition and those gunning for Raj?' questioned a senior journalist and editor close to Raj.[35]

The Pune police began investigating the death, and later, on Sheela's request, the case was handed over to the Maharashtra Criminal Investigation Department (CID). Raj was questioned by the CID for almost three-and-a-half hours. Based on an order of the Bombay High Court, the investigation was transferred to the CBI.[36]

Unease was simmering within the Shiv Sena. Shishir Shinde, who was then an MLC, and had tilted towards Raj in the internal power struggle, alleged a 'political conspiracy' and sent his resignation as a legislator to Bal Thackeray.[37]

'While Raj saheb was being interrogated, I sat on the footpath outside the CBI office at Kitab Mahal on D.N. Road. We felt strongly about the police bringing Ashutosh Rane to court in a burqa. The government seemed to be capitulating to the Opposition,' said Shinde, adding it was Uddhav who advised him to be 'patient' after Shinde had threatened to resign.[38]

Thackeray accused Home Minister Gopinath Munde of doublespeak.[39]

In an interview to *Saamna* in August 1996, Thackeray charged that the Kini case was being used 'for political ends' to target the Thackeray family and admitted that it 'had not been handled the way it should have been from the very beginning' by the government.[40]

Mincing no words, he said it was 'outrageous' that Ashutosh Rane had been brought to the court in a burqa. 'The cause of Kini's death is yet to be arrived at. You have not yet recovered evidence. How can arrests begin before this? How can people be arrested if this is just a suicide?' he asked.[41]

Responding to a question from *Saamna*'s executive editor, Sanjay Raut, on whether 'some parties in the saffron alliance' had a role to play in this controversy, Thackeray said 'the question is as tough as the one about the cause of Kini's death . . . You can say both are mysteries'.[42]

Eventually, Raj was exonerated by the CBI, and Joshi and Munde told the legislature that Kini had died due to alcohol consumption and heart disease. Bal Thackeray said his faith in Raj's innocence had been vindicated. *Saamna* called it 'the victory of the truth', while Uddhav said: 'I had said this before, the hands which have carried the saffron flag, will never commit a sin . . .'[43]

Though the CBI exonerated Raj, it booked the Shah duo and Ashutosh Rane. While Ashutosh Rane was discharged by the court, Laxmichand and Suman Shah were acquitted of charges including criminal conspiracy (Section 120-B of the Indian Penal Code, 1860), abetment of suicide (Section 306 of IPC) and putting a person in fear of injury in order to commit extortion (Section 385 of IPC) in August 2002.[44]

Pushpa Bhave said Raj had been let off 'due to want of proof' which was not appealed by the saffron alliance government.[45]

'After the Kini case, I received around eight to nine complaints of people being threatened by Sainiks to vacate their houses, including at Dadar's Parsi colony. They wanted me to fight for them like I did for Kini. However, I was working in a college and had my own constraints. I told them that they could fight the cases and I would offer support. However, no one could summon the courage to do so,' said Bhave.

The clean chit to Raj was not without controversy. Writing in *Hindustan Times* on 23 December 2013, journalist Sujata Anandan claimed that Amitabh Bachchan had played a role in rescuing Raj from the Ramesh Kini case.[46] Attributing the information to her 'unimpeachable sources from inside Matoshree', Anandan claimed that Thackeray had 'virtually gone down on his knees' with Bachchan to use his influence with the then United Front (UF) government to persuade the CBI to lay off Raj. Bachchan then reportedly arranged a secret midnight meeting at his house between Prime Minister H.D. Deve Gowda and the Sena chief, where the former promised not to go out of his way to pursue the case.[47]

Senior journalist and editor, Nikhil Wagle, whose Marathi eveninger *Mahanagar* had exposed the Kini story, said that in those tumultuous days, rumours were that Raj was likely to be arrested by the CBI. He claimed that politician Amar Singh had saved Raj's skin during the episode.[48] Ironically, Raj would later target Singh during his agitation against north Indians launched in 2008.

Deve Gowda was replaced by I.K. Gujral in April 1997. In an interview to *Saamna* the next month, Thackeray admitted he wanted Gowda to continue. Thackeray however denied reports that he wanted to save the government in the Lok Sabha by voting for it but had been stopped from doing so by Atal Bihari Vajpayee.[49]

The exoneration notwithstanding, the Kini case continued to be perceived as the proverbial albatross around Raj's neck even much later.

In May 2009, Uddhav, who was locked in a battle for political supremacy with Raj's MNS, raked up the Ramesh Kini case to embarrass his cousin. Raj had accused Uddhav of claiming to uphold the interests of Marathi speakers but voting for a non-Maharashtrian, Mahesh Jethmalani of the BJP, in the Lok Sabha polls from the Mumbai North-Central constituency. Matoshree falls in this Lok Sabha constituency, where the presence of MNS nominee Shilpa Sarpotdar split the Marathi vote, and contributed to the victory of Congress MP Priya Dutt.

In a statement, Uddhav said that when Raj was embroiled in the Ramesh Kini case, Bal Thackeray had approached senior counsel Ram Jethmalani (Mahesh's father) to bail him out. Uddhav added that they had voted for Mahesh Jethmalani on instructions from the Sena chief as he had helped them during the Kini case. 'But how can one expect a person like Raj to show gratitude?' he asked.[50]

In 2014, Bhujbal, who was the public works department (PWD) minister in the Prithviraj Chavan government, was attacked by Raj for alleged corruption in the awarding of road toll contracts. Undeterred, Bhujbal told reporters that he 'strongly believed' that the Kini murder case was not investigated properly.[51]

During the days that he was under a cloud in the Ramesh Kini case, Raj's associates said he was forced to keep away from politics and spend time at home or with friends.[52]

A senior Shiv Sena leader loyal to Uddhav said he had stood by his cousin during the Ramesh Kini controversy. 'Many meetings, including those with lawyers, happened at the *Saamna* office. Uddhav also accompanied Raj to the CBI court,' he added.[53]

In March 2011, Sheela, who had taken on the might of the Shiv Sena, died at her home of cardiac arrest. Pushpa Bhave recalled that Sheela was depressed at the time of her death. Incidentally, just before her demise, Matoshree Infrastructure, headed by Raj's close friend and associate, Rajan Shirodkar, decided to redevelop the Laxmi Nivas building after securing consents from most tenants.[54] The structure was finally pulled down in 2013 to make way for a nineteen-storey tower.[55]

The reluctant politician

Even before the Ramesh Kini case came to light, Uddhav had begun taking an active interest in politics. His father's heart surgery had restricted his mobility and like Raj, Uddhav too tried to fill in the gap by campaigning for the party in the 1996 Lok Sabha elections, polling for which was held in Maharashtra in May. Speaking at campaign rallies, Raj would deny that either he or Uddhav would join the Maharashtra cabinet.[56]

The Ramesh Kini case threw a spanner in Raj's rise within the Shiv Sena. This, coupled with Meenatai and Binda's deaths within months of each other and Bal Thackeray's failing health, led the Sena supremo to increasingly rely on Uddhav for emotional support.

One of Raj's former business associates claimed that in these times, some people had tried to influence his uncle's opinion about Raj by alluding to factors like his flamboyant lifestyle. Raj was gradually pushed to the margins and beyond. Soon, he was asked to stop coming to the *Saamna* office.[57]

This led to his estrangement and eventual break from the Shiv Sena to form his own party in 2006.

'The treaty of Versailles [between the Germans and the Allied powers in 1919 to end the First World War] laid the seeds for the rise of Adolf Hitler and the Nazi regime and consequently, the Second World War. Similarly, Raj being forced to a subordinate position within the Shiv Sena eventually led him away from the party,' noted an associate of Raj from his college days.[58] However, on the record, Raj denied any differences with Uddhav.

'Raj was the focal point of allegations in the Ramesh Kini case. This may have led Balasaheb to think that there were risks involved in pitching as his number two a man who was seen as being tainted. Doing so would have had an obvious effect on the Shiv Sena and his own image. This led to Uddhav gradually gaining importance within the ranks,' noted former Shiv Sena Rajya Sabha MP and senior journalist Bharatkumar Raut.[59]

This coincided with Uddhav developing strong political ambitions. 'Uddhav is a reluctant politician,' said Raut, adding that his wife, Rashmi, who is politically ambitious, may have influenced his decision.[60]

A former MNS MLA, who has since split from Raj, noted that his leader was forced to lower his profile during and after the Kini case. 'He was very upset and angry those days and remained aloof from the Shiv Sena's functioning. It was felt that the party had deliberately dragged its feet in ensuring damage control.'[61]

Another Shiv Sena leader, who quit the party with Raj but became disillusioned soon after, added, 'The Kini case damaged the public perception about Raj. There was a simmer within the party about the government not standing by him the way it should have. The home department was held by the BJP and some saw this shoddy handling as its way of cornering the Shiv Sena. Moreover, the burqa parade of Ashutosh Rane was seen as an affront to the Thackeray family and Raj in particular.'[62]

However, Raj Thackeray loyalists who have stuck with him since their days in the BVS, claim that there was a design to undercut their leader even before the Kini case surfaced.

'The process of clipping his wings within the Shiv Sena was launched much earlier,' admitted a former MNS MLA who had worked with Raj in the BVS. 'There was an unwritten policy against giving any importance or respect to BVS leaders and cadre in the Shiv Sena. Even BVS state general secretaries were not given space to sit by local shakha pramukhs when they visited their offices.'[63]

'There was a group within the Shiv Sena that wanted to corner us. BVS office-bearers and those loyal to Raj saheb had no standing in the larger party organization. We were not being given importance in local politics. Shiv Sena leaders and office-bearers were cagey about even putting up banners on Raj saheb's birthday or visiting his residence to greet him,' said MNS leader Yashwant Killedar.[64]

He said Raj would support grass-roots workers at the receiving end of petty politics by some leaders, leading to a pushback.

Killedar alleged that while Sena workers from the suburbs had vandalized the office of the Board of Control for Cricket in India (BCCI) in Mumbai in January 1999 to protest against a proposed India–Pakistan cricket match, Raj loyalists from Dadar were picked up by the police. 'We were arrested at 4 a.m. from our houses like terrorists. We were taken to court under tight security. Our own Shiv Sena–led government was using the police to intimidate us,' he said.[65]

Raj loyalists also clashed with their rivals from the Uddhav camp across the city.

'Raj is a shrewd leader. Through the BVS, he cultivated a parallel Shiv Sena. These BVS leaders owed their loyalties to Raj, and not Balasaheb,' noted Bharatkumar Raut, who has written about the party during his days as a reporter and later, as an editor.[66]

Gradually, two factions emerged even within the BVS. One that stayed loyal to Raj, and the other that chose to align itself with Uddhav and the old guard for 'better career prospects'. Many such leaders were later accommodated within the parent party.[67]

A senior journalist noted that after the Shiv Sena–BJP alliance came to power, Raj and Uddhav were pushing for their own men to be nominated to various state-run corporations. The appointments were announced suddenly, mostly favouring Uddhav's loyalists.[68]

'In 1997, Raj wanted his men to contest the BMC elections. Balasaheb decided to nominate Praveen Darekar, then a general secretary of the BVS and a Raj loyalist, from Dahisar. He even put a tilak on Darekar's forehead to bless him. But by the time Darekar reached Dahisar from Matoshree, he had been replaced with a candidate from the rival camp,' said the former Raj Thackeray associate, adding that this sparked a war between the two camps.[69]

Haji Arafat Shaikh, who was with the BVS, and later pitched himself as a Muslim face of the MNS, said four BVS leaders, including Darekar and himself, were asked by Raj to meet his uncle at Matoshree to seek a nomination for the 1997 BMC elections. 'A senior leader told us we were still kids and should buy a movie ticket instead of angling for an election ticket. It was obvious that the insult was not aimed at us but at Raj saheb.'[70]

'In other parties, office-bearers of the youth front are gradually accommodated in the parent party. However, for BVS functionaries and cadre, the Shiv Sena's doors were shut unlike their competitors from the ABVP and NSUI. This led to them stagnating in the BVS even after the age of forty,' said an MNS functionary.[71]

'In the BVS, we had only three tasks to complete—tree plantation during the monsoons, pushing for admissions in schools and colleges and celebrating Raj Thackeray's birthday,' jokes Shaikh who is now with the BJP and is now the chairperson of the Maharashtra State Minority Commission.[72]

Uddhav, who was clearly looking at manoeuvring himself into the driver's seat, plunged headlong into the 1997 BMC campaign. He called for cooperation between Shivshakti and Bhimshakti—the latter alluding to the Buddhist Dalit-dominated Republican Party of India—in a public meeting at Worli's Jambori maidan.[73] 'By 1997, Uddhavji had assumed power within the party. In the civic polls, his word carried weight and Balasaheb accepted his suggestions during nominations,' said Shishir Shinde.[74]

Whenever reports about differences between the two cousins surfaced, Raj chose to play them down, calling them a 'figment of the media's imagination'.[75] The media, meanwhile continued to write about the emerging and fast-widening cracks in the Sena.

A profile of Raj in *India Today*, written by V. Shankar Aiyar, quoted Congressmen calling Raj the 'Sanjay Gandhi' of the Shiv Sena.[76]

In 1996, Raj launched his Shiv Udyog Sena (SUS) to provide jobs to 27 lakh youth. The front was unveiled at his Dussehra rally by Bal Thackeray, who also inaugurated its head office at Shiv Sena Bhawan on 9 April 1997.[77]

Already smarting from the Kini controversy, Raj provided more fodder to his critics.

He organized a Michael Jackson concert in Mumbai in association with event organizers Wizcraft to raise funds for the Shiv Udyog Sena. In his only tour of India, the 'King of Pop' was welcomed by Raj, wife Sharmila, son Amit, and actress Sonali Bendre at the airport. Shiv Sena's critics questioned how the party, which claimed to uphold the Hindu ethos and Marathi pride, and opposed 'foreign' celebrations like Valentine's Day, could organize a concert by a Western artiste.[78]

Jackson met the Sena chief at Matoshree, where the latter credited Raj with organizing the event. Speaking to Shekhar Gupta much later, he would recount his 'favourite MJ story'—Jackson was accompanied by a lady and several children, and one of them asked where the toilet was. Then, according to Balasaheb, one after the other, all the children went in. 'MJ and the lady joined them,' he said. '*Uske baad*, they bolted the door from inside and did not come out for half an hour,' he said, and asked in what looked like genuine amazement, 'So what do you think they were doing together inside?'[79]

The event was to be held at the Andheri Sports Complex (Raje Shahaji Krida Sankul), but Bal Thackeray's estranged younger brother, Ramesh, who edited a magazine called *Aaroli* (shout) had booked it for a programme, the permission for which was cancelled for Jackson's show. Ramesh threatened self-immolation and was arrested before family friends hammered out a compromise.[80]

Though the police assessed the number of attendees at the 1 November 1996 concert to be 70,000, Wizcraft claimed to have sold only 16,200 tickets.[81] In his *Bal Thackeray and the Rise of the Shiv Sena* Vaibhav Purandare said the SUS was supposed to raise Rs 4 crore from the programme, but Raj admitted they got nothing except criticism.[82] The SUS organized a concert by Lata Mangeshkar at the same venue in 1997, but the organization's plans of providing jobs and livelihood opportunities to Marathi youth eventually did not materialize.

In her book, *The Charisma of Direct Action: Power, Politics and the Shiv Sena*, Julia M. Eckert noted that the SUS revealed a marked change in the Shiv Sena's pitch of jobs for sons of the soil. Eckert noted that the SUS did not serve as a job exchange, but encouraged unemployed youth to start their own businesses. 'Thus, the involvement with jobs changed from the demand-politics of the 1960s and 1970s to the advocacy of self-help. This may be due to the fact that the Sena itself had formed the government to which the demands would have to be addressed. Members of the Sena government considered the government employment exchanges to be inefficient and, rather than improving government services, they chose to form an independent Sena employment unit, through which the "son of soil" politics of the 1960s could be re-articulated.'[83]

The Uddhav camp in the Sena disapproved of such high-profile events which, it is believed, had not led to success for the SUS in delivering on its promise of jobs. On the other hand, Raj's men did not like him being challenged by Uddhav.[84]

In interviews to *Saamna* in 1997, Bal Thackeray denied that Raj was sulking and added that he had 'devoted himself to the Shiv Udyog Sena and would not rest till he made it into a success'. He blamed the media for trying to create a rift within the family and claimed that the duo had made it clear that if politics stood between their relationship as brothers, they would quit politics[85]—something that coming years would disprove.

Raj had his own axe to grind. In 1998, he attacked the government for its failure to tackle rising unemployment and complained that the government's specially created employment department, headed by Chief Minister Joshi and later Pramod Navalkar, had not provided him information on measures taken for employment generation and self-employment. The status report was handed to Raj only after party minister Diwakar Raote took charge of the portfolio.[86]

Though his marginalization in the party was under way, Raj would sometimes dig his feet. Speaking at a rally at Beed in Marathwada, Raj said that if Manohar Joshi was dispatched to the centre, he would become chief minister. However, with Bal Thackeray stating that there was no question of doing away with Joshi, Raj was quick to clarify that this statement should not be taken seriously.[87]

Prem Shukla, former editor of *Dopahar ka Saamna*, claimed that Raj had initially wanted to control BKS after Dattaji Salvi was sidelined, but had floated the SUS after this had failed.[88]

'The SUS did not get any cooperation from the Shiv Sena–BJP government for implementing its agenda for Marathi youth. The SUS secured permissions from the state government to impart vocational and entrepreneurship training only after the Congress–NCP government came to power in 1999. Then, Raj saheb had personally spoken to the minister in charge, the late Patangrao Kadam,' averred Yashwant Killedar, who was superintendent of the SUS administrative office.[89]

Killedar charged that politics within the Shiv Sena and lack of support from the saffron alliance government scuppered the SUS agenda.

The SUS had raised funds primarily through concerts and was making ends meet through interest earned on bank deposits. 'Shiv Sena leaders would ask us to hold career counselling seminars and job melas to get youth support and promise to reimburse the costs. This money rarely came to us. The SUS was hence in financial trouble,' said Killedar.[90]

Bharatkumar Raut said that despite his charisma and aura, Raj had failed to take most of his campaigns and grandiose plans, the SUS included, to their logical end. 'He has failed to make a social, cultural and economic impact . . . Raj's complete emphasis is on his oratory. He can speak well, but rarely are those words followed up by action,' he averred.[91]

Parallel power centres

Meenatai's death had led to the emergence of a new power centre within the Thackeray clan—Smita, the wife of Bal Thackeray's second son Jaidev.

Thackeray had a 'tumultuous relationship' with Jaidev, even going to the extent of saying in an interview for *Saamna* that: 'that boy is a tragedy', according to a report in the *Times of India*.[92] The report added that trouble began in the early 1990s when

Jaidev separated from first wife, Jayashree Kalelkar, daughter of Marathi writer Madhusudan Kalelkar. The couple had a son, and Bal Thackeray felt the separation hurt the family.[93]

Jaidev later married Smita Chitre, who worked as a receptionist and was born into a middle-class Maharashtrian family, in a love match, but separated from her and left Matoshree because of differences in the household. The rift between father and son grew after Meenatai's death.[94] After the Shiv Sena-BJP government came to power, Sena insiders said that Jaidev had tried to assert himself as a power centre for a brief while but was edged out.

Jaidev, a former student of Ruia College, found himself at the centre of controversy after being accused of hunting deer in the Sanjay Gandhi National Park (SGNP) in Mumbai during the Shiv Sena–BJP's rule. Jaidev now lives with third wife, Anuradha, and daughter, Madhuri, in Kalanagar close to Matoshree, collects smoking pipes, paints on black canvases and has also learnt wood carving.[95]

After Smita's emergence as a force to reckon with, Shiv Sena old-timers recall how the battle lines had been redrawn: Manohar Joshi, who was then the chief minister, Uddhav, and the Shiv Sena old guard on one side, pitched against Raj, Smita and Narayan Rane on the other.[96]

However, Raj continued to be friends with Manohar Joshi's son, Unmesh, with whom he purchased 4.8 acre land of Kohinoor Mill number 3 at Shivaji Park opposite the Shiv Sena Bhawan in 2005 when the National Textile Corporation (NTC) auctioned it for Rs 421 crore. In 2009, Raj exited the deal by selling his stake at a profit of Rs 62 crore, though a media report said it was 'at least five times as much'.[97]

In January 2019, a story in the *Mumbai Mirror* said that Unmesh had lost control over the Kohinoor Square project, which consisted of twin glass towers, one housing a five-star hotel and businesses and the other a residential complex, to Sandeep Shikre and Associates (SSA), a Prabhadevi-based architectural firm. This followed the group's inability to repay loans worth Rs 900 crore to a consortium of banks.[98]

Smita, as a July 1999 profile in *India Today* noted, had seen a dramatic rise as a film producer, with her first film being produced by leading diamond merchant, Bharat Shah. It added that when her *Haseena Maan Jayegi* was set for release on 25 June, it was found that *Mann*, a film starring Aamir Khan, was to open on 2 July. The report said Smita had 'gently' persuaded the producers to postpone the release to 9 July to prevent it from clashing with her film.[99]

Joshi, who is hailed as the Shiv Sena's 'great survivor', lived up to this reputation during his chief ministerial tenure, managing the pressures of a coalition government and above all, tackling a mercurial Bal Thackeray, who never let an opportunity slip to show who the boss was.

Thackeray's parallel power structure and the diarchy of power between the government (Joshi) and the Shiv Sena (Thackeray) was fraught with its own tensions.

In November 1995, Rebecca Mark, CEO of the controversial Enron corporation, whose power project in Ratnagiri the Shiv Sena and BJP had promised to 'uproot and throw into the Arabian Sea' if elected, was supposed to meet Joshi in his office. Joshi, a stickler for punctuality, lost his cool when she was delayed and cancelled the appointment without knowing that Mark was with his party chief at Matoshree. Thackeray was told that Joshi was upset because Mark had chosen to meet Thackeray but Joshi 'sir' managed to calm him down.

Thackeray also attacked Joshi in public over a proposed MoU with the Hinduja Group for the construction of an airport and *Saamna* took frequent potshots at the Shiv Sena–BJP dispensation. Vaibhav Purandare notes that Thackeray, who also accused Joshi of corruption, perhaps became the first unquestioned leader of a ruling party to accuse his own chief minister of graft.[100]

After the Shiv Sena's debacle in the 1998 Lok Sabha elections, Thackeray blamed the state government for ineptitude and announced his *sanyas* (retirement) from active politics. This was withdrawn after incensed Shiv Sainiks rushed to Matoshree, also manhandling some Sena ministers and MLAs who were present.[101]

Joshi had to also strike a balancing act in his ties with the BJP and Sharad Pawar. Journalists who covered the state government during the period note that rumours about Joshi's days being numbered would frequently make the rounds before the chief minister placated his boss to live another day.

In his autobiography, Joshi's successor Narayan Rane claims that while Bal Thackeray had promised that his would be a 'remote control' government, it seemed that Joshi had his own agenda and 'didn't respond well to the buttons which the "remote control" pressed'.[102]

Despite weathering many a storm, Joshi's luck soon ran out. 'Apart from resentment against Joshi, there was a sentiment that it was not possible to face the electorate in 1999 with a Brahmin chief minister [Brahmins account for smaller numbers compared to other communities and are politically insignificant]. The BJP was also uneasy at this,' said a former Shiv Sena leader.[103]

A case was filed in the Bombay High Court alleging that a prime plot on Prabhat Road in Pune reserved for a primary school was de-reserved to suit Joshi's son-in-law and builder, Girish Vyas. Joshi was charged with giving his nod to the change in land use. The controversy eventually served as the catalyst for Joshi's exit as the chief minister. In 2011, the Supreme Court indicted Joshi in the case.[104]

Joshi's government was also riven by internal conflicts with ministers like Ganesh Naik, Gulabrao Gawande and Suresh Navale rebelling against the leadership.[105]

On 30 January 1999, a Shiv Sena functionary, Ashish Kulkarni, met Joshi who had woken up after his customary afternoon nap, and handed him a letter from Bal Thackeray seeking his resignation. Joshi submitted his two-line resignation letter to Governor P.C. Alexander. Kulkarni, who helped Thackeray draft the letter with Kiran Wadhivkar and senior leader Subhash Desai, quit the Shiv Sena with Raj in 2005, joining the Congress later.[106]

Julia M. Eckert wrote that the SUS claimed to have organized 2.7 million jobs for the 3.79 million unemployed of Maharashtra, while the Rs 732-crore job scheme initiated by the former chief minister Manohar Joshi floundered, and this was used by *Saamna* to justify Joshi's sacking.[107]

The 1952-born Narayan Rane, a Shiv Sainik who had cut his teeth as a street fighter at Chembur in Mumbai's eastern suburbs, was chosen as Joshi's replacement. Apparently, one of the factors that had swung things in his favour was the support of Bal Thackeray's powerful daughter-in-law Smita.

Second term scuttled

When the Shiv Sena–BJP government was formed, Rane was the animal husbandry and dairy development minister. After Revenue Minister Sudhir Joshi was incapacitated in an accident, the powerful portfolio was handed to Rane. Shiv Sena insiders claim Rane played his cards well in the months preceding Joshi's ouster, impressing upon the leadership how a change was needed and that he was the right candidate.[108]

'The Shiv Sena wanted a Maratha to replace Joshi,' said a Shiv Sena source. Maratha-Kunbis make up over 30 per cent of Maharashtra's population and are the dominant caste. 'Though some names like that of Dattaji Nalawade, who was the assembly Speaker, were discussed, Rane was chosen as he was seen as someone who could get work done and raise funds for the polls.'[109]

Moreover, with his aggressive, scrappy image, Rane fit into the stereotype of the typical Shiv Sainik in contrast with the white-collared Joshi, who, according to an article in *Saamna* on 7 February 1999, by its executive editor Sanjay Raut, functioned more as a 'business executive'.[110]

'Uddhav did not feel the time was ripe to change Joshi. Then, Uddhav, Joshi and Desai were ranged together against Raj, Rane and Smita as their comfort levels with each other were good due to similar temperaments. Uddhav, a quiet and soft-spoken man, had his reservations about Rane, who was aggressive and upfront, but had to eventually go along with the decision to replace Joshi,' a former Sena leader said.[111] 'Things between Raj and Uddhav rapidly started going downhill from 1999 onwards. Things became murkier as leaders from other parties like the BJP and NCP started getting involved in this,' he added.

He said that Meenatai's death had also complicated matters within the family as Uddhav, Rashmi and sister-in-law, Smita, tried to fill the gap. This 'kitchen politics' led to a rift between Raj and Smita on one side and Uddhav on the other.

'Coming to power in Maharashtra turned out to be inauspicious for the Thackerays,' claimed a family friend. 'Ma and Binda passed away, then there was discord within the family. The family began falling apart between 1995 and 1999 when the Shiv Sena and BJP were ruling in Maharashtra,' he added.[112]

Uddhav gradually edged Smita out from the Shiv Sena's internal politics. Said to be in contention for a Rajya Sabha seat in 2008, Smita lost out to Bharatkumar Raut. She also sent out feelers to the Congress in 2009 to enter the Upper House of Parliament, but was rebuffed.

'After Rane's ascension, Raj was in a more comfortable position. The Shiv Sena went with the BJP's insistence for calling polls six months early to coincide with the Lok Sabha elections. However, they had not taken into account the emergence of Sharad Pawar's NCP,' a former Sena leader said. In 1999, Sharad

Pawar had been expelled from the Congress and formed his own party after raising the issue of Congress president Sonia Gandhi's foreign origin, taking with him a bulk of incumbent Congress legislators.[113]

During a Shiv Sena conclave in 1999 at the Rambhau Mhalgi Prabhodhini (RMP) in Uttan on Mumbai's northern fringes, journalist Vageesh Saraswat claimed that Rane had clandestinely prompted him to ask Uddhav about his chief ministerial ambitions. 'For the first time, Uddhav admitted he wanted to become chief minister,' he said.[114]

In the same year, the BJP, which was seeking a fresh mandate for the Atal Bihari Vajpayee government after it lost the trust vote, insisted that the Maharashtra assembly be dissolved, and pre-term polls be held. Though Bal Thackeray was not in favour of this, he eventually agreed.

Raj campaigned hard for Rane. Uddhav too travelled the state, addressing public meetings. The differences between the two cousins came up during the campaign. For a man known to measure his words and be diplomatic, Manohar Joshi's official biography of the Shiv Sena is fairly blunt on several issues. Joshi refers to a 'huge fight' between the cousins during the 1999 campaign. BVS workers threatened Shiv Sena leader Subhash Desai on the phone. Finally, the Shiv Sena chief had to intervene to defuse the situation.[115]

Though the Vajpayee government was re-elected, Shishir Shinde admits the bickering between the Sena and BJP affected their performance in the assembly polls, with them winning sixty-nine and fifty-six seats respectively, compared to seventy-five for the Congress and the NCP's fifty-eight in the 288-member house.[116]

Narayan Rane blames Uddhav for this. In his autobiography, Rane claims after the Sena finalized its list of candidates, Uddhav unilaterally replaced fifteen of them with his choices, catching everyone off guard. He notes that 'interestingly and unfortunately' the candidates who had been replaced by Uddhav were so disgruntled that they went ahead and contested the elections as independents or nominees of other parties, and eleven of them won. If these candidates had been retained by the Shiv Sena, they would have had a tally of 80 seats, helping them come to power.[117]

Many independents, who were former Congress leaders and had supported the saffron alliance, had now joined the NCP. Joshi admits that the Shiv Sena decided on Rane's name as the chief ministerial nominee without consulting the BJP, which upset their ally, jeopardizing their alliance.[118] The BJP's Gopinath Munde, a powerful leader of the OBC Vanjari community and the man credited with the BJP's political and social expansion in Maharashtra, had played deputy to both Joshi and Rane. He now wanted the state's top post.

Rane said as they had 136 seats, including independents, which was eleven short of a majority, he began speaking with smaller parties and other independents and put together a number of 145. He added that meanwhile, Munde was busy with his own politicking, and was speaking to the NCP and others to become the CM. Munde's brother-in-law, the powerful BJP leader Pramod Mahajan told Rane they would not help stake claim as 'we could not form a government based on so many independents'. This was despite the fact that in 1995 the saffron alliance had come to power with the support of independents. BJP state chief Suryabhan Vahadne-Patil refused to sign the list of MLAs supporting them as he had no green signal from Munde and Mahajan.[119]

A former Sena leader said the BJP had sought the chief minister's post or let it be split between it and the Shiv Sena.[120]

A miffed Bal Thackeray later held a press conference saying it was in the best interests of the alliance that the BJP form the government by cobbling the numbers, with the Sena supporting it from the outside.[121]

In his autobiography *Through the Corridors of Power: An Insider's Story*, then Maharashtra governor P.C. Alexander notes that the Shiv Sena–BJP alliance 'had run into problems on the issue of choosing a leader for their legislature group', with the BJP insisting on Munde's claim as the Sena had led the government between 1995 and 1999.[122]

Alexander also refers to 'rumours that the BJP and the NCP had been engaged in secret confabulations about forming the government with a neutral non-political leader . . .' There were also speculations that the Central government would not be averse to President's rule 'if a suitable government could not be formed by the stipulated date'.[123]

Raj would later state that this incident marked the beginning of widening differences between the two parties.[124]

In the prevailing political uncertainty after the 1999 elections, a powerful non-Maharashtrian leader from Khandesh (north Maharashtra) made an offer to the Sena to garner the loyalties of independents and smaller parties in return for the chief minister's chair. This was immediately shot down by the Sena chief.[125]

Eventually, senior BJP leader and Munde's brother-in-law, Pramod Mahajan, who had a special rapport with Bal Thackeray, played peacenik, declaring on 11 October 1999, that the Shiv Sena would retain the chief minister's post.[126] However, it was too late. Pawar put his bitterness with the Congress behind him and the Congress and NCP met Governor P.C. Alexander and staked claim to form the government with the support of 151 legislators.[127]

On 18 October 1999, Vilasrao Deshmukh of the Congress took the oath of office as the chief minister of Maharashtra with the Shiv Sena's old bête noire, Chhagan Bhujbal, as his deputy. Bhujbal also held the crucial home portfolio. Rane had to be content with the position of leader of Opposition.

In 1999, Congress candidate Marzban Patrawala was elected to the state legislative assembly from Colaba on Mumbai's southernmost tip. A lawyer, Patrawala (fifty-two), died of a massive cardiac arrest in October, even before he could be sworn in by the pro-tem speaker. His widow Dinaz tried in vain to secure a Congress or NCP nomination and finally turned to the Shiv Sena, which decided to field her.

The Shiv Sena saw the by-poll as a way to shore up its numbers in the assembly and serve as a morale booster. Moreover, the party could have ensured good optics, by claiming to give representation to a small, yet influential minority group by fielding Dinaz, a Parsi, from the prestigious seat. Dinaz was pitted against Congress corporator Annie Shekhar.

'Balasaheb wanted both Uddhav and Raj to launch Dinaz Patrawala's campaign. But Raj backed out at the last moment. This was seen as a slight,' said a senior political journalist. Eventually, Dinaz retained her husband's seat by a margin of over 2,500 votes.[128]

Raj, who had been keeping away from the Shiv Sena's activities for almost a year by then, chose to attend the party's convention at Amravati in November 2000 in a show of strength, where his supporters drove down from Mumbai in a convoy of around forty vehicles. He also attended party events at Borivali in Mumbai to reassert his presence.[129]

Rane's failed bid

Rane, no stranger to the use of machismo in politics, faced a major embarrassment in his own backyard. In December 2002, angry NCP workers torched his house at Kankavali in the Sindhudurg district after a party worker, Satyavijay Bhise, was allegedly murdered by Shiv Sena activists. A newspaper report described the NCP workers act of burning down the bungalow as a 'violent reaction to the murder . . .'[130]

Prakash Akolkar notes that despite this attack on Rane, the rest of the Shiv Sena was calm with no major leader expressing support or consoling him. This created the impression that Rane was isolated after Uddhav had taken charge of the Shiv Sena.'[131]

Rane's aides alleged that Sena leaders, who were headed to Kankavali to express solidarity, were stopped by the leadership, allegedly at Uddhav's behest. The gloves were off in a full-scale turf war between Uddhav and Rane.[132]

In 2002, Rane made an audacious bid to regain power in the state by toppling the Vilasrao Deshmukh government.

The Peasants and Workers Party of India (PWP) was once the principal Opposition to the Congress in Maharashtra and had leaders, like Keshavrao Jedhe, Shankarrao More, Prabhakar Patil and Madhavrao Bagal, from the Bramhanetar (non-Brahmin) movement. However, years of defections from its ranks to the Congress had shrunk its base. It retained its spunk in the Raigad district neighbouring Mumbai, where it had support among local communities like Aagris and Kolis. The party, which calls itself a Marxist political formation, was led in the district by Jayant Patil, the son of senior PWP leader Prabhakar Patil, and a businessman who owns shipyards in Dubai and Australia, a ferry boat service and a local Marathi newspaper.[133]

In 2002, the NCP's Sunil Tatkare, who was a minister of state in the Deshmukh cabinet, broke his party's understanding with the PWP to elect the Shiv Sena's candidate Apeksha Karekar as the chief of the Raigad Zilla Parishad (ZP) while the NCP took the vice-president's post. Karekar defeated Jayant Patil's wife Supriya. Incensed, Jayant Patil demanded Tatkare's scalp, failing which he would pull his five MLAs out of the government.

With his party cornered, Tatkare resigned as a minister in March, but not before launching a blistering attack against the PWP in the legislature accusing it of 'goondaism' and use of 'muscle power'.[134]

In June, Tatkare was re-inducted at the insistence of mentor Ajit Pawar, the NCP's water resource minister and Sharad Pawar's nephew. The angry PWP pulled out of the government, precipitating a crisis. In all, ten MLAs withdrew support to Deshmukh, including those from the PWP, the Communist Party of India (Marxist) (CPI[M]) and independents, bringing down the thirty-one-month-old Democratic Front (DF) government's bench strength in the assembly to just 145.[135]

This gave the Shiv Sena and the BJP an opening, with Rane claiming they could not spurn an opportunity given to them on a 'silver platter'.[136] Just before three independents were to be sworn in as ministers to mitigate the crisis, Rane and Munde paraded three dissident NCP MLAs before the governor. By the next day, they netted five NCP, one Janata Dal (Secular) (JD[S]) and one Congress legislators. Rane claimed that by 11 June, they had the confirmed backing of twenty MLAs, in addition to open support from a senior Congress MLA.[137] Defecting legislators were kept at Matoshree Sports Club in Jogeshwari, which was managed by the Shiv Sena's Ravindra Waikar. The NCP's Shalinitai Patil, the widow of former chief minister Vasantdada Patil, too withdrew support.[138]

'The operation had the blessings of Balasaheb and Uddhav. It had its roots in the disgruntlement within a section of NCP stalwarts against alleged high-handedness by Bhujbal. Some NCP legislators were also upset at the Congress for trying to undercut them in their constituencies, and were hence more comfortable with the idea of the saffron alliance in power,' claimed a politician from western Maharashtra, who was among the major players in this political tug of war.[139]

The politician claimed that 'huge amounts of money were thrown around'. But the operation failed because of the 'treachery' of some who did not stand by their word and because the PWP's Patil, who had sparked the developments, faced pressure from the party's old guard which was uneasy breaking bread with Hindutva parties.[140]

'Many MLAs were willing to change their loyalties but were apprehensive. They would tell the Shiv Sena's political managers to produce letters from other legislators withdrawing support after which they would take the plunge. This *pehle aap* behaviour caused the plan to fall through,' he claimed.

Bhujbal, who was the home minister, recalls how they airlifted their flock to Indore to prevent them from being poached. 'However, it was a BJP-ruled state and their workers would protest and shout slogans outside the hotel. We brought our MLAs to Mumbai and at the airport, they were asked to board an aircraft for Bangalore that had been parked right next to the plane that had brought them there.' Meanwhile, Congress and NCP strategists were working on the defectors.[141]

A senior Congress leader, who acted as a troubleshooter, recalls how political loyalties had turned fluid in those tumultuous days. 'An independent who had been sworn in as a minister of state was holed up in his constituency and was refusing to come to Mumbai for the trust vote, claiming he was being tailed by Shiv Sainiks. It took some persuasion to ensure his presence on D-day. Similarly, we also took some independents to meet senior Congress leaders in Delhi to ensure their loyalty.'[142]

The mood in the saffron camp was upbeat. Rane seemed to be within striking range of the chief minister's post. Raj visited Matoshree club and met the defecting MLAs.[143]

Rane said Uddhav made his only visit to the club on 8 August when he (Rane) was coincidentally out for a meeting. Uddhav felt 'insulted' that Rane was not available and walked out in a huff.[144]

When Prashant Hire, an NCP MLA from Nashik was on his way to the club, he was waylaid by NCP strongman from Ulhasnagar, Pappu Kalani, and taken to meet Sharad Pawar.

This, said Rane, proved they had a 'mole' among them leaking information to the DF leadership.[145]

The Shiv Sena's bid for power received a jolt, when Padmakar Valvi, a tribal legislator of the Congress from Nandurbar, who was at the club, managed to give his 'captors' the slip. He told reporters that he had been hoodwinked and taken to the Matoshree club by BJP MLA Girish Mahajan and had been trying to escape 'from day one'.[146]

According to a Congress strategist, Valvi's return to the Congress camp blew the bottom out of the Opposition's audacious bid and also caused the BJP to have second thoughts about it.[147]

Narayan Rane claims that on 11 June, defence minister George Fernandes and Munde met Bal Thackeray at his residence, which made him sense some 'foul play'. The next day, Thackeray privately indicated he did not support 'Operation Topple' any more despite his position in public and that the onus of its success and failure would lie entirely on him (Rane).[148]

In the assembly on 13 June, the DF government survived, thanks to some deft manoeuvring. Speaker Arun Gujrathi disqualified seven rebel legislators under the anti-defection law for crossing over to the Opposition. The PWP's five members abstained from voting after the NCP said it would drop Tatkare. PWP and CPI(M) leaders had promised Deshmukh that they would not vote with the Shiv Sena and the BJP.[149] This allowed the government to scrape through with 143 votes against the Opposition's 133.[150]

Though Bal Thackeray called the DF's victory 'one achieved through rape',[151] the Shiv Sena leader claimed that the old guard and Uddhav had gradually come around to the view that if Rane toppled the Deshmukh government, he would be firmly in control.[152]

Rane said 'saheb's (Bal Thackeray)' abandonment had come as a shock to him. 'The more I thought about it, the more I felt that

Uddhavji had much to do with the failure of the operation,' he added, claiming that Uddhav wanted to avenge the 'insult' that he had felt when he didn't find him at the club. Rane alleged that Uddhav had conspired with Munde, who he (Rane) was convinced was the mole, and got Fernandes to persuade Thackeray to withdraw support to the operation.[153] Moreover, even if the plan succeeded. Uddhav would have challenged his bid to become the chief minister, he felt, adding that his heart had now 'stopped beating for the Sena'.[154]

However, Uddhav loyalists said despite Narayan Rane's bravado, Uddhav had his doubts if the exercise would reach its logical end considering the odds stacked against them.[155]

The new working president

'The resolution is that the national executive appoints Shiv Sena leader Uddhav Thackeray to the new post of working president,' announced Raj Thackeray, speaking on a chilly winter day at Mahabaleshwar on 30 January 2003.

A smiling Raj then asked the executive to approve the motion, which, needless to say, was carried through unanimously amidst applause. Raj then invited Uddhav on the dais and garlanded him amid slogans of '*Chhatrapati Shivaji Maharaj ki jai*' and '*Shiv Sena pramukh Balasaheb Thackerayncha vijay aso* (Victory to Shiv Sena chief Bal Thackeray)'.[156]

At the conclave at the hill station, the Shiv Sena's succession battle had finally swung Uddhav's way, with Raj suggesting his name for the working president's post. This meant that Uddhav had been formally anointed as his father's political heir.

Later, after Raj's estrangement, Bal Thackeray would point to how his nephew had suggested his elder cousin's name for the post and claimed he had no knowledge that this would happen.

'He tabled the motion,' said Bal Thackeray, claiming he was not there when it happened. 'I was at a friend's bungalow at

Mahabaleshwar and had told them to call me when the speeches were over. When I went there, I saw a heap of garlands and bouquets, and when I asked, I was told Uddhav had become working president. I was angry and said I did not agree with what had happened, I asked [delegates] to fearlessly tell me if they did not agree with this appointment. I will cancel it immediately,' he said, adding that all those present had given their consent.[157]

However, Raj would later say that his hand had been forced. 'I had no powers to appoint a shakha pramukh, but I appointed an executive president? Even before the Mahabaleshwar conclave, Balasaheb wanted to do this but felt I would be a hindrance. I could understand this,' said Raj, while speaking at a rally at Dombivli in 2010. 'Hence, I said I will declare this if you want it . . . this is your party.'[158]

In 1989, the Shiv Sena drafted its first constitution, with the Shiv Sena pramukh being vested with supreme powers.[159] In 1997, the Election Commission of India (ECI) objected to the constitution which anointed Bal Thackeray as chief for life and threatened derecognition as a political party if organizational elections were not held.[160]

This set the wheels rolling within the Sena for a fresh party constitution and the creation of a new post of working president, who would be 'elected' by the national executive for a five-year period. The working president would be responsible for daily affairs and management of the party.[161]

However, some party leaders, who were against a parallel power centre to the supremo being created, were not amenable to the proposal.[162]

'While framing a party constitution, we were thinking of keeping Balasaheb as party chief for life with a new post of working president, who would be re-elected every five years. Uddhav was an obvious choice. This would formally anoint him as his father's political heir. Raj initially held out against the idea, but had to succumb,' explained the former Sena leader who was involved in the process.[163] 'The logic is simple. I have a son and a nephew and I love both. But when it comes to bequeathing my property, I will naturally choose my son and not my nephew.'[164]

A senior editor from the vernacular press, who is close to Raj, claimed when it came to this incident, Raj, who otherwise venerated and loved his uncle even after forming his own party, was 'slightly bitter'.[165]

Though Raj fell in line, Narayan Rane opposed Uddhav's becoming working president. 'When I reached Mahabaleshwar, the meeting had begun. I directly went to saheb [Bal Thackeray] who was not at the conclave and told him this decision was against the party's interests and would eat into his authority. However, saheb said, "Narayan, the decision has been taken,"' Rane said in 2015.[166]

Raj was given charge of areas like Nashik and Pune while Uddhav was supposed to call the shots in Mumbai and Thane. 'But Uddhav would often call meetings with office-bearers from Pune and Nashik keeping Raj in the dark. Raj felt stifled at Uddhav's interference on his turf,' recalled senior journalist Sandeep Pradhan.[167]

Earlier, the 2002 BMC election were completely Uddhav's show. He sidelined Narayan Rane and Raj and took charge of the nomination process. Apart from the Congress and NCP, the Shiv Sena faced a fresh challenge from underworld don Arun Gawli's Akhil Bhartiya Sena (ABS) and from party rebels.

Raj, who had been privately complaining to his uncle and close friends about no longer being consulted in party affairs, went public with his criticism for the first time and said he had no say in granting party tickets in the Mumbai civic polls.[168]

The Shiv Sena and BJP retained power with ninety-eight and thirty-five seats in the 227-member house. The Congress won sixty seats, while the NCP and Samajwadi Party notched up twelve and ten wins respectively. The Sena's tally fell marginally from 104 in 1997, but the win cemented Uddhav's hold over the party.

Uddhav had risked expanding the Shiv Sena's base vertically, beyond its traditional 'Marathi manoos' electoral catchment. In February 2003, soon after being appointed working president, he reached out to Buddhist Dalits during a ceremony to unveil a portrait of his grandfather at the department of Marathi in the University of Mumbai. He also held a 'Shivshakti-Bhimshakti' rally in Sharad Pawar's stronghold of Baramati, where he called on Dalits to stop voting for the Congress.[169]

The symbolism was significant as the Shiv Sena had crossed swords with Buddhist Dalits in the past. In the 1974 riots at Worli, the Sena clashed with the militant Dalit Panthers and had opposed renaming the Marathwada University after Dr Babasaheb Ambedkar (the Namantar [renaming] movement as it was called, ran from 1978–94) and the Maharashtra government printing Ambedkar's book, *Riddles in Hinduism*, with its controversial references to Hindu deities (1987).[170]

The Shiv Sena had a base among Hindu Dalits, who resented the dominance of Buddhist Dalits in the larger Dalit movement; and Marathas and the intermediate classes, who found it difficult to come to terms with their upward mobility. In the Buddhist Dalits, the Sena had found a social force capable of standing up to them in the use of raw muscle power on Mumbai's streets and was hence hostile towards them.

Uddhav's campaign saw an old Sena foe—Dalit Panther leader Namdeo Dhasal—bite the bait. One of the most charismatic Dalit leaders in Maharashtra, Dhasal was among those who birthed the Panthers, modelled along the lines of the Black Panthers in the United States. Formed in 1972, the thrust of the Dalit Panthers was to 'universalise the dalit identity as proletarian experience', and according to scholar Gail Omvedt, sparked a series of such protests across India.[171]

However, by 2003, the Panthers and Dhasal, a Sahitya Akademi Award–winning poet and avant-garde writer, who had once written angry poems with lines like '*Tyanchi sanatan daya Falkland Road chya bhadwyahun uncha naahi* (Their ancient sense of pity is not taller than the pimp in the flesh trade district)', were pale shadows of their former selves.

Similar attempts to forge unity between these two forces had failed earlier. On 26 February 1978, Bal Thackeray had sketched the Shiv Sena's tiger and the Black Panther on the cover issue of *Marmik*, seeking that the two forces unite for the assembly elections that year. Though the social outreach was swept away in the Janata wave that followed the Emergency, J.P. Ghatge of a Panther faction was later elected to the BMC from Bhandup in an alliance with the Sena.[172] In the official biography of his party, Joshi admits that if the two social forces of 'Shivshakti' and 'Bhimshakti' were to join hands, the scenario in Maharashtra would have changed.[173]

The other effort by Uddhav was more audacious. Hindi speakers had emerged as a formidable force in and around Mumbai with the Maharashtrians, who were the Shiv Sena's natural catchment, being gradually outnumbered.

'Uddhav may be a non-charismatic leader and a poor orator, but he is open-minded, liberal and a believer in inclusive politics,' said Sanjay Nirupam.[174] 'I had been stressing the need for *berjeche rajkaran* [a term popularized by late Congress stalwart Yashwantrao Chavan which means politics of inclusion] by the party. The Shiv Sena had alienated Muslims and sections of the Dalits and north Indians. It was necessary for it to rope in new voters considering that Marathi speakers were being gradually outnumbered by others in Mumbai. The non-Maharashtrians were contributing to population growth.

'North Indians, Gujaratis and Jains were staying in Mumbai for generations and there was no chance that they would just "disappear" because the Shiv Sena rejected them for its politics,' said Nirupam.

With a year to go for the 2004 state assembly polls, Uddhav launched a campaign termed 'Mee Mumbaikar' to reach out to people across linguistic denominations. It was perched precariously from its very inception—reaching out to north Indians, who competed with Maharashtrians for access to jobs and resources—and stood the risk of the Sena drifting away from its core vote base.

'Mumbai served those who came here . . . hence, it is essential to dump narrow identities like religion and caste to work for Mumbai and ensure that it regains its past glory,' said Uddhav. Bal Thackeray too urged everyone to join hands in the struggle to save Mumbai.[175]

After the Shiv Sena embraced hard-line Hindutva in the late 1980s and took an aggressive stance during the Ram temple movement and 1992–93 Mumbai riots, Bal Thackeray was projected as a Hindu Hriday Samrat (Emperor of Hindu hearts), which necessitated the need for the party to create an auxiliary constituency among non-Marathi Hindus. The Shiv Sena had launched a Hindi eveninger *Dopahar Ka Saamna*, in 1993, with Nirupam, who had been brought in from the Express Group's *Jansatta* as executive editor.

This also required a delicate balancing act between the interests and aspirations of its core Maharashtrian constituency and non-Marathi voters including Hindi and Gujarati speakers.

Though Ghanshyam Dube was the first north Indian to become its MLC in the 1990s, the Shiv Sena's outreach towards a growing number of Hindi-speaking migrants from states like Bihar and Uttar Pradesh picked up after Uddhav became working president.

Sachin Parab, who covered the Shiv Sena as a reporter during this period, noted that Uddhav was trying to give the party a liberal image through campaigns like 'Shiv Shakti-Bhim Shakti' and 'Mee Mumbaikar'.[176]

'The launch of "Mee Mumbaikar" at Bandra saw a massive response. Shiv Sena shakhas in Mumbai and Thane saw at least one non-Maharashtrian deputy shakha chief being appointed. The Shiv Sena was finally in the process of getting a long-overdue makeover,' said Parab.[177]

Parab explained how a Shiv Sena leader had told him that the party was affected at the hustings when the 'majority of the minority', namely, north Indians, Muslims and Buddhist Dalits, voted tactically to defeat them. 'The Sena leader said they had no problems with these sections not voting for them, but it was this tactical voting that hurt them. "Mee Mumbaikar" was a strategy by Uddhav to blunt the opposition of these linguistic and religious minorities,' he said.[178]

Kamlesh Rai, who was the Shiv Sena's first north Indian shakha pramukh and corporator from Andheri in Mumbai's western suburbs, recalled how they pasted 'Mee Mumbaikar' stickers on vehicles. 'The idea was that those who had arrived in Mumbai by 1995 are naturalized Mumbaikars. The response of north Indians towards the campaign was gradually picking up,' said Rai, who was elected as a corporator from a ward in Andheri that was a north Indian–dominated Congress stronghold.[179]

However, a section of the hardliners within the Shiv Sena was uneasy at this dilution in the party's core Marathi manoos agenda. Sanjay Nirupam admitted that during a party meeting attended by Uddhav, his 'Mee Mumbaikar' campaign was derided by a senior party leader. He added that the idea had also found an opponent in Raj.[180]

A key charge by the Shiv Sena, and later the MNS, had been that the recruitment process in the railways, which is among India's biggest recruiters, and other Central government units, was tweaked to suit candidates from north India. They accused railway officials of not publishing advertisements in local media, which ensured Maharashtrian youth were unaware of recruitments in their own region.[181]

Raj, seen as a hawk within the party, seemed uneasy with the campaign, and his absence at its launch at Rangasharada Hall in Bandra raised eyebrows.

On 18 November 2003, activists from Raj's BVS attacked and vandalized the Railway Recruitment Board (RRB) office at Mumbai Central, demanding priority for local youth in recruitments. The police countered them with a lathi charge. Haji Arafat Shaikh, who was part of the mob, recalled protestors throwing cupboards from one of the top floors of the building.[182]

In the same month, BVS cadre sprung a surprise, attacking candidates from north India who had come for the Railway recruitment exams at Kalyan. Raj warned that they would 'strike down any attempt to recruit outsiders'.[183] This attack sent shock waves among north Indians, who organized a protest at Kalyan railway station and the railway police station seeking action against the Shiv Sena and protection for candidates from outside states. The Shiv Sena, in turn, warned that any talk of a *muqabla* (confrontation) would be met with excessive force. BVS workers tore up call letters of Railway Board examinees at Vasai.[184]

Raj later claimed that the assault happened because a railway official had abused Maharashtrians.

The violence led to a war of words between Rashtriya Janata Dal (RJD) chief Lalu Prasad Yadav and Bal Thackeray.[185] Uddhav was forced to relent on the Mee Mumbaikar campaign.

Though similar protests had happened in the past, the context of the Kalyan attack was important as it came at the time when Uddhav was reaching out to Hindi speakers, a year before the 2004 assembly polls. It also revealed the undercurrent of resentment within the organization towards efforts to 'secularize' and broad-base the Sena, which could eventually alienate it from its core agenda and socio-electoral catchment.

Joshi's official biography of the Shiv Sena is again uncharacteristically candid on the issue, admitting that this turn of events caused the attempts to bring the Marathi manoos and the north Indians together falling through, leading to 'Mee Mumbaikar' being shelved. The Shiv Sena continued to tread the beaten path, abandoning attempts to unite Maharashtrians and non-Maharashtrians, he writes.[186]

Inflamed passions

On the morning of 5 January 2004 around 150 workers of a little-known Maratha group called 'Sambhaji Brigade' vandalized the Bhandarkar Oriental Research Institute (BORI) in Pune. Named after Ramkrishna Gopal Bhandarkar, an Orientalist and social reformer, the institute housed a large collection of rare manuscripts. The Pune police arrested seventy-two men.

The group—the youth wing of the virulently anti-Brahmin Maratha Seva Sangh (MSS) founded by Purushottam Khedekar, an engineer with the state government's PWD—was angered at the allegedly demeaning references to Chhatrapati Shivaji and his mother, Rajmata Jijabai, in American author James Laine's book, *Shivaji: A Hindu King in Islamic India*. The book mentioned that some Maharashtrians 'tell jokes naughtily' about Shivaji's parentage.[187]

This allusion to Shivaji's Brahmin guardian, Dadoji Konddeo, was seen as a plot hatched by the Brahmins to co-opt Shivaji and denigrate his legacy, leading to widespread anger. However, after the controversy, Laine told author Martha C. Nussbaum that according to his notes, he had heard the jokes in 1987 but made it clear that he did not accept this account, which he called a 'piece of malicious gossip'.[188]

The BORI attack sent ripples across the state. Dnyanesh Maharao, editor of the Marathi magazine *Chitralekha*, who was the first to write against these references, said he had spoken at a number of public meetings across the state to generate awareness, which led to the formation of a 'Shivbhakta Andolan Samiti' (Committee of Shivaji's devotees).

'Why aren't such things said about [Brahmins] like Lokmanya Bal Gangadhar Tilak? Making insinuations about the character of people while trying to underplay their achievements is heinous,' he said.

While pointing to how Brahminist interpretations of history had distorted and suppressed lives and works of icons from the Bahujan Samaj, Maharao said that the reference in Laine's book was a symptom of a larger disease. Maharao questioned why none of the people whose help was acknowledged by Laine, including BORI and its senior librarian, V.L. Manjul, had objected to these references, and how 'naughty jokes' could possibly be used to write a historical work.[189]

On 22 December 2003, a group of Shiv Sainiks led by Rambhau Parikh, then Pune city unit chief of the party, blackened the face of Sanskrit scholar Shrikant Bahulkar, who was among those the author had thanked in the book. A week later, Raj arrived in Pune to personally apologize to Bahulkar, who had also worked as a co-author with Laine on *The Epic of Shivaji: A Translation and Study of Kavindra*, which was the translation Kavindra Paramananda's Sanskrit work, *Shivbharat*.[190]

'I was expecting Balasaheb and the Shiv Sena to speak up against this insult of Shivaji Maharaj as the Sena extracted the highest political capital using his name. However, at a function on 16 January 2003, Balasaheb kept mum as then prime minister Atal Bihari Vajpayee spoke on the controversy claiming that countering the views in a book by another good book is understandable. But there was no intellectual view in the offending sentence. The irony was that Vajpayee was speaking at a function to unveil the statue of the warrior-king at Mumbai's Chhatrapati Shivaji International Airport (CSIA)!' said Maharao.[191]

The state government declared it would seek Laine's arrest for the remarks.[192]

Though the Supreme Court lifted the ban on Laine's book in 2010, the publisher, Oxford University Press (OUP), declared they would not reprint it.[193]

In December 2010, the Pune police wire-tapped a conversation between Uddhav Thackeray's controversial personal assistant, Milind Narvekar, and Shiv Sena MLC and incumbent Maharashtra legislative council deputy chairperson, Neelam Gorhe, where Narvekar purportedly instructed Gorhe to cause violence during a Pune bandh. The bandh had been called after the Pune Municipal Corporation (PMC) removed Dadoji Konddeo's statue from Lal Mahal (a replica of the palace where Shivaji Maharaj had stayed during his childhood in Pune) after protests by Maratha groups.[194]

Gorhe and Narvekar were booked by Pune police under the IPC sections 153 (promoting enmity between different groups and doing acts prejudicial to maintenance of harmony) and 120 (b) (hatching criminal conspiracy). In October 2017, a Pune court accepted the government's plea to withdraw the case.[195]

After the controversy and attack on BORI, the ruling NCP latched on to the opportunity, deploying one of its star speakers, then home minister, late R.R. Patil, who used the issue to canvas support for his party.

Cornered, the Shiv Sena tried to use one thorn to extricate another. Thackeray attacked Marathi writer R.R. Borade, a Maratha by caste, who headed the state board for literature and culture. The board had published the Marathi translation of a book, *Marathyanchi Prashasan Vyawasta* (The Administration System of the Marathas) in 2003 with allegedly derogatory references to Shivaji. This led to Shiv Sena workers attacking Borade's residence in Aurangabad.[196] However, this issue was overshadowed by the Laine controversy.

With its barely disguised anti-Brahmin undertones, the campaign led to the dominant Marathas mobilizing in the NCP's favour. They were helped by the caste politics in Maharashtra, which is the womb of the non-Brahmin movement. The Brahmins, though miniscule, are an articulate cultural elite with an influence far beyond their numbers and are regarded by the other castes as perpetrators of centuries of caste oppression.

Saffron setback

In the 2004 Lok Sabha elections, the Atal Bihari Vajpayee government faced a shock defeat. The Shiv Sena and BJP lost five of six seats in Mumbai, barring Mumbai South Central represented by Mohan Rawle. Manohar Joshi, then the Lok Sabha speaker, was trounced by the Congress' Eknath Gaikwad, allegedly because of opposition from within his own party.

In the 2004 state assembly elections, the NCP, which was on a weaker footing, rode on the back of this Maratha consolidation to edge out the Congress to emerge as the single largest party with seventy-one seats compared to its ally's sixty-nine.

This Maratha polarization, coupled with factionalism within the Shiv Sena and the BJP, led to the saffron alliance getting just 106 seats (sixty-two for the Shiv Sena and fifty-four for the BJP). The Congress replaced incumbent Sushilkumar Shinde, a Hindu Dalit, with Vilasrao Deshmukh, a Maratha. In January 2003, Deshmukh had stepped down in Shinde's favour.

Insiders say the Shiv Sena was unable to manage its factional feuds during this period as Uddhav's loyalists tried to deny nominations to those inimical to them or who were close to the Raj and Rane camps.

Raj Thackeray's loyalist and two-term MLA Deepak Paigude (who later joined the MNS), lost from his Bhavani Peth seat in Pune to the NCP's Kamal Dhole Patil by a wafer-thin margin of around 300 votes. His supporters claimed this was because Shiv Sainiks loyal to Uddhav stayed away from his campaign.

The western Maharashtra politician quoted on page 106 claimed that Narayan Rane had decided to honour the commitments given to dissident NCP MLAs who had tried to dislodge the Congress–NCP government in 2002. For instance, while Narsing Gurunath Patil from Chandgad in Kolhapur wanted to join the Shiv Sena, cooperative baron Vinay Kore-Savkar wanted the Sena to help him get votes from Vaibhavwadi taluka in Sindhudurg that was part of his Panhala constituency in Kolhapur.[197]

'Uddhav may have been insecure about Rane's leadership and turned down these demands as he feared Rane would have become stronger within the legislature party. This led to Shiv Sena and BJP losing at least twelve to twenty seats. Perhaps, the Sena–BJP alliance may have come to power if this had been avoided,' he said.[198]

Congress leaders state that the Laine controversy, coupled with the pushback by north Indians after the assault by Raj's men, also helped tilt the scales in favour of the Congress–NCP alliance.

'If Raj's men had not assaulted north Indians, these votes may have gone with them [the Shiv Sena] due to the Mee Mumbaikar campaign. The Shiv Sena and BJP were in striking distance of power,' admitted Congress leader Kripashankar Singh, a first-generation migrant from Jaunpur in Uttar Pradesh, who became the powerful minister of state for home during Vilasrao Deshmukh's first chief ministerial stint.[199]

Before the state assembly elections, Bal Thackeray refused to declare the Shiv Sena's chief ministerial face if elected to power, calling it a 'secret'. Incidentally, a readers' poll by Marathi newspaper *Loksatta*[200] identified Raj as a popular choice for the chief minister's post, with the others being Sharad Pawar, Manohar Joshi and Gandhian social activist Anna Hazare. The unwell Shiv Sena chief could address just two rallies during the assembly campaign—at Mumbai and Thane, and Uddhav and Raj led the charge for the party.[201]

Speaking at a rally, Raj said he would 'surely like to be the chief minister of Maharashtra'.[202]

The loss may have come as a rude reminder for one man—Narayan Rane, who would have a bitter parting with the Shiv Sena the very next year.

'The Shiv Sena faced two back-to-back setbacks in 1999 and 2004. Factionalism within the Shiv Sena and its tussle with the BJP were also responsible for the debacle. Rane realized that despite his best efforts, the Shiv Sena had been unable to form its government. He did not foresee a future for himself in the party,' said a former Shiv Sena leader.[203]

With Uddhav's star on the rise, and their best-laid plans coming apart, Rane and Raj had hit a glass ceiling in the party.

6

Raj's Estrangement and the Birth of MNS

> Time present and time past
> Are both perhaps present in time future,
> And time future contained in time past.
> If all time is eternally present
> All time is unredeemable.
> What might have been is an abstraction
> Remaining a perpetual possibility
> Only in a world of speculation.
> What might have been and what has been
> Point to one end, which is always present.
>
> T.S. Eliot, 'Four Quartets'

By 2004, with his ageing father retreating from an active role and Raj sidelined, Uddhav was firmly in the saddle. Gradually, complaints about his being inaccessible for party leaders and cadre, almost like a modern-day Lady of Shalott, began making the rounds. Senior BJP leaders and journalists claimed there were times when even the likes of Pramod Mahajan and Gopinath Munde found it tough to access the Shiv Sena working president.

The relationship between Rane and Uddhav, which was never rosy to begin with, was deteriorating further. Shiv Sena insiders claimed Rane was being slighted in small but significant ways, like being made to wait before meeting the party chief or his son, or his phone calls going unanswered. Vageesh Saraswat, then a reporter on the political beat, said there were unwritten instructions to the Shiv Sena cadre against inviting both Raj and Rane to any local-level party functions.[1]

The Shiv Sena's monolithic structure makes the party supremo rely on regional and subregional satraps to run the party. Matoshree loyalists felt Rane was becoming powerful and a threat to this familial control over the party, and hence, tried to clip his wings.[2] Congress leader Vijay Vadettiwar, who was then a Rane loyalist and quit the Shiv Sena with him, claims there were fears in the ranks of Uddhav loyalists that 'Rane and Raj would hijack the Sena'.[3]

In his autobiography, Rane admits he had lost control over the party apparatus just before 'Operation Topple', and was not being invited to important meetings. He charged that the troika of Uddhav, Manohar Joshi and senior leader Subhash Desai wanted to 'bring him down'.[4]

Uddhav's private secretary, Milind Narvekar, emerged as a power centre at Matoshree due to his ability to grant and deny appointments and access. Uddhav's preference for not readily associating with people beyond his immediate circle meant that Narvekar soon became entrenched as his gatekeeper.

The tall and lanky Narvekar, who was a *gatpramukh*, the lowest post in the party organization at Liberty Gardens at Malad, is reputed to have met his future boss in the early 1990s seeking the post of shakha pramukh. He was however chosen by Uddhav to work as his assistant.[5]

With his boss preferring his own company at times, Narvekar's clout rose in the Sena. He was also blamed by leaders ranging from Bhaskar Jadhav (in 2004) to Narayan Rane (in 2005) and Mohan Rawle (in 2014) for their decisions to quit the party.

Today, though Narvekar tails Uddhav in public, Sena insiders claim he no longer has the kind of clout that he once had a decade ago, due to the emergence of other power centres and gatekeepers at Matoshree.

Narvekar was said to be in the race for a Rajya Sabha or state legislative council nomination but had to settle for the party secretary's post instead in January 2018.

Rane's exit

Unlike many party leaders, Narayan Rane, called Dada or NTR (an abbreviation of his full name Narayan Tatu Rane) by his supporters, had a mass base in Sindhudurg and the loyalty of some Sena legislators.

In a closed-door meeting of office-bearers on 14 April 2005, Rane's anger boiled over. 'Positions in the Shiv Sena were being bought,' he alleged. 'A bazaar for these posts happens in the party.' It was obvious he was pointing fingers at Uddhav and his coterie.[6]

Bal Thackeray and Uddhav were not present at the meeting. Thackeray, who was informed of Rane's allegation, arrived at the meeting and asked Manohar Joshi, Rane and others if anyone had asked them to pay money when they were nominated to a post. 'If it is proved that Uddhav or Raj has taken money, I will not keep them in the Shiv Sena and if these charges against me are proved, I will quit the Shiv Sena and take sanyas,' he said.[7]

In June 2005, Sheshrao Girhepunje, the Shiv Sena's district chief in Bhandara, some 900 kilometres from Mumbai, was a troubled man. Booked in around forty cases of organized protests, he had been served a notice by the local subdivisional police officer (SDPO) for externment from five districts—Bhandara, Nagpur, Gadchiroli, Chandrapur and Gondia—for two years.

A resident of the communally sensitive Sadak Arjuni town in Bhandara, Girhepunje had been working for the Sena since 1987.

He decided to go to Mumbai to meet Narayan Rane and appeal for succour. Rane, who was leader of Opposition at the time, was travelling abroad and asked him to approach Uddhav instead.

'The police were trying to frame me. These cases were political. When I went to Matoshree, I was told Uddhav was in a meeting. On my second trip a couple of days later, a policeman on duty said Uddhav was upset as a fish worth around Rs 1.25 lakh brought from abroad had died and hence, would not meet visitors,' Girhepunje alleged.[8]

On his return, Rane heard the story from Girhepunje. Journalist Sandeep Pradhan, who was then working for the Marathi daily *Loksatta*, said Rane told reporters about this incident, using it to illustrate how the common worker was being slighted by the leadership.[9] Uddhav denied the incident and called it an attempt to defame him.

'Contrary to popular notion, it was not Milind Narvekar who turned me away,' admitted Girhepunje, who later followed Rane into the Congress. Girhepunje, who admits to having 'traces of the *bhagwa* [saffron flag]' even now, said he had no way to confirm if what he was told about the fish was true or not. Girhepunje says that Rane decided to quit the Shiv Sena after that incident.[10]

Rane, who calls Uddhav and his wife Rashmi 'great human beings', said he felt guilty as Uddhav and his father quarrelled because of him. This guilt, he claimed, was a major reason behind his decision to leave the Shiv Sena. Rane said he wrote an informal letter to his party boss, stating he would leave the Sena and sit at home.'[11]

Rane said after submitting that letter, he went abroad for a fortnight, and on his return, was surprised to see media reports 'sown' by Narvekar, Joshi and Desai, stating he was leaving the Shiv Sena and joining the Congress–NCP alliance.[12]

Later, Rane met party supremo Bal Thackeray and handed over letters resigning from the Sena, as the leader of Opposition and from the assembly. Rane claimed when Uddhav learnt of his father's efforts to make amends with him (Rane), he threatened to leave Matoshree with his wife Rashmi. This broke the conviction of the late Sena chief, who had already lost one son and was estranged from another.[13]

On 28 June 2005, Rane flew to Goa en route his constituency in neighbouring Sindhudurg. In an apparent show of strength, he was received by supporters in around 250 vehicles, shouting slogans like '*Narayan Rane angaar hai, baaki sab bhangar hai*' (Narayan Rane is an ember, all others are riff-raff).[14] Rane is said to have addressed his followers and shared his anger at Uddhav's style of functioning.

Meanwhile, Bal Thackeray asked party cadre to 'stop believing rumours which aim at creating divisions', and that Rane was a hard-core Shiv Sainik who would never betray the Sena.[15]

On 2 July, Rane held a press conference in Mumbai and announced his resignation from the Shiv Sena. He said he was quitting because his seniors in the party were not happy with him, and that he would remain a Sainik regardless.[16]

On the same evening, Bal Thackeray announced Rane's expulsion at the Rangasharada Hall in Bandra. The Shiv Sena chief charged Rane with betraying the organization. He dared Rane to quit as an MLA if he had any self-respect, and said he would not tolerate such 'gangsterism'.[17]

According to a senior Congress leader, Rane, as leader of Opposition, had been uncomfortable with the growing clout of Goregaon MLA Subhash Desai in the Shiv Sena legislative party. It was rumoured that Uddhav would eventually replace Rane with Desai.[18]

Media reports said that in an emergency meeting called by Bal Thackeray on 6 July, where fifty-two MLAs were present, Raj suggested that Uddhav resign as working president to placate dissenters. Some MLAs even suggested Manohar Joshi as working president as a compromise between the warring cousins.[19]

Rane claimed he had been victimized by Uddhav for speaking out at the party convention and that he could present people who had paid money for party tickets in the previous elections. He alleged that Uddhav's personal assistant had brokered the deals. Writing in *Outlook*, Smruti Koppikar said Rane and his supporters had 'made a public mockery' of Bal Thackeray's decision to anoint Uddhav as the Sena's working president.[20]

'Cut-outs of Raj put up for his birthday had to be pulled down . . . Raj Thackeray is also a sufferer like me,' Rane declared. He also accused Bal Thackeray of putting his love for his son above everything else.[21]

Rane informed his followers that he would not join any party and quit politics. But, a group of thirty-eight Shiv Sena MLAs, led by Raj Thackeray aide Bala Nandgaonkar, urged him to reconsider.[22] Finally, Rane received support from ten Shiv Sena legislators.

After being wooed by the Congress, NCP and even the BJP, Rane finally joined the Congress. One reason for the choice was that the party had the chief minister's post and the party high command was eager to replace incumbent Vilasrao Deshmukh.[23]

Rane made a startling claim that in July 2005, after he quit the Shiv Sena, Raj came to his house at night and said he wanted to do likewise. Raj suggested they must align their interests and start a new party, which would attract loyal Sainiks. However, Rane refused, as he knew how the 'Thackerays operate' and didn't think he wanted to work with one again.[24]

However, a former Raj Thackeray aide, who is now with the BJP, claimed otherwise. 'Rane was in touch with Raj, insisting they quit the Shiv Sena together. Raj instead wanted them to stay on and fight. Rane refused to continue in the Shiv Sena as matters had come to a head for him.'[25]

Raj too was feeling cornered within the party, but could not have walked away with Rane, who was seen as a *gaddar* (traitor) by the party faithful, affecting his claim to the Thackeray legacy.[26] Neither could he work as anyone's second-in-command.[27]

Vijay Vadettiwar, who is the leader of Opposition in the Maharashtra legislative assembly, said while Raj and Rane were in touch, it was tough to say who made the first move. 'Both of them were unhappy, and the reasons for their grief were the same. However, both have their reasons to say that the other person took the initiative to join hands, one that was short-lived for obvious reasons.'[28]

In his co-authored book, Harshal Pradhan, Uddhav's media adviser, notes that 'it was not a mere coincidence' that both Rane and Raj quit the party within a few months of one another.[29] The duo had realized that 'after Uddhav Thackeray's appointment as the Shiv Sena's working president in 2003, they would not be able to have their writ run large and fulfil their political ambitions,' Pradhan claimed.[30]

In contrast to another high-profile dissenter—Chhagan Bhujbal—who had been made a target of the Shiv Sena's backlash, Rane seemed to have the upper hand.

For years, the slogan, *Aavaz kunacha? Shiv Senecha!* (Whose voice rules? That of the Shiv Sena!), had underlined the Shiv Sena's pre-eminence in Mumbai, especially when it came using muscle power. At this point, however, the Shiv Sena was forced on the back foot, as Rane's men attacked party offices. The Sena found itself at the receiving end of the very forces it had unleashed. The party seemed to be imploding like the proverbial 'snake that ate its own tail' to quote an article.[31]

A former Maharashtra cabinet minister recalls how Rane all but charged at two Sena MLAs who were shouting slogans against him in the state legislature premises but was restrained by a Congress legislator from Vidarbha.[32]

Shiv Sena leaders recall that there had developed an atmosphere of mutual distrust where 'one person found it tough to trust another in the fear that he could be Rane's mole'.[33] Rane boasted to the media about some attendees at a Shiv Sena meeting at Rangasharada Hall at Bandra shouting slogans in his favour![34] Rane's loyalists had also tried to wrest control of the Shiv Sena's unions in five-star hotels and, the Brihanmumbai Electric Supply and Transport Undertaking (BEST), of which Rane had been chairman during his days as a BMC councillor. He also challenged the Shiv Sena in its own den by holding a public meeting outside the *Saamna* office at Prabhadevi!

To prevent any more defections, Shiv Sena legislators were kept at a five-star hotel in suburban Mumbai. Apart from the police, a security ring of Shiv Sainiks was formed to prevent these legislators from jumping ship or being poached.

Rane, who controlled the Shiv Sena legislature party with an iron fist during his tenure as leader of Opposition, tried to catch his erstwhile party in a pincer by seeking the disqualification of twenty-five Sena MLAs.[35]

Later, Rane resigned as leader of the Opposition and Shiv Sena's Ramdas Kadam, a legislator from Khed in Ratnagiri, was elected in his place. Like in 1991, the BJP waited in the wings to wrest the position from the Sena if its numbers dipped below its own due to defections to Rane's fold.[36]

The Sena also worked hard to ensure that corporators in the BMC did not defect to Rane, with both Bal Thackeray and Uddhav making an emotional appeal to ensure that the flock stay together.

In an interview to *Saamna* in January 2006, Bal Thackeray claimed that Rane had once admitted that he (Rane) would have been bumped off in a police encounter had he not joined the Shiv Sena.[37]

On 26 July 2005, Mumbai faced torrential rains, paralysing the city. Railway services were disrupted as was road traffic. People were stranded either in their offices or on roads as the city saw a record 944 mm of rainfall. Electricity supply was cut off and operations at the Mumbai airport were disrupted due to flooding. Over 500 people died.[38]

Kalanagar being a low-lying area, where Matoshree is located, was also flooded. Bal Thackeray was shifted to Raj's house at Dadar. The Shiv Sena-controlled BMC faced flak for the poor state of civic infrastructure.

'Raj nursed a vain hope that when it came to his successor, Balasaheb may finally choose him. However, during the time when Balasaheb was at his house, he realized that he was mistaken. This may have led him to decide to quit the Shiv Sena,' said Vageesh Saraswat, who as a journalist working on the Shiv Sena beat, had gradually come close to Raj.[39]

Finally, Rane joined the Congress in July 2005 and was appointed revenue minister. His supporters claimed he had been promised by the leadership that he would be appointed as chief minister within six months.

A senior Congress leader said that before making his disgruntlement against the Shiv Sena public, Rane had contacted NCP chief and then Union agriculture minister Sharad Pawar, seeking an entry into the party. 'However, Rane was looking at the chief minister's post or an important portfolio that incumbent NCP ministers were not too comfortable to part with. Finally, it was senior Congress leader, late Balasaheb Vikhe Patil [a cooperative sector bigwig with interests spanning sectors like education and sugar mills who shifted from the Congress to the Shiv Sena and back], who took the initiative to bring him into the Congress. Though state Congress chief Prabha Rau and general secretary in charge of Maharashtra, Margaret Alva, were in favour of getting Rane to join the party, then chief minister Vilasrao Deshmukh was uneasy because he saw Rane as a claimant for his chair.'[40]

The Marathi manoos from the Konkan region accounted for a significant number of Maharashtrians in Mumbai. The Konkan region was once described as a remittance economy surviving on the earnings of migrants from Raigad, Ratnagiri and Sindhudurg, who worked in Mumbai mostly in blue-collar jobs. Though things had changed for the better thanks to tourism, the famous Alphonso mango and marine fishing, the coastline retained a strong emotional bond with Mumbai.

Conversely, people from the Konkan region who had settled in Mumbai also cherished the association with their roots. As Konkani people revel in saying—any style or fashion statement that takes hold among their brethren in Mumbai is soon replicated in their region.

Hence, for the Shiv Sena, losing the Konkan to Rane would go on to mean repercussions in Mumbai.

Faced with a challenge to its control over the region, the party fell back on Raj Thackeray, who began his tour of the region on 9 August 2005, in the backdrop of the floods. But he left it midway after K.M.M. Prasanna, superintendent of police of Sindhudurg, requested him to do so, considering the repercussion on law and order.[41]

'This was a difficult time for the Shiv Sena and we left for the Konkan with vehicles full of workers. The cavalcade included supporters from Muslim areas like Behrampada, Bhendi Bazaar and Govandi. We would move a few kilometres ahead of the main cavalcade to check if things were safe. However, we turned back from Sindhudurg after the police warned us of a likely fallout,' said Haji Arafat Shaikh.[42]

Amid reports of disagreements between the cousins, Bal Thackeray met Uddhav and Raj on 17 August with Manohar Joshi and Sanjay Raut in attendance. *Saamna* front-paged the photo with the caption '*Hum Saath Saath Hain* (We are united)'. Bal Thackeray issued a statement claiming that 'after healthy discussions, the cobwebs of misunderstandings had been burnt away', and henceforth, Raj, Uddhav and other leaders would take decisions based on consensus. He warned against groupism.[43]

On 26 August, Uddhav and Raj released a joint statement claiming that 'Shiv Sainiks will not believe in baseless reports of a split'.[44]

The Shiv Sena faced its litmus test, when the 19 November 2005 by-election to Rane's Malvan constituency was announced after his resignation as Sena MLA. The Shiv Sena fielded Parshuram Uparkar, a former Rane associate, and the party deployed its most potent weapon for the campaign—Shiv Sena chief Bal Thackeray who came to the constituency despite his poor health and advanced years.

'Those were tough days as Rane's men virtually had a carte blanche. They ensured that Shiv Sena leaders got no hotels or even bread-and-breakfast facilities to stay in. Four Shiv Sena MLAs from Marathwada were asked to vacate their hotel the very next morning after their identities were revealed. Vehicles of Shiv Sena leaders were denied petrol at fuel pumps,' said the former Raj Thackeray associate.[45]

A senior journalist from Sindhudurg district claimed that when Raj arrived to campaign, some of Rane's supporters standing by the wayside welcomed him with slogans of '*Ye andar ki baat, Raj hamare saath hai* (This is a secret, but Raj is with us)'.[46]

Raj campaigned and even addressed a public meeting at Kankavali but left the tour midway, claiming to suffer from backache. In a press conference, Bal Thackeray said that he was now in an advisory role, leaving most of the decision making to Uddhav.[47]

In a public meeting at the ASD Topiwala High School grounds at Malvan, Bal Thackeray made an emotional appeal to voters to stand by the Shiv Sena, but it was in vain. When the results were announced on 22 November 2005, Rane defeated

Uparkar with 78,616 votes against his adversary's tally of 15,224. Adding insult to injury, the Shiv Sena lost its security deposit.[48]

Two years after quitting the Shiv Sena, Raj made a sensational claim.

Speaking at a public meeting at Thane on 29 October 2007, Raj alleged that a plan had been hatched to eliminate him during the by-election. Raj claimed he had been warned by the police about a threat to his life, causing him to return to Mumbai halfway through the campaign.[49] Bal Thackeray denied the claim, calling it 'unfortunate' and questioning how Raj could stoop so low.[50] He spoke about how the Shiv Sena and Uddhav had stood by Raj during the Ramesh Kini case.[51] Deputy chief minister and home minister R.R. Patil too refuted Raj's charges.[52] However, Raj's associates claimed that this incident was the last straw in Raj's relationship with the Shiv Sena, prompting his decision to quit the party.[53]

The final split

On 27 November 2005, Raj Thackeray addressed his supporters outside his home, 'Krishnakunj', at Shivaji Park.

'My quarrel is not with my Vitthala [Lord Vithoba] but with the priests around him,' he said as a crowd of thousands of supporters clapped and cheered and raised slogans of '*Raj saheb aage badho hum tumhare saath hain* (Raj saheb, move ahead, we are with you)'.

'There are some people who do not understand the ABC of politics. Hence, I am resigning as a leader of the Shiv Sena. Balasaheb Thackeray was, is and will continue to remain my God,' he announced.[54]

Raj had earlier skipped a meeting of Sena leaders called by Bal Thackeray. Before addressing his supporters, he had faxed a letter to his uncle resigning from party posts and questioning the party's electoral setbacks in the past three years.[55]

One of Raj's personal friends, who would join the MNS later, said Raj had become emotional after resigning from the Shiv Sena, even breaking into tears in a closed-door meeting.[56] He claimed Raj's attempts over the years to bridge differences had been slighted. 'That phase was very traumatic for Raj, around 1 per cent of his sorrow was linked to him quitting the Sena, while 99 per cent was for his estrangement from his uncle,' said a senior editor close to Raj.[57]

Raj's resignation letter was said to have been drafted by Sanjay Raut. 'The letter was balanced in its tone and laid down the reasons why he was quitting the party. Balasaheb had one look at it and told Raut that this was his handiwork!' said a senior Shiv Sena leader.[58] Sanjay Raut, who joined *Saamna* as its executive editor in 1990, was among the Sena chief's favourites and was considered almost his alter ego due to his aggressive editorials and columns in the paper.

Ironically, Raut's car was damaged by Raj's supporters when he, along with Manohar Joshi, was sent as an emissary by Bal Thackeray.[59] On the day Raj made this formal announcement, *Maharashtra Times*, the Marathi daily from the Times Group, had front-paged a story about Raj's plans to quit the Shiv Sena.[60]

'I had met a senior Shiv Sena leader close to Raj at the party office. This man was literally tearing into Uddhav loyalists like Subhash Desai during our conversation. This set me thinking if Raj, whose disgruntlement was very obvious, was planning to go Rane's way. Later, I called Raj and asked him point blank if he was planning to quit the Shiv Sena. His cryptic reply was very revealing. Raj did not deny this outright, but just said let's speak later,' said Sachin Parab. He filed the story after speaking to his sources, who confirmed his hypothesis.[61]

After the story appeared in *Maharashtra Times* and the *Times of India*, incensed Shiv Sainiks burnt copies.[62] However, Raj's loyalists started trooping to his Dadar residence.

Much later, in 2018, in an interview with his friend and actor, Atul Parchure, Raj recounted an incident about his favourite scriptwriters—Salim–Javed (Salim Khan and Javed Akthar). 'I once asked Salim saheb, how did your partnership break? He said, every product has an expiry date,' said Raj.[63]

Perhaps like the partnership of the famous scriptwriter duo, Raj's association with the Shiv Sena too had outlived its utility.

Nikhil Wagle said earlier, several attempts to bring about a reconciliation between the two by their maternal uncle, Chandrakant Vaidya, history writer Babasaheb Purandare and Jayant Salgaonkar, an astrologer and businessman who launched the iconic *Kalnirnay* calendar, had failed.[64]

Among those upset with the turn of events was Chhagan Bhujbal. Despite his bitter parting, Bhujbal still had an emotional attachment with the Shiv Sena. 'I had not spoken to the Shiv Sena chief, Uddhav or Raj after leaving the Sena. But, after reports of their estrangement surfaced, I called Raj and Uddhav and asked them to take it easy and rethink their positions. But the inevitable happened,' he said.[65] Even today, Bhujbal feels that the cousins would have 'ruled Maharashtra, single-handedly' if they had stayed together. 'Raj is an aggressive leader and an orator in Balasaheb's mould, while Uddhav is a great planner with an understanding of situations.'[66]

One of Raj's former associates claimed his leader was also toying with the idea of quitting politics altogether and focusing on his business and his passion—cartooning. Raj, during his college days, had nursed an ambition to work at the Walt Disney Studios. He agreed to remain in politics at the behest of his followers, who by now were straining at their leashes in the Shiv Sena.[67]

A senior Shiv Sena leader, who is close to both Uddhav and Raj, said the younger Thackeray cousin had often spoken to his uncle about his plans to quit politics altogether. 'Raj contemplated this at least twice or thrice and told Balasaheb that if he was the cause of discord within the party and family, he would rather call it a day,' he added.[68]

His former business associate claimed that Raj had little option but to take the plunge at that point. For one, the Shiv Sena was being weakened and for Raj, it made sense to walk out with some of its support base before things went further downhill.[69] 'There are some decisions that have to be taken at the right time. Raj had age on his side and did not want to lose that advantage. He had told Balasaheb about his decision to quit. Balasaheb may have known that this situation was brewing, but after all, blood is thicker than water.'[70]

Raj had been asking for sweeping changes in the party's organization, with much of his ire being directed against Subhash Desai, whom he accused of hatching conspiracies against him, as Bal Thackeray admitted in an interview to *Saamna* in January 2006. Later, the Sena chief blamed Raj's acolytes for poisoning his ears.[71]

Desai is the industries minister in the Fadnavis government and the only leader from Bal Thackeray's times to be part of Uddhav's inner circle. 'Earlier, Raj would rarely broach the topic of quitting the Sena or express himself when his associates exhorted him to do so. However, after Raj returned halfway from the Malvan by-polls, he held a meeting with some of his very close confidants, wherein he said it was over. He would quit the Shiv Sena at the opportune time,' claimed a journalist, who is part of Raj's inner circle.[72]

Sachin Parab noted that Rane, who was the first Shiv Sena rebel to put the party on the back foot, had created a situation where questions were being raised about the future of the party.

'Things were so bad for the Sena that there were times when they would have to bring in muscle from Thane for a confrontation with Rane's men. There was speculation if Rane would edge out Vilasrao Deshmukh to become the chief minister,' he said.[73]

In Raj's camp, the only question was the timing of the split. 'Some wanted to break away immediately, while others wanted to bide their time till Bal Thackeray was alive. Finally, the first school of thought prevailed,' said Parab.[74]

In an interaction with the *Loksatta* newspaper in 2012, Raj said the decision to quit the Shiv Sena had been brewing for almost a decade. He admitted he had two options, either quit politics altogether or form his own party.[75]

Vageesh Saraswat, a Hindi speaker born in Uttar Pradesh and who later joined the MNS, recalls when he had invited Raj to launch his book of poems, *Ekalavya ka Angutha* (Ekalavya's thumb), at the Indian Merchants Chamber (IMC) auditorium in Mumbai on 21 July 2005.

The titular poem drew from a popular story from the Mahabharata. Ekalavya was a tribal prince who was self-taught in archery, but he considered Dronacharya, teacher of the Pandavas and Kauravas, his guru, despite the Brahmin warrior refusing to teach him because of his 'lowly' origins. However, in this poem, Ekalavya, instead of doing his guru's bidding by cutting off his right thumb (which would affect his archery skills), he chooses to rebel against his guru.

'Raj saheb asked for the book and read the poem. He later attended the book release and spoke in Hindi saying he had no objection to the language. After he walked out of the Shiv Sena, Raj claimed that my poem and Eklavya's defiance in it had played a part in his decision,' said Saraswat.[76]

'Till the very end, Balasaheb felt, albeit in an innocent or as some may say, in a naive manner that Uddhav and Raj would continue to stay together as his heirs, somewhat like a modern-day version of Luv and Kush,' says a veteran editor. 'He perhaps did not feel that the confrontation between the two would reach such a disruptive level.' He added that Thackeray senior perhaps wanted 'Raj's charisma' but Uddhav as the Sena's next in command.[77]

'Balasaheb was depending heavily on Uddhav and it was obvious that he was his choice as his political heir. Perhaps, Balasaheb felt that like his younger brother Shrikant, who stayed in his shadow despite his immense talents, Raj would do likewise,' said one of Raj's friends.[78]

Those close to Bal Thackeray often recounted how hurt their leader was at 'Raja's' decision to quit the party. Thackeray made this clear in an interview in 2012 to Nikhil Wagle on IBN Lokmat, where he said, 'How can I forget him, he is from our family. He grew up in this very Matoshree. Ma [Meenatai] fed him with her own hands. He played with me, I used to show him the flickering lights of planes from Matoshree's terrace. Leave aside our relationship, I was shocked at the way in which he was behaving. Why did he do this?'[79]

In an interview to IBN Lokmat a year after Bal Thackeray's death, his second son Jaidev claimed he had suggested to his father that two posts of working presidents, namely one for urban and one for rural Maharashtra, be created in the Shiv Sena. While Uddhav could take charge of the urban areas, Raj could handle rural Maharashtra. Jaidev claimed while Bal Thackeray and one of the warring cousins had agreed to this, the other cousin had not. He however refused to state who (Uddhav or Raj) had refused to toe the line.[80]

On 18 December 2005, three days after he met his uncle with Manohar Joshi, Raj finally announced his decision to quit the Shiv Sena and form a new political party. In a crowded press conference at the Shivaji Park gymkhana, Raj said he would tour Maharashtra from 17 January 2006 onwards, after darshan at the Siddhivinayak Temple.[81] Then Union agriculture minister and

NCP chief, Sharad Pawar, taking a dig at Raj, said that to be active in politics, one had to wake up early!

On 19 March 2006, history seemed to repeat itself.

Exactly forty years after his uncle held the Shiv Sena's first rally at Shivaji Park grounds, Raj was doing likewise, addressing the maiden public meeting of his own political outfit—the Maharashtra Navnirman Sena (MNS).

Raj had announced the formation of the MNS a few days earlier, on 9 March. The nomenclature made it clear that he had no pan-India aspirations and would remain a regional player. The three colours in the party flag—saffron, green and blue—highlighted his aspiration to build a broad-based social coalition of Hindus, Muslims and Dalits.

One of Raj's friends said after quitting the Shiv Sena, he was undecided on forming his own political party. 'When the plan was finalized, names like Lok Sena were being considered. But, Maharashtra Navnirman Sena was decided upon as Raj said he wanted the party to be restricted to Maharashtra and have the term 'Sena' in the name. He chose Navnirman because of Jayaprakash Narayan's Navnirman movement, which he wanted to recreate in Maharashtra,' he said. The party's tricolour flag with the saffron green and blue colours, and strips of white in between, was drawn by his childhood friend and schoolmate Jay Kowli, who is also an artist.[82]

At his first rally, recalling how his grandfather, Prabodhankar, had announced that he was dedicating his son Bal to Maharashtra in the Shiv Sena's first public meeting at the ground in 1966, Raj said he was similarly 'dedicating himself to Maharashtra from this very moment'.[83]

On that muggy day in March, Raj's speech touched mostly on brick-and-mortar and bread-and-butter issues of development such as poor-quality education that made students unemployable, and Mumbai's bad roads. He questioned the benefits to the taxpayers from governments in terms of infrastructure like gardens and announced that he was working on a blueprint for the state's development.[84]

More importantly, Raj seemed to be moving away from the emotional issues that established political parties, the Shiv Sena included, had championed. He questioned if renaming the Marathwada University after Dr Babasaheb Ambedkar and V.T. railway station after Shivaji Maharaj served a larger purpose.

'The family members of my activists must feel proud that he is with Raj Thackeray,' Raj said, adding that he would not disappoint them like the others. He also declared that henceforth, no one would touch his feet in salutations and that a simple 'namaskar' with folded hands would do.

If Hindutva was nationalism, he agreed more with nationalism, he declared, and that while he had visited a dargah at Miraj in Sangli district during his statewide tour, he was against the kind of 'pseudo-secularism' he accused the Congress of practising. Pointing to how he had told a delegation of Muslims that while drawing cartoons of Prophet Muhammed to insult a religion was wrong, Muslims should also protest against M.F. Hussain's images of naked Hindu goddesses.

Dr Deepak Pawar, associate professor, department of civics and politics, University of Mumbai, noted how Raj's maiden speech was full of clichés and trivialized important issues. 'In his rally, Raj spoke about how he wanted to see farmers wearing T-shirts and jeans driving tractors. However, he did not speak about the crux of agrarian distress—lack of remunerative pricing and failed crops due to the vagaries of nature.'[85]

Setbacks for the Sena

While Raj was striking out on his own, Uddhav was trying to fend off challenges from his bête noire, Narayan Rane.

On 4 November 2005, three Shiv Sena legislators who were Rane's supporters from the Konkan region—Subhash Bane, Ganpat Kadam and Shankar Kambli—resigned their seats and joined the Congress. The by-polls to their seats, Lanja-Sangameshwar, Rajapur and Vengurla, took place in January 2006, where these newly minted Congressmen comfortably defeated their Shiv Sena rivals.[86]

In the next month, Rane loyalist Kalidas Kolambkar retained his Naigaum seat in Mumbai defeating the Shiv Sena's Shradda Jadhav, a BMC corporator. However, the Shiv Sena had some succour when its nominee from Srivardhan in Raigad, Tukaram Surve, trounced Shyam Sawant, who like the others had followed Rane into the Congress.[87] There was a similar sense of déjà vu for the Sena in April 2007 when its Prakash Jadhav defeated former Shiv Sena MP and ex-union minister Subodh Mohite, who had quit his Ramtek Lok Sabha seat near Nagpur, and defected to the Congress, necessitating a by-poll.[88]

In June 2006, the Shiv Sena suffered yet another blow as twelve of its MLAs cross-voted, leading to the defeat of its nominee Vijay Loke in the legislative council elections. Narayan Rane's confidant Rajan Teli (who would fall out with him in 2014) was elected to the Upper House.[89]

Uddhav's associates note that this period, when both Raj and Rane had quit the Shiv Sena, was the most trying for him. Questions were being raised about the very existence of the party and there was talk that Raj would walk away with a chunk of the support base in the post–Bal Thackeray era.[90]

A senior Shiv Sena leader said Bal Thackeray had advised Uddhav to make fundamental changes in the way he functioned if the party was to survive, something he took to heart.[91]

'When Raj decided to quit the Shiv Sena, his uncle was in charge of the party and despite his poor health, was in full elan and spirit. Quitting the Shiv Sena and confronting Bal Thackeray at this point required enormous mobilizing abilities, courage and confidence,' said the senior editor and Shiv Sena critic quoted earlier.[92]

'Uddhav had to rise above this rebellion and show equanimity in the face of this confrontation which had split the Sena. Raj was also popular with the media, which backed him and not the Shiv Sena. Uddhav's only asset was his father, whose twilight was apparent after the 2005 Malvan by-poll defeat. At this point in time, Uddhav was like the Shiv Sena's *pappu* [loser].' He added that Uddhav gradually changed his personality to become more outgoing.

The Shiv Sena–BJP alliance suffered another body blow on 22 April 2006, when senior BJP leader and former Union minister, Pramod Mahajan's younger brother, Pravin, shot the former at his Worli residence.[93] Three bullets hit Pramod Mahajan, damaging his vital organs.[94] He was rushed to the Hinduja Hospital at Mahim, where he passed away on 3 May.[95]

Pramod Mahajan was seen as the architect of the Shiv Sena–BJP alliance in 1989 and worked as a troubleshooter. 'Balasaheb was fond of Pramod. Trust was implicit in their relationship. When the Shiv Sena and BJP would release joint statements to the media, Balasaheb would not have a second look if Pramod was in the loop,' remembered a senior Shiv Sena leader.[96]

Though the Shiv Sena and the BJP were natural allies due to their common agenda of Hindutva, their alliance had its own undercurrents of tension. The two parties had an overlapping political base and the BJP perceived it to be a hindrance to its social expansion in Maharashtra and tried to catch it in a bind wherever it could.

The differences between the two parties came to a head in 2006 over a by-election to the Chimur assembly segment in Chandrapur district. Shiv Sena MLA Vijay Vadettiwar, who quit the party to join the Congress, had resigned his seat and the BJP staked claim to it. The BJP said a majority of the Sena's cadre had followed Vadettiwar to the Congress. The BJP poached the Sena's probable candidate Dr Ramesh Gajbe, and hence claimed that the Sena could not pose a tough challenge to Vadettiwar.[97]

A furious Shiv Sena threatened to snap ties with its ally, but eventually caved in. However, Vadettiwar trounced Gajbe while his party colleague Prakash Patil Bharsakhale, who had also defected to the Congress, defeated the Shiv Sena's Balasaheb Hingankar from Daryapur in Amravati in the 4 December 2006 by-election.[98]

A jubilant Rane, whose chief ministerial ambitions were an open secret, rose several notches in his new party, whose bench strength in the assembly had reached seventy-five, surpassing that of the NCP's seventy-one.[99]

Equations of power

In 2007, the Congress-led UPA government sprung a surprise by nominating a little-known Congress politician from Maharashtra, Pratibha Patil, as its nominee for president.

Patil, who belonged to a Rajput family settled in north Maharashtra's Jalgaon, was leader of the Opposition between 1978 and 1980 during Sharad Pawar's first chief ministerial tenure, when she controversially called for those with hereditary diseases like diabetes to be sterilized.[100] She was also deputy chairman of the Rajya Sabha and a Lok Sabha MP. Patil was involved in controversies ranging from allegations of murder against her brother and mismanagement in her cooperative bank.[101] She was governor of Rajasthan at the time of her nomination. Her one major qualification seemed to be her loyalty to the Gandhi family.

Though the name of another Gandhi loyalist from Maharashtra—then Union home minister Shivraj Patil—was making the rounds, the Congress high command decided on Pratibha Patil after the left opposed the former. The announcement put the Shiv Sena in a bind. While Bal Thackeray was friendly with the BJP's candidate, Bhairon Singh Shekhawat, the incumbent vice-president, the Shiv Sena had to vote for the Congress nominee because she was a woman and a Maharashtrian to boot.

The Shiv Sena finally decided to support the Congress, breaking ranks with the BJP like in the 1997 presidential polls, when it had backed former chief election commissioner (CEC) T.N. Seshan against K.R. Narayanan.

The same year, in 2007, the Shiv Sena had another litmus test in store—the BMC elections.

The cash-rich BMC played an important role in helping the Shiv Sena nurture its networks of power and patronage in Mumbai. Winning the elections was crucial if the party was to survive at this delicate moment. The elections were due on 1 February, and the Congress and the NCP were exploring the possibility of a pre-poll alliance. According to a senior NCP leader, the deal collapsed because a section of Congress leaders in Mumbai were 'overconfident' about their chances.[102]

The NCP leader who was part of the negotiations said, 'We were in talks for an alliance, but they fell through at the last minute with the Congress declaring its candidates for all 227 seats. The 2004 Lok Sabha elections had seen the Congress sweep five of the six seats in Mumbai and it also had fifteen legislators. With the Shiv Sena weakened after Rane and Raj's desertions, the Congress felt it had a better chance of wresting the BMC.'[103]

However, a senior Indian Administrative Service (IAS) officer, who has worked in the Sena-ruled BMC, had a contrarian view. He added that a section of the Congress leadership in Maharashtra had a soft corner for the Shiv Sena. The Sena could also be used by this faction to settle its scores with rival groups in the Congress, like in the 1985 BMC polls. 'The Shiv Sena may also be a dangerous foe when out of power,' said the official, while recounting how a former chief minister of Maharashtra, who is no more, would often say in half jest, '*Tyanna khush thewa* (Keep the Shiv Sena happy).'[104]

During the campaign, Uddhav went back to the issue that had helped the Shiv Sena win the BMC elections in 1985—the threat of Mumbai being severed from Maharashtra by the Congress if the Sena was defeated.[105] A senior Congress leader from Mumbai said that the MNS leaders had approached them for an 'understanding' in the 2007 BMC elections, which was the party's first shot at the hustings.[106]

'The MNS sent feelers to me,' he said. 'They proposed that we help them indirectly in the Maharashtrian-dominated Dadar–Mahim belt to take on the Shiv Sena in return for similar cooperation elsewhere. Some of Raj's men travelled to Bengaluru and Pune to meet a senior All India Congress Committee [AICC] leader who was in charge of Maharashtra. However, we were a divided house and the plan was sabotaged by a senior Mumbai Congress leader, who is no more.'[107]

When Raj formed his MNS, Shiv Sena leaders were wary at the chances that he was likely to walk off with a large section of the middle-rung and cadre. However, that did not happen, which according to a veteran journalist on the Shiv Sena beat, could be attributed to 'the Indian mentality, where people do not like to disturb the status quo'. Raj, who was then in his late thirties, was seen as young, inexperienced and untested. Moreover, Raj did not try hard to ensure defections from his parent party as he wanted to start from a clean slate.[108]

When the results were declared, the Shiv Sena secured eighty-three seats and the BJP twenty-eight. The Congress saw its tally rise marginally to seventy-one, followed by the NCP's fourteen. Raj's newly minted MNS won only seven seats.[109]

7

The MNS Tastes First Blood: The Shiv Sena's Fortunes Decline

> Turning and turning in the widening gyre
> The falcon cannot hear the falconer;
> Things fall apart; the centre cannot hold;
> Mere anarchy is loosed upon the world,
> The blood-dimmed tide is loosed, and everywhere
> The ceremony of innocence is drowned;
> The best lack all conviction, while the worst
> Are full of passionate intensity.
>
> W.B. Yeats, 'The Second Coming'

The insipid result of the 2007 BMC elections was a rude jolt for Raj. In an interview to *Loksatta* in 2012, he admitted he was shocked to see a headline in an English daily about the MNS. The headline read, 'The party is over.'[1]

'Electoral success can rarely be achieved on the basis of a developmental agenda. For that you need something else,' says Shishir Shinde (who had followed Raj when he left the Shiv Sena and joined the MNS), explaining how the MNS shifted its agenda to parochialism by latching on to the Shiv Sena's nativist plank and using it against north Indians.[2]

With Bal Thackeray donning the saffron garb of a 'Hindu Hriday Samrat' in the late 1980s, the Shiv Sena went for a larger constituency than the Marathi manoos to align itself with the city's changing demography. It was one which included voters of other linguistic groups. This led to resentment among Marathi speakers, who felt their concerns were being ignored. According to Chhagan Bhujbal, Raj, who would come to be hailed as 'Marathi Hriday Samrat' (emperor of the hearts of the Marathis) by his supporters, tapped into this dormant anger of Maharashtrians.[3]

Vageesh Saraswat, who was the 'north Indian face' of the MNS, claimed that after his statewide tour, Raj had felt confident about being able to upstage the Shiv Sena, and was shocked when confronted with the ground reality.

On 9 March 2007, the first foundation day of the MNS, Raj spoke at the Shanmukhananda Hall, launching a broadside at the Shiv Sena. 'But he referred to the 2003 attacks at Kalyan and said if Biharis insulted Maharashtrians, they would be slapped for breakfast, lunch and dinner,' said Saraswat, calling this a 'turning point' in the history of the MNS, which till then had a largely development-centric agenda.[4]

The statement was picked up by the media and flayed by parties like the Congress, NCP and north Indian politicians like Lalu Prasad Yadav who was railway minister at the time. Bihar chief minister Nitish Kumar went to the extent of calling for Raj to 'be tried as a traitor' for trying to break 'the unity of the nation'.[5]

Uddhav Thackeray ridiculed his estranged cousin, saying it was Raj who had wrecked Marathi unity by leaving the Sena and forming his own party.[6]

Saraswat felt that such knee-jerk reactions laid the ground for the aggressive anti-outsider agitation of the MNS that would follow, with the party realizing the potential the issue had in terms of polarizing the Shiv Sena's politically aware voters.[7]

Moreover, as a former Raj aide claimed, the demand to control migration to Mumbai, which was already bursting at its seams, was a natural corollary of the MNS's development agenda. 'The rising influx into the city, sea-locked from three sides, will negate any infrastructure addition. So, there must be restrictions on its population growth,' the aide explained.[8]

Raj wanted to arrive with a bang on the political stage. And he chose a high-value target. This was a strategy that could never come a cropper.

Recalibrated strategy

At a rally on 2 February 2008, at Vikhroli in Mumbai's working-class, Maharashtrian-dominated eastern suburbs, Raj attacked superstar Amitabh Bachchan, a family friend of the Thackerays and his own favourite actor.

A day earlier, while speaking at a function in Dharavi, Raj had flayed Bachchan for taking 'more interest' in his home state of Uttar Pradesh than in Maharashtra, or even Mumbai, the city that had made him a star.[9] Though Raj was repeating his criticism of the 'Chhora Ganga Kinarewala' (the boy from the banks of the Ganga) at Vikhroli, the public meeting at Kannamwar Nagar had more television crews in attendance.

Raj said Amitabh had made his fortune in Mumbai and Maharashtra. However, the superstar had chosen to contest a Lok Sabha election (in 1984) from Allahabad in his home state of Uttar Pradesh, rather than the state which had made him what he was today. Also, the star had agreed to become the brand ambassador of Uttar Pradesh rather than Maharashtra.[10] Raj asked why Bachchan had not spoken about distress suicides by farmers in Maharashtra considering the heft that his word carried. Also, the actor had started a school for girls named after his daughter-in-law, Aishwarya, in Uttar Pradesh and not Maharashtra.[11]

'Aren't there any girls in Maharashtra, Gujarat or Tamil Nadu? . . . I only said that if a superstar like him can love his state, can't a small man like Raj Thackeray love Maharashtra and the Marathi manoos?' he questioned.[12]

Raj also attacked controversial Samajwadi Party leader Abu Asim Azmi, who had threatened to distribute lathis to north Indians for their 'protection', and north Indian leaders like Kripashankar Singh, Lalu Prasad Yadav and Amar Singh, then the powerful general secretary of the Samajwadi Party (SP).[13]

'If Abu Azmi distributes lathis in Mumbai, Maharashtra, I will distribute swords across Maharashtra,' Raj thundered, while warning Azmi against 'coming from 2,000 miles away and threatening us'.[14]

Referring to his opposition to Chhath puja (a festival observed mostly by people from Bihar and parts of Uttar Pradesh) Raj said he only opposed *nautanki* (drama) in the name of the rituals and claimed the festival was a 'show of strength' by north Indians. Raj also opposed celebration of the foundation day of Uttar Pradesh in Maharashtra and questioned how he could be labelled 'narrow-minded' for speaking about interests of his own state.[15]

'. . . You will not be able to come to Maharashtra without the permission of Marathi manoos,' he threatened Amar Singh, saying Maharashtra did not need lessons in nationalism as it had always upheld the interests of the nation unlike other states. The MNS chief sought that people from other states living in Maharashtra integrate with local culture.[16]

Two days later, a rally of the short-lived United National Progressive Alliance (UNPA) saw MNS activists clash with workers of the SP. There was tension around the Shivaji Park area where the public meeting attended by Mulayam Singh Yadav, Farooq Abdullah, Chandrababu Naidu and Babulal Marandi, was held. The rally saw verbal attacks against Raj for his 'petty politics'.[17] Lalu Prasad Yadav was heckled during a function at Dombivli near Mumbai earlier in the day.[18]

'Some of Raj saheb's friends insisted that we take an aggressive, hard-line, pro-Marathi stand as just speaking about development will not yield votes. The Thackerays choose their targets carefully. Picking on a man of Amitabh's stature would obviously yield dividends,' chuckled a former MNS MLA.[19]

One of Raj's then advisers said, 'Faced with the risk of becoming another NGO, which seeks gardens and open spaces for Mumbai, he then took on an aggressive, nativist agenda, which yielded dividends immediately.'[20]

Azmi, who was the target of Raj's ire along with Bachchan, has been a deeply polarizing personality. Born in Manjeer Patti in Uttar Pradesh's Azamgarh, he came to Mumbai in 1973 to help his ailing father, Haji Niyaz Ahmad Azmi, in his business of embroidering garments meant for export. One of Azmi's aides once claimed that his leader had come to Mumbai 'with a few hundred rupees in his pocket', and gradually built an empire of hotels, supply of skilled workers to the Middle East, construction, shoe stores and an export firm.[21]

Azmi was arrested for allegedly booking air tickets for people involved in the 1993 Mumbai bomb blasts but was subsequently discharged by the apex court after spending some time in jail. Azmi once told the author that was his life's 'turning point', for he realized how minorities can be framed in the country.

He later joined Mulayam Singh Yadav's Samajwadi Party (SP), gradually sidelining other leaders in the state and crossing swords with the Maharashtra government on issues like the Ishrat Jahan encounter case in 2004 and the Malegaon bomb blasts in 2006.

In 2000, Azmi, who pitched himself as the leader of north Indian Muslims in Maharashtra, gave a provocative speech at Mastan Talao in Mumbai where he warned that if there was any interference in matters of religion, 'rivers of blood would flow'. Azmi was convicted in this case in 2012, but his conviction was suspended by a sessions court in 2014.[22]

In 2004, Azmi fought the assembly elections from the communally sensitive textile town of Bhiwandi near Thane, where he lost to the Shiv Sena's Yogesh Patil. Some residents of the constituency claimed local Muslims had voted for Patil to prevent Azmi's election from the town, which was once known for its communal violence.[23]

Raj targetting Azmi was certain to lead to a polarization of Marathi and Hindu voters in favour of the MNS. On the other hand, Azmi stood to gain by projecting himself as a champion of Muslims and Hindi speakers.

Uddhav, who had attended an Uttar Pradesh Day rally in 2008, had been trying to expand the Sena's reach away from the narrative of polarization, which was ironically the very direction that Raj had now chosen for the MNS. After his 'Mee Mumbaikar' outreach failed in 2003 following the attack by BVS workers on north Indians at Kalyan, Uddhav had launched a fresh attempt after Raj quit the Shiv Sena.

Prem Shukla, former editor of the Sena's *Dopahar Ka Saamna*, said that in 2006, the Shiv Sena organized a *Bhojpuri sammelan* (a convention of Bhojpuri speakers) at Thane, which was attended by around 1.5 lakh people from the region settled in and around Mumbai. This was followed up the next year by Lai Chana (a mix of puffed rice and chana popular in Uttar Pradesh and Bihar) sammelans.[24]

Uddhav had also tried to broad-base the Shiv Sena's urban-centric focus to cover issues like agrarian distress, power cuts and rural indebtedness. Shukla added that in the 2007 civic elections in Mumbai and Thane, north Indian voters had tipped the scales for the Sena in several wards and helped offset losses caused by Raj and Rane's exit.

However, like in 2003, Raj would once again pose a stumbling block for his cousin and attempt to eat into the Shiv Sena's core Maharashtrian vote base in Mumbai and neighbouring areas.

An NCP functionary Mangaleshwar (Munna) Tripathi had lodged a case against Bal Thackeray and others for certain communally provocative remarks during the Shiv Sena's foundation day programme at the Shanmukhananda Hall at Sion in 2006 and for the speech that was reproduced in *Saamna*. The case, which was registered in the Andheri court, saw the Sena chief being arrested and released on bail in a matter of minutes.

Tripathi, who headed the Uttar Bharatiya Vikas Parishad, withdrew the case after Uddhav attended an event to mark the establishment of Uttar Pradesh on 24 January 2008 and referred to him as his 'brother'.[25] Prem Shukla said he had prevailed upon Uddhav to attend a programme organized by him and BJP leader Amarjit Mishra at Vile Parle on the same day.

This gave Raj ammunition with which to attack Uddhav and the Shiv Sena, claiming that the party's core Marathi identity and agenda were being diluted. Raj questioned why the Uttar Pradesh *sthapana diwas* (foundation day) was being celebrated in Mumbai when it was not commemorated in the former state.

For the first time after launching the MNS, Raj was arrested by the police in Mumbai later that month for incitement and promoting enmity between groups, after his remarks sparked off violence.[26] His arrest led to MNS workers taking to the streets in places like Nashik, where the MNS had some base to boast of. Since his days in the Shiv Sena, when he had been given charge of the district, Raj would frequently visit the city, located around 180 kilometres from Mumbai.

In the 2007 elections to the Nashik civic body, the MNS had secured twelve seats in the 108-member house, forcing the Shiv Sena—its numbers dropping to twenty-five from thirty-six—join hands with diverse political parties to get its mayor elected.

'The biggest agitation by the party in Maharashtra was at Nashik,' said Raj's former associate Vasant Gite, who was elected to the state assembly in 2009 from Nashik as an MNS MLA. 'The number of paraprantiyas [outsiders] had gradually risen in the industrial belts around the town like Ambad, Sinnar and Igatpuri. These people would work at rates less than the minimum wage, undercutting locals, and depriving them of employment. Our agenda appealed to the youth, who joined us in large numbers.'[27]

After Raj's arrest in February 2008, Vinod Singh Fauzdar Singh (forty-two), a security guard at Igatpuri's Jindal Steel unit, and Ambadas Haribhau Dharrao (fifty-six), an employee of Hindustan Aeronautics Limited (HAL) at Ozar, were the first casualties of the anti-outsider campaign.

Singh, who was from Aurangabad district in Bihar, was assaulted by thirty-five people near his factory in the Gonde industrial estate. He died at a private hospital later. Dharrao, who was returning from work in a company bus, was fatally hurt in the head by a stone flung by the agitators.[28]

The irony was inescapable. Dharrao, a Marathi manoos was the victim of a political campaign that claimed to uphold the interests of the sons of the soil. He became an apt metaphor of how the common man stands to lose in the games that politicians play. As a reporter for the *Indian Express*, I remember visiting Dharrao's family house at Niphad, the ancestral village of one of Maharashtra's social reformers, Justice Mahadeo Govind Ranade. Ambadas's younger brother Madhukar, a sugar factory employee, did not mince his words while criticizing the hate campaign. 'Have you ever heard of the leaders being hurt in the violence? Stopping such hate campaigns is the only way to pay tribute to my brother,' said Madhukar.[29]

Raj ups the ante

The years 2008 and 2009 clearly belonged to Raj Thackeray. The media blitz and controversies generated by his anti–north Indian statements were clearly swaying the Shiv Sena's hard-bitten loyalists, especially the young, towards the MNS. From opposing the 'imposition' of Hindi, protesting 'demographic invasions' from northern states and ensuring around 1900 sacked staff members of the beleaguered Jet Airways were reinstated, Raj managed to project himself as an alter ego of the Marathi manoos who was feeling undermined in Mumbai.

In April 2008, the Shiv Sena too seemed to go with the flow when a front-page report in *Saamna* pointed to actor Rajinikanth's solidarity with Tamil Nadu on the Hogenakkal water dispute with Karnataka. It added that Rajinikanth, a Maharashtrian who grew up in Karnataka, had overshadowed Amitabh with this act of loyalty despite being an outsider.

After a media frenzy, Bal Thackeray tried to underplay the controversy over these comments and called Amitabh Bachchan his family friend.[30] The MNS was aggressively encroaching on the Shiv Sena's turf. The Sena, in turn, was fumbling for a political strategy.

'Marathi or Hindutva? This was a Catch 22 situation for the Shiv Sena. Faced with the prospect of losing its core voter to Raj, it finally reverted to using the Marathi identity for mobilization, often repeating things that the MNS had done,' said Prem Shukla.[31]

In September 2008, Amitabh's wife and SP Rajya Sabha MP, Jaya Bachchan, gave Raj another opportunity to attack them. At the music release of son Abhishek's film, *Drona*, she said, '*Hum UP ke log hain, Hindi mein baat karna chahenge. Maharashtra ke log hum logonko maaf karein.* (I would like to speak in Hindi since I am from UP. People from Maharashtra, forgive me).'[32]

Incensed MNS workers took to the streets, blackening Amitabh's image in advertisements. Bal Thackeray too warned Jaya against provoking Maharashtrians, and Amitabh sought 'forgiveness'.[33] Raj accepted the apology and withdrew the agitation against the Bachchans, adding, '*Guddi buddhi zhali tari akkal yet nahi*' (Referring to one of Jaya Bachchan's roles—*Guddi*—he said that wisdom had eluded her despite her age). Raj, who had earlier been issued a gag order by the Mumbai Police, also attacked Joint Commissioner of Police (Law and Order) K.L. Prasad for saying, 'Mumbai does not belong to anyone's father.'[34]

In May 2008, Raj relaunched his anti-outsider tirade, repeating his criticism against Bachchan, the celebration of Uttar Pradesh and Bihar statehood days, and Chhath puja. Speaking at the second anniversary rally of the MNS, he claimed he was being targeted as he had 'foiled the plans of people from Uttar Pradesh and Bihar to take control of Maharashtra'. He also questioned why the media was silent on the killings of north Indian migrants in states like Manipur.[35]

'Let Lalu [Lalu Prasad Yadav] come and perform Chhath puja outside my house. He will not go back,' added Raj in this rally at Shivaji Park on 3 May 2008. Lalu had earlier dared Raj, claiming he would come to Mumbai for the festival.[36]

'There are Punjabis, Sindhis, Parsis and all kinds of people [in Maharashtra]. Why don't we feel threatened by them? But these north Indians are showing their strength [through events like Chhath puja],' Raj said. He also claimed antisocial elements in Mumbai hailed from north India. Raj dared the government to arrest him saying only the celebration of Maharashtra Day would be allowed in the state.[37]

'Maharashtra united after I spoke as I voiced something that they suffered every day. This is nothing but demographic invasion,' Raj declared.

The Shiv Sena was in a quandary as public celebrations of Chhath had been launched on a mass scale by its former member, Sanjay Nirupam's 'Bihari Front' in 1998. Nirupam, who left the Sena in 2005, admitted that at that time there was unease at north Indians flocking to Juhu beach to celebrate the puja under his Front's banner, with his party chief upbraiding him on one occasion.[38]

With the stage set for his aggressive brand of politics, Raj took up emotional issues that would serve as good optics, thanks to the electronic media, especially Hindi channels. This included issuing diktats in July 2008 to shopkeepers to have signboards in Devanagari (July 2008), which was mandatory as per rules of the Shiv Sena–run BMC.[39] Raj warned the defaulting shopkeepers of the wrath of his cadre. Incidentally, the Shiv Sena too had been taking up the issue of Marathi boards on shops since 1966 as Bal Thackeray recalled in a 2000 interview with *Saamna*.[40]

In October 2008, after MNS workers attacked Railway Board examination centres and north Indian candidates appearing for these tests in Mumbai, Raj was arrested from Ratnagiri in the Konkan where he was on tour. This led to sporadic incidents of violence across Mumbai.[41] Raj was later released on bail in multiple cases in Mumbai and Thane, including those for his activists damaging the Kalyan railway station premises, and returned home to a hero's welcome.[42]

The anti-outsider agitation led to ripples in Mumbai with tensions between the Maharashtrians and Hindi-speakers almost reaching a tipping point. The long-hailed cultural osmosis and cosmopolitan nature of the city were gradually coming apart.

Residents of Maharashtrian localities like Parel, Lalbag, Dadar and Vile Parle (East) found that non-Maharashtrian taxi and rickshaw drivers would often think twice before accepting rides to these areas due to the fear that had set in.

Such was the controversy generated by Raj's protests, that twenty-three-year-old Rahul Raj Kundan Prasad Singh, a gun-toting youth from Patna, hijacked a double-decker bus heading to Kurla station from Saki Naka in Mumbai, injured a passenger and claimed he wanted to kill Raj Thackeray. He was protesting the attacks on north Indian candidates appearing for a railway recruitment examination. The Mumbai Police eventually shot him dead.[43] [44]

Rahul was cremated at Gulbighat on the banks of the Ganga where those in attendance chanted slogans like '*Raj Thackeray murdabad* (Down with Raj Thackeray)' and '*Rahul raj amar rahe* (Long live Rahul Raj)'. The Bihar government sought a judicial probe into the killing.[45]

The MNS also hijacked the Shiv Sena's agenda and demanded that locals get preference in at least 80 per cent jobs in industries and the private sector. The state government issued a revised notification to ensure the implementation of the rule, which dated back to 1964. Chief Minister Vilasrao Deshmukh said they would create an enabling mechanism to ensure that this rule, which defined a local as a person domiciled in Maharashtra for fifteen years, was implemented.[46]

Nikhil Wagle is of the view that though Raj had struck a different note while speaking at the first public meeting of the MNS, he remained a Shiv Sainik at heart. 'I often doubt if he had any convictions in the thoughts expressed in this speech. Initially, he showed a different side, but since he was competing with Uddhav and the Shiv Sena, there was no bigger credo that he could adopt. Like Balasaheb, his politics was based on emotional issues,' he added.[47]

Dr Deepak Pawar, associate professor, department of civics and politics, University of Mumbai, noted how issues raised by Raj during this period were typical of his formative years in the Shiv Sena.[48]

'Like Bal Thackeray, Raj too adopted a stance that is superficial. For instance, the Sena and MNS insist on shops having signboards in Marathi but are not bothered by who owns the shops. The Shiv Sena and MNS are unable to reconcile themselves to the need for *Marathikaran* (influence of Marathi and Marathi speakers in all walks of life), which is a complex matrix involving language, society and culture. This type of politics can be done without assaulting others.'[49]

In a column on rediff.com, senior journalist Mahesh Vijapurkar blamed the media for blowing up Raj Thackeray's comments. He noted that in his February 2008 Vikhroli speech, Raj had not criticized Bachchan but presented the strength of his love for his own state. He added that newspapers had reported that the MNS chief had criticized Bachchan and news channels used voice-overs with content akin to the contentions in print. 'The media thus created a Frankenstein, revelling in its own doing,' said Vijapurkar.[50]

He added that Raj seemed to have smartly co-opted the misreportage into a political campaign. 'Here, the Indian media's obsession to shape—or sex up—a story to its worst distortion has come to the fore. And without anyone even batting an eyelid in concern.'[51]

History of migration

In Mumbai, the north Indians are referred to as 'bhaiyas', which literally means 'elder brother'. However, its Mumbai usage is as a contemptuous term. It has a historical context. As the Marathas expanded militarily into north India, *Purbaiya*s—as people from the eastern Uttar Pradesh belt were called—joined them as soldiers, with some even migrating to the Peshwa capital at Pune.

In the Peshwa era, the Marathas virtually emerged as masters of Hindustan and Marathi speakers dispersed to north and east India. Maratha generals like Malharrao Holkar, Ranoji Scindia and others settled in the north, taking with them several people from Maharashtra.

After the British defeated the last Peshwa, Bajirao II, he was exiled to Bithoor near Kanpur. His foster son, Nanasaheb, played a pivotal role in the First War of Indian Independence of 1857 with fellow Marathis like Tatya Tope and Rani Lakshmibai. The family of Govind Ballabh Pant, the first chief minister of Uttar Pradesh who later became the Union home minister, hailed from Karad in Maharashtra. Baburao Paradkar, one of the doyens of journalism in Hindi, was from Sindhudurg.

In his 1994 book, *Bambai ke Uttar Bharatiya*, journalist-turned-politician, Ram Manohar Tripathi, who was a minister of state in Maharashtra, notes that the dhobi (washerman) community from the north was the first to migrate to Mumbai before 1857 as domestic servants of the British. Similar competing claims are also made by those from the Purvanchal and Braj regions.[52] Tripathi records that in 1858 or 1860, two north Indians were blown off using cannons at Azad Maidan in south Mumbai for crimes that have not been recorded in the annals of history.[53]

After the great war of 1857, many from north India, mostly Muslims from Varanasi, Allahabad, Jaunpur, Barabanki and Fatehpur, fled to Mumbai and other areas in Maharashtra to escape the wrath of the British.[54]

In *India Moving: A History of Migration*, Chinmay Tumbe notes that de-industrialization in the early nineteenth century, due to cheap machine-made British cloth flooding the Indian market, led to weaving communities migrating from eastern Uttar Pradesh to Mumbai, Bhiwandi and Malegaon in Maharashtra.[55]

Kolkata was a stronger magnet for economic migrants in north India. However, they chose to migrate to Mumbai as it grew into an industrial city, after the establishment of the railways, textile mills and engineering units and development of its port after the opening of the Suez Canal in 1869. Some like the Yadavs trooped into Mumbai to meet the demands of the rising population and began supplying milk and started *tabela*s (dairies) in areas like Grant Road, Pila House, Parel, Colaba, Tardeo and Agripada.[56]

Tripathi writes how migrants from north India initially launched businesses that required low capital investment like selling groundnuts, paan (betel leaf) and coal. They gradually forayed into other sectors like running flour mills and driving taxis. Those from the 'Braj' area of Uttar Pradesh like Hathras, Aligarh and Mathura, started shops selling bhelpuri that Mumbai is famous for. They also gave Mumbai another culinary trademark—kulfi.

From 1930 onwards, the number of north Indians in Mumbai, especially those from Uttar Pradesh, increased. Migrants from Uttar Pradesh, Bihar, Uttarakhand, Himachal Pradesh gradually ordered themselves into organizations based on their states, or their castes like Bhumihar, Yadav, Pasi and Pal.[57]

Today, while migrants from Jaunpur are in the milk and security businesses, those from Azamgarh, Deoria and Pratapgarh largely work as security guards, sell vegetables and drive taxis. The milk business has significant numbers from Varanasi and many paan vendors are from Mathura.[58]

According to Ram Manohar Tripathi, Asoka Mehta, the socialist leader, promoted north Indians in his Praja Socialist Party (PSP) to take on S.K. Patil, who was the undisputed boss of the Congress in Mumbai. As the younger generation of north Indians in Mumbai was swayed by the leadership of socialist leaders like Jayaprakash Narayan, Ram Manohar Lohia and Acharya Narendra Dev, Patil too reached out to this constituency.

In 1951, Pandit Bhagirath Jha of the Socialist Party became the first north Indian MLA in the Bombay legislative assembly, from the Chinchpokli-Lower Parel-Love Grove constituency, awakening the political ambitions of this linguistic group.[59] Gradually, areas like Shaitan Chowki, Andheri, Kurla and Malad developed significant north Indian populations. Hindi speakers like Tripathi and Ramesh Dubey (who was elected to the Maharashtra assembly from Andheri and became a minister) forayed into politics.[60]

Mill economy

India is believed to have been the country where cotton originated. The cotton textile industry drove the Industrial Revolution in the West and also played a role in India's industrialization, with Mumbai, Ahmedabad, Coimbatore, Malegaon and Bhiwandi competing for the moniker of 'Manchester of India'. As has been noted in an earlier chapter, textile units were responsible for the industrialization of Mumbai.

From the 1970s onwards, Mumbai saw its biggest economic disruption as around sixty cotton mills, which employed about 2.5 lakh workers, went into terminal decline for reasons like lack of modernization. Workers who distrusted the Congress-led Rashtriya Mill Mazdoor Sangh (RMMS), the sole representative body under the Bombay Industrial Relations Act, 1946 (BIR Act), persuaded the militant labour unionist, Dr Datta Samant, to take up their leadership. In 1982, Samant called an indefinite strike for demands like increase in salaries and bonus.[61]

Gradually, these sunset mills were shut down by their managements, who found it more lucrative to sell their lands. The proud *girni kamgar* (mill worker), who had ensured that Mumbai remained within Maharashtra, was dispossessed. The same fate befell other factories and engineering units.

Though Gillian Tindall, a biographer of the city, argues that the industry in Mumbai followed with a time lapse the 'classic pattern of the developed world in moving from the centre to the outskirts, or to other towns in the region such as Poona and Nashik',[62] the changes were sudden and disruptive and the stakeholders had little time to prepare for them.

As Darryl D'Monte notes, the de-industrialization of Mumbai began with the decline of the textile industry.[63]

The service and financial sector industries that came up on land once occupied by these units were unable to absorb the labour that was dispossessed by the decline of the manufacturing sector as they required a different skill set. The jobless workforce was pushed into informal trades like hawking, driving taxis and rickshaws and contractual labour, where they had to compete with the north Indians, who worked for cheap.

Working-class mill areas like Parel and Lalbag underwent a transformation as plush-gated housing complexes, some of them boasting of 'exclusively vegetarian residents', sprang up. The cultural shift and influx of upper-class residents also meant a rise in costs of living for others.

Sociologists like Jan Brennan have studied how the closure of textile units in Ahmedabad after 1985 affected the social fabric and led to the communalization of the city.[64] Kapil Patil, the journalist-turned-politician, noted how the textile strike and shutdown of mills caused a vacuum that the Shiv Sena filled. 'Workers were jobless and frustration was mounting. The youth was going astray. The Sena stepped in and gave them a sense of identity, rallying them through the ideology of Hindutva,' he said.[65] For instance, this was evident in the 1992–93 Mumbai riots.

The Shiv Sena's turn to Hindutva, which was also meant to broaden its appeal to non-Maharashtrian communities and grow beyond Mumbai, and its subsequent 'Congressization', as some called it, had led to a sense of status quo and hobbled its pro-Marathi agenda. It was unable to respond to the frustration of working-class Maharashtrians regarding the changing economic, social and cultural landscape, which they felt threatened their very existence and identity. The MNS, the new kid on the block and a product of the post-globalization era when Mumbai was changing economically, politically and culturally, occupied the gap.

'The issues responsible for the formation of the Shiv Sena in the 1960s were still relevant when Raj launched his anti-outsider protest. There was an intense competition for jobs and resources due to an increase in migration. There were similar protests in states like Gujarat, Assam and south India. However, those leaders were never dubbed as parochial. Raj had a point when he stressed on primacy for the sons of the soil in Mumbai,' said Girish Kuber who is the editor of *Loksatta*.[66]

'The Shiv Sena lost its raison d'être when it took up the cause of Hindutva. This is also Raj's conviction,' explained Kuber, adding that there was nothing wrong if a political party sought that the interests of its state be protected.[67]

Kuber observed that while there were charges that the MNS was being used by the Congress and NCP to undercut the Shiv Sena and BJP, similar allegations had been made against the Shiv Sena in its heydays. 'The Congress leadership in Maharashtra had always used the Shiv Sena as a tactical weapon in their fight against the high command. The Shiv Sena was derisively called Vasant Sena (after then Congress chief minister Vasantrao Naik), and Congress chief ministers like Vilasrao Deshmukh and Ashok Chavan gave Raj a long rope. This was changed to an extent by Prithviraj Chavan,' he added.[68]

Academician and political analyst, Dr Deepak Pawar, pointed out that the Shiv Sena's turn towards Hindutva signalled an incongruence with its core Marathi agenda. 'Hindutva and pro-Marathi politics cannot go hand in hand. As then, one has to turn a blind eye towards assertion by linguistic groups like Gujaratis, Marwaris and north Indians,' he explained.[69]

Prowling on this frontier, the MNS chose to articulate the 'cultural disenfranchisement' among the Marathi people,[70] who felt they were being pushed beyond the margins in a fast-changing city.

Pawar said the assertion of Hindi at the cost of other regional tongues had also led to anger. 'Many working-class Marathis had lost their jobs in the organized sector after the advent of globalization. Now, they had to compete with the bhaiya, who was omnipotent in the informal economy. The influence of the north Indians was on the rise and the cultural arrogance of those from the north Indian upper castes like Brahmins and Thakurs manifested itself in slums and lower-income housing, adding to resentment.[71]

'This was a bit like the *Deewar* syndrome,' said Pawar, pointing to how workers cheer Amitabh Bachchan—who plays Vijay in the blockbuster, after he emerges, bruised and tired, after bashing up goons inside a godown—but do not join him in his fight. 'The larger Marathi community wants a revolution without them participating and feeling the pinch. This includes the middle-class and the intelligentsia,' he laughed, adding that these sections were happy if Raj were to do the dirty work.[72]

'The average lower- and lower-middle-class Marathi manoos were angry at north Indians taking away their jobs and livelihood opportunities. They were seething with resentment against bhaiyas who came to work in the city's tabelas but gradually acquired economic clout, edging them out,' admitted Congress leader Kripashankar Singh.[73]

The MNS took a page out of the Shiv Sena's book, which, in the words of T.B. Hansen in the 1970s, set out to 'domesticate the city's public spaces by Marathi names, posters . . .' This expressed 'a yearning for a wholly vernacular public—a marking of space that would make the cosmopolitan public culture of the city less strange, more domesticated, welcoming, and comfortable to Marathi speakers'.[74] Hansen calls the Sena 'stylistically the most urban of all the populist movements in India . . .'[75]

Political commentator Mahesh Gavaskar notes that after its ascendancy, the Shiv Sena realized the political limits of its monocultural, ethno-linguistic agenda and that a taste of power in the 1990s lulled it into a 'self-congratulatory pose' of complacency, much like the Congress of the 1960s.[76]

This explains the popular support to the MNS when it trained its guns on the north Indians, cast them in the mould of the 'other' and insisted on shopfronts having signboards in Marathi.

Migrants vs Maharashtrians

Maharashtra saw a rise in urbanization, from 42.4 per cent in 2001 to 45.2 per cent in 2011 according to the census. With Mumbai gradually being saturated, many north Indians shifted to smaller cities, towns and even villages, where they also worked as seasonal labour on farms.

A story in the *Indian Express* said a 2011 census report on the mother tongue of residents in the city has shown that respondents identifying Hindi as their mother tongue has grown by around 40 per cent from 25.82 lakh to 35.98 lakh in Mumbai from 2001.[77]

The report said though individuals claiming Marathi as their mother tongue were Mumbai's largest ethno-linguistic group, followed by Hindi, Urdu and Gujarati speakers, their numbers declined from 45.24 lakh in 2001 to 44.04 lakh in 2011. In the same period, the number of Gujarati speakers fell marginally from 14.34 lakh in 2001 to 14.28 lakh in 2011. The number of Urdu speakers fell from 15.87 lakh in 2001 to 14.59 lakh in 2011. However, numbers of Hindi speakers rose from 25.82 lakh to 35.98 lakh (up 39.35 per cent). This demographic shift was also seen on Mumbai's periphery, with both Thane and Raigad districts showing an over 80 per cent increase in numbers of Hindi-speaking residents.[78]

In 'Population Change and Migration in Mumbai Metropolitan Region: Implications for Planning and Governance', Ram B. Bhagat, Department of Migration and Urban Studies, International Institute of Population Sciences, India, and Gavin W. Jones and J.Y. Pillay, Comparative Asia Research Centre,

Global Asia Institute, National University of Singapore, noted a significant change in source populations of migrants to Mumbai.

'The most noticeable change over the last fifty years was a considerable increase in the share of migrants from the northern state of Uttar Pradesh, which shows an increase from 12 per cent in 1961 to 24 per cent in 2001, and from Bihar, from 0.2 per cent to 3.5 per cent,' it added. However, the increase in interstate migration was paralleled by a decline in migration to Mumbai from within Maharashtra—41.6 per cent in 1961 to 37.4 per cent in 2001. The paper notes that the resurgence in anti-migrant agitations through the emergence of the MNS was associated 'not with increasing migration in Mumbai but with the shift in the migration pattern in favour of inter-state migration'.[79]

While south Indians were the Shiv Sena's original target, migration from these states decreased due to their economic development. The MNS chief at times referred to the southern states as an exemplar when it came to upholding their regional pride.

In December 2018, while speaking at a programme organized by a north Indian organization in his first such outreach, Raj asked people from Uttar Pradesh and Bihar to take their politicians to task for failing to develop their states that led to job seekers migrating elsewhere. Raj justified his nativist stance and, more importantly, blamed the migration to Mumbai on the erstwhile Shiv Sena–BJP government's decision to grant free houses to slum dwellers through Slum Rehabilitation Authority (SRA) projects.[80]

According to Prem Shukla, migration from Uttar Pradesh and Bihar to Mumbai and Maharashtra rose in the 1980s, hastened by the gradual decline of the manufacturing sector in Uttar Pradesh, like tanneries and textile mills in Kanpur. Mumbai and emerging growth centres in the Mumbai Metropolitan Region (MMR) served as magnets for them as they crowded into the decrepit slums and chawls that have become Mumbai's distinguishing feature, housing around 60 per cent of the population. Some of these new arrivals who lacked a roof over their head, had to be content with space on footpaths and shopfronts.[81]

Since the 1980s, as the Hindi heartland states degenerated into lawlessness, the migration into Mumbai and Maharashtra for better livelihood opportunities increased.

'Before the 1980s, few north Indians purchased houses in Mumbai, choosing to buy land and property back in their villages. In Mumbai, around twenty-five to forty people were crammed into a small room, where they slept in shifts. However, this changed gradually,' Shukla noted. He added that areas in eastern Uttar Pradesh like Jaunpur, Azamgarh, Sultanpur and Bhadoi, had no village where at least one member of a family had not migrated elsewhere for work.

Even those in the government admitted that Maharashtra, being a developed state, was bearing the brunt of backwardness in the northern states. In May 2008, finance minister and NCP leader, Jayant Patil, demanded that developed states like Maharashtra get more funds in the devolution of taxes by the centre. Patil complained that despite performing at standards lesser than the average, Uttar Pradesh and Bihar were getting more of these funds.[82]

'Hindi speakers were the most visible migrants in Mumbai due to their presence in labour and public transport and lack of cultural and linguistic integration. The working woman who was harassed by a roadside bhaiya vendor or the youngster at the receiving end of the rickshaw driver's arrogance, were happy that Raj was standing up to them. They were the strongest constituency of the MNS,' explained a Shiv Sena leader.[83]

Though the Shiv Sena had attacked south Indians in its early days, Bharatkumar Raut noted that the prime difference between them and north Indians was that the latter had political ambitions, adding another layer to the resentment of Marathi speakers.[84]

Raj would often point to how migrants would create their own political constituencies in Mumbai.

In his book, Ram Manohar Tripathi admits that while migrants from Punjab and Rajasthan migrated to Mumbai and gradually made it their home, those from Uttar Pradesh continued to maintain a dual citizenship, maintaining their presence in voters lists back home in their villages and also in Mumbai![85]

Chhagan Bhujbal noted that as migrants, north Indians had an economic advantage compared to the locals. 'They were unencumbered by any family responsibilities and did not need leave for festivals that any local worker normally does,' he said, adding that since these people came from poorer backgrounds, they were also willing to work for lesser wages.[86] After the MNS hit out at them, they fled for their states, affecting work in industries and even the construction sector.

'Trains were full of migrant workers fleeing Nashik and surrounding areas. We then ensured that our boys secured these jobs, which was a win-win situation for them and factory owners who were afraid they would have to close down their units due to the manpower crunch,' explained Vasant Gite.[87]

'Raj has an impeccable sense of timing. The average age profile of the Shiv Sainiks was around forty to fifty years, while the MNS had younger cadre. Many children of Shiv Sena leaders and cadre had followed Raj as he launched his party. Raj understood that he had to encash on this by taking up issues that mattered to the young,' explained his former business associate.[88]

He added that the choice of north Indians for vilification as the 'other' was obvious considering the lower- and lower-middle-class Maharashtrian was competing with them economically.

In October 2006, Shiv Sena and MNS clashed at Dadar, with Raj Thackeray's men finding themselves at the receiving end of the Sena's muscle. The MNS leader, Vageesh Saraswat, added that this underlined that they had to rope in the rough-and-ready working-class Marathi manoos, who was a bulwark of support for the Shiv Sena. This was being done through mobilization against north Indians.

When the MNS launched its anti-outsider agitation, there was seething resentment against members of mercantile communities like the Gujaratis and Marwaris, the more affluent of whom were gradually populating gated colonies and 'vegetarian only' towers in traditional Marathi-dominated areas. Shiv Sena and MNS cadre spoke in hushed tones about how flats in these new constructions were sold or rented only to buyers from these communities. Moreover, many leaders from the Shiv Sena and MNS were said to have financial stakes in these constructions.

Even Shiv Sena men found themselves on the back foot when faced with the new form of linguistic and culinary apartheid seeping into the working-class, Marathi-dominated areas. Parag Chavan, a Shiv Sena corporator who later defected to the Congress and son of the Shiv Sena's MLA from Parel, late Vitthal Chavan, recounted his experience of trying to buy a flat in a tower in the locality. 'Initially, the developer was reluctant and quoted a high price running into crores. I said I would arrange the money. Then, the penny dropped and they started saying the flats were meant to be sold to buyers from just one community,' Parag alleged.[89] The most striking irony was that Parag was allegedly denied a flat in a building that had come up on a road named after his late father!

The Maharashtrian proprietor of a famous masala shop at Lalbag made similar allegations. 'The development of mill lands has made real estate prices shoot through the roof. Even those Maharashtrians who can afford to buy flats have been turned down. Needless to say, the *zendewale* [the Shiv Sena and MNS] are doing nothing,' he complained.[90]

'North Indians are soft targets. They are poor and rarely hit back. The Gujaratis and Marwaris are more organized, control the business world and can starve parties of funds at will,' admitted the Uttar Pradesh-born and Haryana-educated Vageesh Saraswat who moved to Mumbai in 1991 for work, but speaks impeccable Marathi.[91]

As his anti–north Indian campaign gathered steam, Raj even demanded that a permit system be imposed in Mumbai to prevent the influx of outsiders.[92] Incidentally, this demand had been raised by the Shiv Sena since its first rally in 1966.[93]

'Who gave these intellectuals the right to call Mumbai the financial capital. It is first the capital of Maharashtra,' Raj told journalist Manu Joseph, adding that while non-Maharashtrian migrants could live here, they needed to respect Marathi heritage.[94]

Shiv Sena leaders admit that the years between 2008 and 2014 were tough for the party because of the MNS's aggressive expansion into their electoral catchment. The MNS was also setting the agenda for the Sena, by hijacking its original agenda.

In 2008, perhaps in an attempt to outmanoeuvre the MNS, the Shiv Sena's mouthpiece carried an editorial '*Ek Bihari Sau Bimari* (One Bihari causes thousand illnesses)', which quoted part of a text message to claim that Biharis were like an affliction. This drew immediate condemnation from parties like the Rashtriya Janata Dal (RJD) and Janata Dal (United) (JD [U]).[95]

During my visit to the residence of Ambadas Dharrao, who lost his life in the MNS protests at Nashik, his nephew Dr Sanjay, who practised medicine at Lasalgaon, questioned if politicians fanning the anti-migrant campaign would take responsibility for retribution against Maharashtrians living outside Maharashtra.[96] In November 2008, the *Times of India* reported that a group of armed men had barged into the house of a Maharashtrian family at Karnal in Haryana and gave them a 'deadline' to return to their native places on the pain of death.[97] Vijay Singh Suryavanshi and his wife, Kalpana, who hail from Jalgaon in north Maharashtra, had migrated to Karnal around fifteen years ago. Their children were born in Haryana, which has around 15,000 Maharashtrians.[98]

Eventually, the Haryana government and local residents stepped in to ensure that the Marathi families stayed put.[99]

Similarly, the residence of S.B. Borwankar, a Marathi official of Tata Motors at Jamshedpur, was ransacked by the little-known Bharatiya Bhojpuri Sangh (BBS).[100] A woman IAS officer hailing from Maharashtra was also targeted by an angry mob that surrounded her office and shouted slogans in Bihar's Purnia district. The reason? Ashwini Thakare's surname![101]

Misalliance in the making

With the MNS snapping at its heels, a section of the Shiv Sena and the NCP was planning to join hands. They believed that an alliance with their allies (the BJP and Congress respectively) had outlived its utility.

These Sena leaders felt that if the 2009 Lok Sabha elections threw up a hung Parliament, they could support NCP chief Sharad Pawar, a fellow Marathi manoos, as a consensus candidate for the country's top post. Sanjay Raut, the Shiv Sena Rajya Sabha MP and executive editor of party organ *Saamna*, was viewed as being close to Pawar.

'Pawar has nursed prime ministerial ambitions since the 1990s. Though the NCP's seats in the Lok Sabha have never crossed a single digit, he fancies his chance at the head of a coalition of regional forces considering his experience in public life,' explained a senior politician from the sugar bowl of western Maharashtra, the NCP chief's stronghold.[102]

He claimed Pawar wanted to replicate the Progressive Democratic Front (PDF) experiment at the national level. In 1978, Pawar (thirty-eight), toppled the Vasantdada Patil regime in Maharashtra to form a government with Congress defectors and the Janata Party to become the youngest chief minister of the state.

The Shiv Sena was also upset at the BJP's attempts to corner it wherever possible after Rane and Raj's defections like during the 2006 Chimur by-poll. Hence, some leaders from the NCP and Shiv Sena were looking at allying for the 2009 Lok Sabha polls by ditching their respective partners. 'However, the idea had to be junked as there was a risk involved. The NCP associating with the Shiv Sena would have led to secular regional parties moving away. Muslims and Dalits would have also spurned Pawar, who always projected himself as a progressive,' the leader noted.[103]

NCP sources admitted that the move was counter-intuitive as the Shiv Sena and NCP cadre were ranged against each other in local politics.[104]

Writing in *Wagache Panje*, a compilation about Bal Thackeray by Canada-based Vijay Dhawale, former three-term Shiv Sena MP from Shirur, Shivajirao Adhalrao Patil, reveals the tale of the Sena's stillborn alliance with the NCP.

Born into a family of marginal farmers at Landewadi at Manchar near Pune, Adhalrao shifted to Mumbai where his father was a vegetable vendor. He stayed in a slum at Ghatkopar, washing cars, working as a casual labourer and an usher in movie halls, and attending night school.[105] He became an entrepreneur, launching his company, Dynalog, which went on to supply components for India's missile programme. He struck up a friendship with senior NCP leader Dilip Valse Patil. After a power tussle with Valse Patil, an MLA from Ambegaon in Pune, Adhalrao joined the Shiv Sena and became a Lok Sabha MP from the Khed constituency in 2004.

The constituency's name and boundaries were changed in the delimitation exercise. Adhalrao writes that he had asked Uddhav to hold a public meeting in the constituency to reach out to new voters. The date was fixed for 8 October 2008, but he was suddenly informed by Milind Narvekar that Uddhav would have to cancel the engagement and asked him to speak to Sanjay Raut.[106]

'The Shiv Sena is talking to the NCP for an alliance,' Adhalrao quotes Raut as saying, adding that Sharad Pawar was seeking the Shirur constituency for himself as it consisted of areas that were earlier part of his Baramati seat. 'You take any other constituency. There is ambivalence about Shirur and hence Uddhavji cannot come,' said Raut.[107]

Adhalrao said these reports made his workers uneasy. There was no progress in the parleys between the two parties. Finally, he was told that Uddhav would come for the rally, in which he lashed out at the Congress without mentioning the NCP, which was the Shiv Sena's main adversary there.[108]

In his piece, Adhalrao claimed surveys commissioned by Pawar indicated he could lose to the former from the seat in a photo finish. He said Pawar called him to the Taj in Mumbai on 24 November 2008, just two days before it was attacked by Pakistani terrorists, and said he wanted Shirur. Pawar offered Adhalrao the chance to contest from Beed or take his daughter Supriya Sule's Rajya Sabha seat. Instead of rejecting his proposal outright, Adhalrao said he would get back to him after speaking to his wife, who was in the United States. 'The NCP realized I would not budge. Pawar gave up on his plans for an understanding with the Sena and his demand for Shirur,' wrote Adhalrao.[109]

The Shiv Sena's alliance with the BJP continued, and Pawar contested and won from the Madha constituency, leaving Baramati for his daughter.

Adhalrao contested the 2009 Lok Sabha election against NCP MLA Vilas Lande, and scored a win by over 1.80 lakh votes, the fifth highest in Maharashtra.

Raj's former business associate claimed that his protests had come as a manna from heaven for the ruling Congress and NCP government, which saw the chances of the MNS eating into the votes of the Opposition Shiv Sena and BJP. 'The government went out on a limb to support Raj. Permissions for his rallies were granted easily and the police went soft on his workers when they took the law into their hands,' he claimed.[110]

The political boundaries of the Lok Sabha and assembly constituencies had been redrawn by the Delimitation Commission, altering the balance of power from the rural to urban areas. The delimitation of assembly constituencies also saw assembly seats in the fast urbanizing Mumbai–Thane region rise from forty-seven (thirty-four in Mumbai and thirteen in Thane) to sixty (thirty-six and twenty-four respectively). The Lok Sabha seats also increased from eight to ten. It was in this belt that the MNS agitation had maximum impact. In what hurt the Sena, many of its traditional assembly constituencies like Opera House were either wiped out or merged (like Dadar and Mahim).

The Shiv Sena, which saw an existential threat from the MNS, alleged that the party was being promoted clandestinely by the ruling Congress and NCP combine. The former Maharashtra cabinet minister claimed the 'government had extended help to the MNS wherever it could' with some powerful developers acting as go-betweens.[111]

'There is nothing wrong in dividing the votes of our opponents. The MNS was growing at the expense of the Shiv Sena and it was obvious that we would go soft on it,' admitted a senior NCP leader.[112]

After the 26/11 terror attacks, when Pakistani terrorists rampaged in Mumbai killing over 160 people, Chief Minister Vilasrao Deshmukh found himself in the throes of a controversy when he visited the ravaged Taj hotel with actor son Riteish and film-maker Ram Gopal Verma in tow and was accused of prompting 'terror tourism'.

To successfully force the Congress to claim Deshmukh's scalp, NCP chief Sharad Pawar, who was Union agriculture minister, asked Deputy Chief Minister and Home Minister R.R. Patil, who was from his own NCP, to quit.[113] MNS sources admitted

Deshmukh was said to be among those from the ruling coalition who were aiding and abetting the MNS behind the scenes to fracture the Shiv Sena and BJP's vote base.[114]

In an off-the-record conversation soon after quitting office, Deshmukh admitted that a factor that led to his resignation was the opposition of leaders from north India like Lalu Prasad Yadav who were reportedly upset that the state government had failed to reign in the MNS, which would have an adverse impact on their political prospects in their home states.[115]

Ashok Chavan, son of Deshmukh's political guru and former Union home minister, Shankarrao Chavan, replaced him in Maharashtra. Deshmukh, who was later inducted in the Manmohan Singh–led government, passed away in in 2012.

Lok Sabha 2009

The MNS fielded twelve candidates for the Lok Sabha elections in 2009 even as the Shiv Sena and BJP hyperventilated against what they claimed was an attempt to divide the Maharashtrian and anti-incumbency votes.

Political reporters covering the elections were surprised to note the groundswell of support for the MNS, especially among the youth and women in Maharashtra.

Journalist Sachin Parab noted that Raj found support among first-time voters and women due to his 'macho image', and also the upper castes, for whom the BJP and its then leadership held little attraction. He said the sister of a senior BJP leader, who has a strong base in the RSS, had admitted she would vote for the MNS rather than the BJP![116]

An MNS candidate noted how they had received support from non-Maharashtrians like Gujaratis and Sikhs. 'The anti–north Indian campaign had struck a chord with them. We had the upper-middle-class Marathi manoos, who was not a traditional

Sena supporter, giving us an encouraging response. Voter fatigue with the Shiv Sena–BJP alliance was obvious. The anti-incumbency vote was gained by the MNS, which was seen as an alternative to established parties and had no legacy baggage.'[117]

When the results were declared, it was clear that the presence of the MNS had helped the Congress and NCP sail through all six Lok Sabha segments in Mumbai. In nine of the eleven seats that it was in the fray, the votes polled by MNS nominees were more than the victory margins of the Congress and NCP candidates, ensuring it had played the spoiler.

For instance, in Mumbai North-east constituency, Sanjay Dina Patil of the NCP won by just 2933 votes against Kirit Somaiya of the BJP. Shishir Shinde of the MNS cornered over 1.95 lakh votes. In Mumbai South, Shiv Sena MP Mohan Rawle was pushed to third place with just 1.46 lakh votes as Bala Nandgaonkar of the MNS edged him out as a runner-up against Milind Deora of the Congress. In Mumbai North, the BJP's veteran warhorse Ram Naik lost to Sanjay Nirupam (Congress) by a 5779-vote margin with Shirish Parkar of the MNS walking away with 1.47 lakh votes. Speaking to the author later, Naik admitted they had underestimated the MNS factor. In Maharashtra, the Congress and NCP had secured seventeen and eight seats and the BJP and Shiv Sena trailed at nine and eleven respectively. Independents and smaller parties had won three seats. When it came to number crunching in terms of leads secured in assembly segments, the results were even more startling.

The Congress led twenty-three assembly segments in Mumbai including Sena–BJP strongholds like Worli, Malabar Hill, Vile Parle and Goregaon and the NCP was ahead in one. The Shiv Sena and BJP could neck ahead in just two and five, respectively. The MNS had stolen a march in five constituencies. For the saffron alliance, this was a dip compared to the 2004 assembly poll results where the Congress and NCP won fifteen and four assembly seats respectively, followed by the Shiv Sena (nine) and BJP (five), with alleged underworld don turned politician Arun Gawli winning one seat.

A jubilant Raj, ever the movie buff, mouthed a dialogue from the movie *Amar, Akbar, Anthony*: '*Usne apun ko mara . . . apun ne sirf do mara, lekin solid mara ke nahin* (You beat me so much, I hit you just twice, but hard).'[118] Ironically, this dialogue was delivered by Amitabh Bachchan, who played Anthony in Manmohan Desai's blockbuster.

State Assembly 2009

In the state assembly elections due a few months later, the MNS strategy was clear.

'Our target was the Shiv Sena. We divided assembly seats into the A, B and C categories based on our chances. A category seats included those which could be won by us, B were those where we could defeat the Shiv Sena–BJP, if not win ourselves, and in C category seats, we chose to fight just to energize the local cadre,' admitted MNS leader Vageesh Saraswat.[119]

While the Shiv Sena and BJP put up 160 and 119 candidates respectively, the MNS fielded just 143.

A veteran of the Dalit Panthers movement remembers how he saw some Buddhist Dalit youth from a slum located in Mumbai's eastern suburbs canvassing for the MNS. 'I asked them why they had chosen to throw in their lot with the MNS, with whom they shared almost no ideological affinity. They replied that Raj's protests would see Marathi youth like them being placed in railway jobs. This showed there were too many expectations from Raj due to the high-octane publicity for his protests.'[120]

An SP politician noted that some Muslim youth in south Mumbai's Dongri, which has attained infamy as the place where the city's dreaded underworld was born, had joined the MNS and started a party shakha. 'Muslims who had been settled in Mumbai for generations felt they were being elbowed out by newer arrivals from northern India. By starting an MNS shakha in a polarized Muslim area like Dongri, the MNS achieved something that even the Shiv Sena could not all these years,' he added.[121]

Writing in the *Economic and Political Weekly* (*EPW*), Mumbai, on 3 October 2009, Maya Lalvani ('Regional Variations and Impact of Delimitation in Maharashtra') pointed to the potential threat that the MNS posed for the Sena. According to Lalvani, the urban belt of Mumbai, adjoining satellite townships, Nashik and Pune, that earlier had fifty-two seats in the assembly would now have seventy-three seats, ahead of the sugar belt, which had a reduced number of constituencies from seventy-five to sixty-three.

With nearly 100 out of the 288 assembly seats in Maharashtra now predominantly urban, the BJP–Shiv Sena alliance had an advantage over the ruling NCP–Congress, at least on paper. But much depended on how each party played its cards as well as on the emergence of new 'spoilers', she noted.

Lalvani pointed to how the Congress had a silver lining, as most new constituencies in the suburbs had a significant non-Maharashtrian population, in addition to a sizeable north Indian influence, in at least one-third of these seats, which would make things difficult for the Shiv Sena–BJP. More importantly, the trends in the 2009 Lok Sabha indicated that the strongest factor favouring the Congress was the MNS factor.

The MNS won thirteen seats in the assembly, of which six were from Mumbai. This performance in the first assembly election after it was formed far exceeded the Shiv Sena's historic performance—the party crossed single digits only in 1990. In Mumbai, MNS candidates like Bala Nandgaonkar (Shivdi), Shishir Shinde (Bhandup West), Ram Kadam (Ghatkopar West), Pravin Darekar (Magathane), Nitin Sardesai (Mahim) and

Mangesh Sangle (Vikhroli) trounced their opponents from the Shiv Sena and BJP.

Among those who were defeated was Pramod Mahajan's daughter, Poonam Mahajan Rao, who lost to Ram Kadam. For the Shiv Sena, the most humiliating defeats came in Mahim, which included Dadar, the 'epicentre' of the Shiv Sena earthquake,[122] and Shivdi, which covered the Girangaon belt, and which gave the Sena its first MLA in 1970.

MNS nominees Vasant Gite, Nitin Bhosale and Uttamrao Dhikale swept three of the four seats in Nashik, with Babanrao Gholap (Deolali) serving as the sole face-saver for the Shiv Sena.

After Raj's success in the 2009 state assembly elections, his uncle is said to have sent him a bouquet and letter to congratulate him.[123]

A senior Mumbai Regional Congress Committee (MRCC) leader said that as the presence of the MNS helped the Congress and NCP win six Lok Sabha seats in Mumbai, it had helped them sweep Mumbai's assembly segments later that same year.[124] 'In the state polls, we put up weak candidates against the MNS on seats where they had strong chances of victory and they returned the favour. Transfer of votes between the Congress–NCP and the MNS ensured that the Shiv Sena and BJP were left with a bloody nose,' he admitted.[125]

Shishir Shinde, elected to the state assembly from Bhandup after defeating the Shiv Sena's Sunil Raut, Sanjay Raut's younger brother, said the most significant achievement of the MNS was to show that a party could achieve electoral success in Mumbai purely on the votes of Marathi speakers. 'Raj's expectation that he could walk away with half of the Shiv Sena was belied. But he had captured the sentiment of the Maharashtrians. Moreover, a rebel always attracts sympathy,' he added.[126]

The MNS secured 11.88 per cent votes (25,85,597) in the 143 seats it contested compared to the BJP's 33.56 per cent (63,52,147 in 119 seats) and Shiv Sena's 29.90 per cent (73,69,030 in 160 seats).

The Shiv Sena won forty-four seats and BJP forty-six. Adding insult to injury, the Shiv Sena, which by now was at number four in terms of bench strength in the assembly, lost the leader of Opposition's post and the status of the principal Opposition party to the BJP.

The BJP's Eknath Khadse, a legislator from Muktainagar in north Maharashtra's Jalgaon, became the new Opposition leader. Shiv Sena's Subhash Desai had to be content as his party's group leader.

As senior BJP leader late Gopinath Munde said two years later at a party conclave in Aurangabad, the MNS won thirteen seats but damaged the prospects of the saffron alliance in fifty-three. If the Sena–BJP tally of ninety was combined with sixty-six (fifty-three plus thirteen), it would be more than that of Congress–NCP and mooted an alliance between the three parties.[127]

'These results were a severe setback to us. Many were writing the Shiv Sena's political obituary. Our position was worse than in 1990,' a Shiv Sena strategist admitted.[128]

On their part, Raj and other MNS leaders denied that they had helped the Congress and NCP romp home by splitting Marathi votes. They pointed to how the saffron alliance had been trounced in 1999 and 2004 when the MNS was nowhere on the horizon.

Moreover, the Shiv Sena–BJP government had come to power in 1999 due to support from independents. 'Doesn't the Marathi manoos in Maharashtra have his own opinions on whom he is supposed to vote for?' Raj asked in an interview to *Loksatta*.[129]

The SP secured four seats in the state assembly. Azmi, who had declared Rs 122 crore worth assets when he contested the Lok Sabha elections from the Mumbai North-west constituency, was elected from two seats—Mankhurd Shivajinagar in Mumbai and

Bhiwandi East. Later, Azmi quit his Bhiwandi seat and fielded his son, Farhan, who was defeated by the Shiv Sena's Rupesh Mhatre.

Azmi was seeking to project himself as a leader of the north Indians and not just Muslims. Raj often claimed that non-Marathi leaders like Azmi were creating their own political constituencies in Maharashtra.

As the Shiv Sena fumbled for a response, an editorial in *Saamna* showcased the party's precarious state of mind. It alleged that the Marathi manoos had 'stabbed the Shiv Sena in the back' by voting for the MNS.[130] After an outrage, Thackeray Senior distanced himself from the offending statement in a meeting of party legislators.[131]

The Shiv Sena was clearly caught between a rock and a hard place.

8

The Downfall of the MNS: The Shiv Sena Holds Its Own

> This is the way the world ends
> This is the way the world ends
> This is the way the world ends
> Not with a bang but a whimper.
>
> T.S. Eliot, 'The Hollow Men'

After the 2009 assembly polls, the old bête noire of the MNS, Abu Asim Azmi, declared that he would take his oath of office in Hindi. Holding a red rag to a bull in an already politically charged environment, Azmi sought that the agenda and communication of the legislature be given to him in Hindi.

Raj immediately countered this. 'Every MLA will have to take oath in Marathi. If they take oath in any other language, the legislature will see what my MLAs will do,' he warned.[1]

As newly elected legislators were being sworn in on 9 November 2009, the very first day of the session, Azmi came to the lectern with a flourish as his name was announced. As he started reading out the oath in Hindi, Ramesh Wanjale of the MNS, who was elected from Khadakwasla in Pune, rushed to the well of the house. The house watched, stunned, as the well-built

Wanjale, a wrestler, lifted the lectern. Armed with placards, MNS legislators too came to the well, as those from the treasury benches rushed to protect Azmi, who took oath standing next to pro tem Speaker Ganpatrao Deshmukh.

Perhaps perturbed at the MNS walking away with its sons-of-the-soil agenda, Shiv Sena members too started sloganeering against Azmi with some holding pro-Marathi placards.

After stepping down from the dais, Azmi entered into a verbal duel and scuffle with the MNS contingent. He was slapped by MNS MLA Ram Kadam before being whisked away to safety. Four MNS legislators—Wanjale, called 'Gold Man' due to the copious amount of jewellery that he wore, Kadam, Shishir Shinde and Vasant Gite—were suspended for the assault, which had resulted in widespread condemnation.[2]

Incidentally, while Azmi was the target of MNS's ire, the party kept mum over Congress MLAs from Mumbai, Baba Siddique, Ramesh Singh Thakur and Amin Patel taking their oath in English and Hindi. After the attack, Ram Kadam gave sound bites to the electronic media in Hindi![3]

In his weekly column in *Saamna* on 15 November 2009, Sanjay Raut alleged that there was an arrangement between Azmi and the MNS and, ironically, claimed this controversy had divided Hindus along the lines of Hindi speakers and Maharashtrians.

Raut pointed out that while the three Congress legislators had taken oath in languages other than Marathi, no one from the MNS had objected. 'Because this had not been decided between the two parties,' charged Raut. He also called the spat between the SP and the MNS 'politics of mutual convenience'.[4]

Azmi continues to deny that his confrontations with the MNS before and after the state assembly polls were stage-managed. 'The lathis that I was seeking to distribute were the symbol of the one used by Mahatma Gandhi. But they could be used to beat attackers here,' he claimed.[5]

Azmi said he had decided to take the oath in Hindi as it was an official language and was spoken by the largest number of people across India. 'There was no *noora kushti* [fixed fight] involved. I am willing to transfer all my property to those who can prove my business dealings with Raj Thackeray,' he averred.

Anti-toll campaign

The two issues that catapulted Raj Thackeray and the MNS to public attention between 2009 and 2014 were a morcha in Mumbai after violence by Muslim groups and the party's agitation seeking transparency in road toll contracts.

In 2012, aided by Right to Information (RTI) activist Sanjay Shirodkar, Raj alleged massive corruption in toll agreements. He charged that contractors continued to collect toll even after recovering the road's construction cost and projected returns on their investment, and fudged traffic numbers for windfall gains. MNS activists also attacked toll nakas across the state, including Mumbai, to protest the policy.

The public private partnership (PPP) model for constructing roads was launched with the 12-kilometre road linking Indore to Pithampur in Madhya Pradesh, which was opened to traffic in November 1993.[6] Around the same time, Maharashtra introduced road development through private participation and the first toll road in the state was Jaisingpur bypass between Kolhapur and Sangli.

Gradually, a resource-crunched state government involved private parties for constructing roads in return for collecting toll from vehicles. Toll collection rights at the five entry points to Mumbai were also securitized. The Maharashtra State Road Development Corporation (MSRDC) also entered into a concession agreement to maintain the iconic Mumbai–Pune expressway along with the old Mumbai–Pune highway.[7] Even senior ministers in the erstwhile Congress–NCP governments admitted that these concession agreements and toll contracts left much to be desired.

'Most of these charges are collected in cash and hence, figures can be manipulated. Everyone in the system had their hands in the till. Rules regarding the minimum distance between two toll posts were manipulated to ensure certain contractors could benefit,' admitted a former Congress minister.[8]

Though Chhagan Bhujbal, who was the PWD minister between 2009 and 2014, claimed there was nothing amiss,[9] the Congress minister quoted earlier, admitted agreements were loaded in favour of contractors with some even lacking a buyback clause.[10]

In his book, *Toll Ek Jhol Aani* . . . (Toll, a scam), Sanjay Shirodkar pointed to how road users were forced to pay toll despite shelling out thirteen types of taxes like motor vehicles tax, cess on petrol and diesel and passenger goods tax.[11] Shirodkar claimed that vehicle numbers were under-reported in traffic surveys and project costs were inflated. He charged toll operators pocketed money by claiming they had allowed a certain number of 'unpaid' and 'exempted' vehicles, including those of VIPs, to pass.[12]

In 2017, the Comptroller and Auditor General's (CAG) audit report for public sector undertakings (PSUs) for the year ended 31 March 2016, may have touched the tip of the iceberg. It pointed to how the MSRDC failed to verify the traffic data provided by the contractor and recover its share of excess toll revenue worth Rs 54.59 crore from a collection contractor on the Mumbai–Bengaluru national highway.[13]

In June 2012, Raj ordered MNS workers to launch a round-the-clock, fortnight-long survey at forty major toll posts to record the number of vehicles paying toll and check if there were any deviations in claims about vehicular traffic made by contractors.

MNS leaders had claimed that vehicular traffic surveys conducted before granting the toll collection rights were manipulated in favour of contractors to give them a sweet deal.

MNS functionaries said the campaign had struck a chord with the middle class, with many motorists, including non-Maharashtrians, stopping to encourage the around 10,000 activists who sat in shifts to record these numbers.[14]

In November 2008, the state government securitized toll collection rights at the five entry points to Mumbai (Vashi, Mulund, Airoli, Dahisar and LBS Marg) for just Rs 2100 crore till 19 November 2026 to MEP Infrastructure Developers Ltd.[15] Transport sector experts alleged that an undervaluation of vehicle numbers and longer duration of the contract was expected to cause a Rs 10,000 crore loss to the exchequer.[16]

After the survey was completed in July 2012, Raj made a sensational claim that the five entry points to Mumbai saw daily collections of Rs 1.37 crore, which even when rounded off to Rs 1.25 crore, meant yearly collections of Rs 456.25 crore. He added that the operator had collected Rs 3934.64 crore by then, which worked out to Rs 14,524.79 crore till the completion of the concession period (considering the projected annual increase in vehicle numbers).[17]

Raj claimed their survey showed that collections at the Khalapur toll naka on the Mumbai–Pune expressway were around Rs 1.75 crore daily or Rs 638.75 crore annually and the old highway (NH4), had collections of Rs 45 lakh daily or Rs 164.25 crore annually. Put together, this worked out to an annual Rs 803 crore.[18]

In August 2004, MSRDC and Mhaiskar Infrastructure Private Limited (MIPL), a special purpose vehicle of IRB Infrastructure Developers Ltd, signed a concession agreement to develop, operate and maintain the Mumbai-Pune expressway and the NH4 for a fifteen-year period. The cost of the project was Rs 1301 crore.[19]

Raj said that considering a 5 per cent annual increase in vehicles, the toll operator had managed to collect over Rs 5915 crore so far by spending just Rs 1301 crore.[20] He and MNS leaders further alleged that while toll was collected from road users, they did not get facilities like service roads, toilets, breakdown vans and ambulances.

Raj asked people to stop paying toll till the state government ensured transparency in these contracts. He later met then chief minister Prithviraj Chavan to discuss the lacunae in the system and the way forward.[21]

Though Raj announced MNS workers would also keep a vigil at these nakas to ensure that people were not pressured to pay up, the agitation gradually fizzled out.

A former MNS MLA from Mumbai said he had rallied around 3000 of his supporters to protest at a toll naka in Mumbai, when the region's additional commissioner of police (ADCP) asked him to wind up as he (the officer) had discussed this with 'Raj saheb'. The IPS officer then called Raj who asked the MLA to take it easy. The message to step back was delivered, albeit not in so many words, he claimed.[22]

In an interview, Raj had spoken about how he chose to wind down his agitations when they reached a crescendo to prevent matters from escalating further. He said this was also necessary to ensure that the cadre did not become 'arrogant'.[23]

In February 2014, Raj suddenly renewed the anti-toll protest, courting arrest with party MLAs Bala Nandgaonkar and Nitin Sardesai at Chembur in Mumbai's eastern suburbs. But, by then, the campaign had lost its credibility.[24]

'We took up issues like corruption in toll contracts that had not been touched by other political parties, but failed to take them to their logical end,' admitted Vasant Gite, who was then an MNS MLA from Nashik and general secretary. Gite, who quit the MNS later after differences with Raj, said this caused the party to be seen as having capitulated, which in turn caused it immense electoral damage.[25]

The sharpest attack came from Uddhav in June 2012. Soon after Raj began his campaign, Uddhav charged his cousin for using the protests to 'extort money' from toll operators.[26] However, even MNS's detractors admit that the party achieved something by the dint of its campaign—it brought the issue into mainstream political discourse.

In 2014, senior BJP leader late Gopinath Munde promised to make Maharashtra 'toll-free' if elected to power in Maharashtra and the promise was repeated ad nauseam by BJP leaders. But, other voices, like that of Union transport minister Nitin Gadkari, who was seen as Munde's rival in the BJP, claimed this would be difficult to implement economically. Gadkari, whose tenure as PWD minister in the Sena-BJP regime had seen a massive expansion in road infrastructure, did admit to flaws within the system.[27]

After coming to power in Maharashtra in 2014, the BJP government led by Devendra Fadnavis shut down twelve toll plazas and waived off toll on light vehicles like private cars at fifty-three locations in a move that warmed the hearts of the politically resurgent middle class. This happened when Maharashtra was reeling under a debt of Rs 3.33 lakh crore and Rs 27,663 crore interest servicing cost. The move cost Rs 799 crore for the buyback and toll waiver in 2014–15 alone.[28] Social activists and farmer leaders pointed to the dichotomy—the state subsidizing the middle- and upper-middle classes through its limited resources while glossing over the plight of distressed farmers and the cash-strapped social sector.[29]

Shishir Shinde, who was then an MNS MLA, however claimed that the party could not be blamed for failing to take the road toll issue to its logical end. 'Everyone, be it politicians, bureaucrats and contractors, have stakes here. It is not so easy to break this nexus,' he said.[30] 'There is a point in every agitation where you reach a plateau. How long can you protest and beat up people? Once fatigue sets in within the cadre, people can easily claim that the party has been manipulated, said a senior journalist who has covered the MNS at close quarters.'[31]

Raj claimed that his party failed to adequately inform voters of all the 'good work' it had accomplished. 'We could not convince people that the government's decision to shut down sixty-five toll plazas was an outcome of our agitation,' he lamented.[32]

Meanwhile, the Shiv Sena faced a critical test in the 2012 BMC elections. With three successive defeats in the state assembly and Raj's resurgence, the party desperately needed to hold on to the cash-rich civic body for political survival.

As in 1985, when Chief Minister Vasantdada Patil gave the Shiv Sena a political opening to enable it to capture the BMC, one of his successors in the state helped the Sena retain control over the civic body in what was claimed as 'an error of judgement' by his party leaders.

Speaking to the media, Chief Minister Prithviraj Chavan claimed the Shiv Sena would become irrelevant after its defeat in the BMC.[33] This led to a massive mobilization at the grass roots by Sena cadre.

The Shiv Sena and BJP won the elections with seventy-five and thirty-one seats in the 227-member house. The saffron alliance was helped by the inclusion of Dalit leader, Ramdas Athavale, who heads his own faction of the Republican Party of India (RPI), due to an outreach by Bal Thackeray.

The Congress got fifty-two seats while the NCP picked up thirteen. However, it was the MNS that put up a stellar show, notching up twenty-eight wins and winning all seven wards in the Shiv Sena's bastion in Dadar and Mahim, with Sena veterans like former mayor Milind Vaidya biting the dust.

The wins in the Mumbai and Thane civic polls gave the Shiv Sena a much-needed morale booster.

It takes two to reconcile

Ever since the two cousins split, there was a 'will they, won't they' kind of speculation on whether they would finally unite.

On 17 July 2012, Uddhav complained of severe chest pain and was admitted to the Lilavati Hospital in Mumbai for an angiography. On being informed about this by none other than Bal Thackeray, Raj, who was at Alibag in neighbouring Raigad district for a three-day party workshop, rushed to Mumbai, meeting his cousin briefly, and returned to the hospital later in the evening to drive him to Matoshree.[34] This was Raj's first visit to Matoshree after 2008, when he had met his uncle and returned some books, including those on David Low's cartoons.

As images of Raj driving his cousin to the Thackeray family residence hit television screens, there was renewed kite-flying on whether they would overcome their estrangement and reunite. Raj was also present when Uddhav underwent an angioplasty to remove three blockages in his arteries.

A senior Shiv Sena leader told me at the time that the bitterness between the cousins and their immediate families was too deep and intense to be bridged. A BJP leader, who is now a minister in the Maharashtra cabinet, agreed. 'One can make up when the differences are political. Here, there is a lot of personal acrimony,' he explained.[35]

Indeed, in an interview to *Hindustan Times* in April 2014, Raj described Uddhav as a 'misfit' in politics who lacked 'the calibre of being a politician'.[36]

Rumours about a likely political reconciliation between the cousins reached a crescendo after Bal Thackeray's death, when Uddhav said in an interview with *Saamna* that 'one cannot clap with one hand',[37] indicating he was open to breaking bread with Raj. However, both MNS and Sena leaders admitted that a lot of water had flowed under the bridge since 2005. For instance, both the parties had parallel organizational set-ups and merging the two would be troublesome.

Nikhil Wagle, who was then the editor of the Marathi news channel IBN Lokmat, agreed. Before the 2012 BMC elections, Wagle had interviewed Bal Thackeray where the latter had spoken about his love for Raj and replied to questions about whether he and Uddhav would make amends. Thackeray had claimed their egos prevented Uddhav and Raj from uniting. 'There is no use about me feeling so, they must,' he said, when asked about whether the two needed to bury their differences and unite.[38]

'Uddhav was sitting behind me and when the questions about Raj came up, he was signalling to my producer that they should not be asked. Minutes after I left Matoshree, I received a call from Uddhav seeking that the footage not be shown as it would affect the outcome of the polls. Balasaheb also called later. Eventually, we decided to air the footage about Raj after the voting was completed as otherwise, there was a chance that they would ask us to withdraw the entire interview as was their prerogative,' said Wagle.[39]

However, Thackeray Senior had 'blessed' Track-2 efforts to ensure that the two brothers patched up due to 'public pressure'.

In 2006, one of the thousands who turned up to hear Raj speak at Shivaji Park in March as he launched his party was Satish Valanju. A successful entrepreneur, with businesses ranging from pest control, laundry, to namkeen (snacks) as well as an unit manufacturing semen straws for livestock and bio-fertilizers in Mauritius, Valanju grew up at Worli in central Mumbai and was a veteran Shiv Sainik.

'When Raj split from the Shiv Sena, I was among those confused about our loyalties. Many questions were playing on our minds. For instance, was injustice perpetrated upon Raj, who had been launched into politics before Uddhav? There was a perception that the Shiv Sena had kept the interests of the Marathi manoos on the back burner for Hindutva,' said Valanju, while speaking to me at his flat in Mahim.[40]

'I was at the MNS inaugural rally but was soon disillusioned. Even the party flag with shades of saffron, blue and green indicated he was moving away from the Sena's Marathi moorings. I felt the Shiv Sena was better. Plus, I had great attraction for Balasaheb,' he added.

Valanju knew his party chief closely. He handled the pest control at Matoshree. The tone of reverence and awe in Valanju's voice is apparent as he speaks about Bal Thackeray. 'Saheb loved gardening. There were times when he asked me to ensure that necessary treatments were done on spots like the terrace as mice had chewed up the plant leaves.'[41]

After the MNS drew first blood in the Lok Sabha and assembly polls, the sentiment in the two parties' electoral catchment grew for the two cousins to unite. It was felt that their rift helped the Congress and NCP. Valanju was among those who wanted this to happen before the 2012 BMC elections by dint of public pressure.

With six of his friends, Valanju decided to launch 'Majhi Chalval' (My movement) on 16 May 2010, which was Akshay Tritiya, an auspicious day for Maharashtrians. This public movement would seek to unify the two warring cousins. Though Valanju denied that Bal Thackeray had played a role in the launch of this gesture of Track-2 diplomacy, he admitted that the Sena chief had consented to it subsequently.

'Word about my initiative got around and on 14 May, I was invited to a talk show on a Marathi news channel. I called up Balasaheb and asked him to watch it if possible. By then, he had already been told by others about my plans,' said Valanju.

'Balasaheb watched the show and called me the next day from his assistant Ravi Mhatre's phone,' said Valanju, his voice cracking as he fought tears. 'Balasaheb said, may Aai Jagdamba (The mother goddess) bless you. My blessings will always be with you. You are not doing this for Raj or Uddhav but for Maharashtra.'

Majhi Chalval held a series of public meetings at Mumbai, Pune, Nashik and Thane to generate a public push for Raj and Uddhav to unite. Valanju was scheduled to fly to Australia when Mhatre rang him to ask him to keep his mobile phone turned on just in case Bal Thackeray wanted to contact him.

'In my 20 June public meeting at Damodar Hall in Mumbai, I attacked Manohar Joshi and Sanjay Raut. Saheb called me at the bungalow and chastised me. He asked if I was trying to break or mend relationships. I promised him I would not say anything that could mar the prospects of Raj and Uddhav's unification. Saheb was very pleased at the initiative. He wanted this to happen.'

A photograph popularized by the group had Bal Thackeray at the centre with his arms around the shoulders of Uddhav and Raj, who flanked him, with the caption: 'I want to see this picture again.'[42] However, on record, Shiv Sena leaders claimed that the campaign had not been patronized by the party.

On 5 September 2010, Majhi Chalval organized a silent march with around 10,000 participants. Launched from the site of Meenatai's bust at Shivaji Park, it wound its way to Raj's house nearby and later to Matoshree.

'Raj did not meet us to take our bouquet and memorandum which sought that the cousins unite respecting the sentiments of the people. Though we were told that he was in Pune, it was learnt that he was at home. At Matoshree, Uddhav met us and though he did not accept the letter, he took the flowers,' said Valanju.

On 23 January 2011, Bal Thackeray's birthday, Majhi Chalval was dissolved. 'Ever since our first press conference on 9 May 2010, we made it clear this was a time-bound project. We wanted to give saheb a birthday gift,' said Valanju, who laments that if the Thackeray cousins had joined hands, it would have caused a 'political tsunami' to wipe out other parties in its path.[43]

Valanju said their success was in bringing these issues into the mainstream public discourse. 'There were 10,000 people in our silent march. Perhaps we could have achieved our purpose if there were a lakh,' he said, his voice trailing off.[44]

MNS gets a chance to govern

'*Mazhya hatat Maharashtra dya, paha kasa suta sarkha saral karto* (Give me power in Maharashtra and see how I set things right)', Raj would often claim.

In 2012, Raj got an opportunity to translate his promises into reality at Nashik, a town where he had a presence since his days in the Shiv Sena. The anti-outsider protest in the pilgrimage centre had led to the MNS carving out a base of its own with three of its thirteen MLAs being elected from there.

The elections to the Nashik Municipal Corporation (NMC) held in February saw the MNS emerge as the single largest with forty out of 122 seats. The NCP, whose Chhagan Bhujbal had led the charge, was the runner-up with twenty, followed by the Shiv Sena (nineteen), Congress (fifteen) and BJP (fourteen).

The BJP, whose state unit president Sudhir Mungantiwar had earlier called the MNS a 'test-tube baby' of NCP chief Sharad Pawar, sprung a surprise over the Shiv Sena by agreeing to support the MNS. Yatin Wagh was elected the first mayor from the MNS while Satish Kulkarni of the BJP became his deputy.

A senior BJP leader, who is now a minister in Maharashtra, said they decided to back the MNS to blow the bottom out of its claims. 'This was the brainchild of the late Gopinath Munde. He said it was easy to make tall promises but when it comes to implementation, things are not so simple. The MNS reign over the Nashik civic body marked the beginning of its end,' he claimed.[45]

During his Lok Sabha and assembly campaigns in 2014, Raj would point to the Jawaharlal Nehru botanical garden, 100-feet water curtain on the Ahilyabai Holkar bridge, 510 kilometres of durable internal roads, a unit that generated power from waste, plants that processed sewage before it was discharged into the Godavari river, as his achievements in Nashik.

But MNS leaders admitted they had been unable to fulfil the heightened expectations of the people. Moreover, the change in political masters had not improved the civic body's grass-roots administration.

In 2014, the MNS leadership ditched the BJP and joined hands with the NCP and Congress to get its Ashok Murtadak elected as the mayor. Vasant Gite, who led the charge on Raj's behalf in Nashik and a former mayor himself, said this was because the BJP was demanding that its corporator be appointed as chairman of the lucrative standing committee that decides on grant of civic contracts.[46]

The MNS was relentlessly attacking Bhujbal, an MLA from Yeola near Nashik.

'Just days before the MNS and NCP joined hands, Raj saheb had attacked Chhagan Bhujbal in a public meeting. This was not lost on the people. Our credibility was eroded further,' said Gite, who quit the MNS to join the BJP after the 2014 assembly elections.[47]

In the 2017 Nashik civic polls, the MNS saw its numbers dip to just five as the BJP surged past the halfway mark with sixty-six of 122 seats. The Shiv Sena captured thirty-five seats and the Congress and NCP six each.

Shiv Sena's Agnipariksha

Shiv Sena leaders admit that the years between 2009 and 2014 were tough for the party, which was made to undergo an agnipariksha (test by fire) as it faced a series of successive political setbacks.

In June 2010, in an election to the legislative council that saw rampant horse-trading, the Shiv Sena's Anil Parab was defeated by a Congress-backed independent candidate, Vijay Sawant, with the MNS dividing its votes between the Congress and NCP nominees.[48] This revealed that members of the Sena's legislature party were amenable to shifting loyalties, a far cry from the days when its corporator was murdered in Thane for the same 'offence', noted a former Maharashtra minister.[49] The soft-spoken Parab, who is close to Uddhav, and is one of the party's key strategists, was elected to the council later.

The Shiv Sena, after losing Raj and Rane and failing to come to power in the state, was gradually trying to regain its pre-eminence on Mumbai's streets. In 2010, actor Shah Rukh Khan, who owned the Kolkata Knight Riders IPL team, spoke in favour of including Pakistani players in the series. An incensed Shiv Sena threatened to disrupt shows of Khan's movie, *My Name Is Khan*, but the actor remained defiant.[50]

Not to be outdone, Raj questioned why the Shiv Sena was silent when actor Amitabh Bachchan had shared the dais with Pakistani personalities in a poetry reading session organized by a media group, and said if Shah Rukh had to apologize, so did Bachchan.[51]

As Shiv Sainiks launched protests, and tore posters of Khan's film, many of them, including women, were beaten up by the police. Chief Minister Ashok Chavan threatened to withdraw Uddhav's security cover and around 2000 Shiv Sena workers were placed under preventive detention. In a symbolic gesture, Chief Minister Chavan and Home Minister R.R. Patil watched the movie.[52]

Ranged against the might of the state, the Shiv Sena was forced to wind down its agitation. This had come on the back of another setback for the party.

The Shiv Sena had declared war on Rahul Gandhi, who was then the Congress general secretary, after he said in Bihar that India belongs to all Indians and that commandos from Bihar and UP fought to save Mumbai during the 26/11 terror attacks. Though Congress leaders admitted that the statement was somewhat over the top, considering Maharashtra's presence in the armed forces, they said Rahul had only chosen to stress that every citizen of India had the right to migrate for better opportunities.

Rahul was scheduled to visit Mumbai in February 2010, interact with students at Vile Parle and then visit the Ramabai Ambedkar slum in Ghatkopar, where ten Dalits were killed in firing by the police during the Sena–BJP regime. The 1997 incident, that happened during protests against the desecration of Dr Babasaheb Ambedkar's statue, had caused widespread anger and consolidation of Dalit voters.[53]

The Shiv Sena announced that Rahul would be greeted with black flags and this was followed by a police crackdown. The Congress leader travelled to Vile Parle under a massive security cover and later, withdrew cash from an ATM and travelled in second-class compartments of local trains to Ghatkopar, leaving the Shiv Sena, whose cadre were looking to protest on the roads, nonplussed.[54]

The Shiv Sena's antipathy towards the MNS was skilfully used by the BJP to plant reports about the party's plans to tie up with the Raj Thackeray–led outfit if the Sena asserted itself beyond a point. However, a senior BJP leader admitted that though the Sena was going through a tough phase, the MNS was more of a flash in the pan as was subsequently proved. Raj's anti-migrant position would have hurt the BJP in north India if the two had joined hands.[55]

According to journalist Sandeep Pradhan, some BJP leaders used the MNS to mischievously needle the Shiv Sena by playing on its insecurities, almost deriving vicarious pleasure from its ally's discomfort.[56]

On 21 December 2010, Raj, who visited the Life Insurance Corporation of India (LIC) office at Nariman Point, went to the

BJP's Maharashtra headquarters located across the road and had a cup of tea with its leaders. An incensed Shiv Sena took umbrage at the MNS chief breaking bread with its ally and threatened to abstain from a rally of the BJP-led National Democratic Alliance (NDA) to be held the next day.[57]

End of an era

> 'At least the Marathi manoos should not stand against the Shiv Sena. In the Dadar area where the Shiv Sena was born [in 1966], where the Shiv Sena Bhawan stands proudly, in that Dadar the Shiv Sena had to bite dust. [By those who] split the Shiv Sena into two. Why has this happened? . . .'
>
> Bal Thackeray's swansong at
his party's Dussehra rally in 2012

In 2012, there were reports that Bal Thackeray's health was taking a turn for the worse. In July, soon after Uddhav's discharge from Lilavati Hospital after his angioplasty, his father had to be admitted there upon complaining of breathlessness, inflammation and constipation.

There was speculation whether the Sena patriarch would be able to attend the Shiv Sena's annual Dussehra rally in October. Finally, Thackeray had to skip the public meeting, where a book of his cartoons was to be released, and addressed the party faithful in a twenty-five-minute pre-recorded speech.

Thackeray, who was looking frailer, said he wanted to come and address his cadre but could not as 'his health had collapsed'.[58]

In his speech, which touched an emotional chord with the party faithful, the Sena chief made a strong emotional pitch to stand by his son Uddhav, and grandson and Yuva Sena chief, Aaditya.

Without naming either Raj or the MNS, Thackeray rued that the Maharashtrian votes were being split causing defeat in the Marathi heartland of Dadar. 'The Shiv Sena has not given up on Marathi [identity]. Marathi is our base,' the Sena chief, dismissing charges that the Sena's focus on Hindutva had diminished its focus on the Marathi agenda.[59]

During Diwali, reports of Bal Thackeray's deteriorating condition leaked out after lanterns at Matoshree and other Shiv Sena strongholds were taken down. Shiv Sainiks from across Mumbai and Thane thronged to Kalanagar.

Over the days, several high-profile visitors including Raj, Amitabh Bachchan, Sharad Pawar and Lata Mangeshkar visited the Thackeray household as hundreds of Shiv Sainiks and media crews kept a vigil outside Kalanagar's main gate.

After reports of him being put on ventilator support, an editorial appeared on 12 November in *Saamna* that was attributed to the Sena chief and scotched rumours about his failing health.[60] On 17 November, the Shiv Sena chief, the original angry young man of Maharashtra's politics, passed away.

Mumbai, reputed to be the city that never sleeps, came to a halt as Shiv Sena workers took to the streets and shopkeepers hastily downed shutters. Heavy police deployment ensured that despite being on edge, the city's law and order situation did not deteriorate. As journalists were herded into the compound of the Maharashtra Housing and Area Development Authority (MHADA) building across the road from Kalanagar, where Matoshree is located, to protect them from restive Sainiks, I found myself with Bal Nare, Bal Thackeray's former bodyguard. As a Class 10 student, Nare, who stayed in Parel where the communist flag used to flutter proudly, bunked school to attend the Shiv Sena's first public meeting on 30 October 1966.

'His speech was so captivating, his words went straight to our hearts,' said a moist-eyed Nare, who joined the party and became an informal bodyguard for the Sena chief. 'If Saheb had not formed the Shiv Sena, there would have been no place for the Marathi manoos in Mumbai. He taught us to fight injustice,' said Nare, a former corporator.

The memories tumbled out as an emotional Nare spoke—how Thackeray stood by his men through thick and thin, bailed them out when they were in trouble and even warned a dreaded criminal from touching a hair on Nare's head when he shut down his *matka* (gambling) business.[61]

As the Mumbai police were preparing to handle the funeral procession, an unexpected problem surfaced. A senior Congress minister in the Prithviraj Chavan government said the family and some Shiv Sena leaders were insisting that the cremation be conducted in public at the Shivaji Park grounds and not at the nearby Dadar crematorium.[62]

'According to the law, cremations have to be performed at designated spots [crematoriums]. The police too were insisting on the Dadar cremation ground. Chavan was uncomfortable with the demand for the funeral to be held at Shivaji Park as this would have set a precedent and led to other such demands. However, since this was a sensitive issue, a via media was arrived at by designating Shivaji Park as a temporary cremation ground,' the minister said.

On 18 November, Thackeray's mortal remains encased in a glass box were transported to Shivaji Park from Matoshree. The cortège, which stretched 2 kilometres, is believed to have drawn a crowd of nearly one million from across Maharashtra.[63]

Raj fuelled speculation when he chose not to travel on the truck carrying the body with Uddhav and other family members but walked alongside it. A few hours later, when the hearse was about to reach Mahim Causeway, he left the procession. This led to conjecture about whether Uddhav had not allowed Raj to board the truck or if the MNS chief backed off fearing ire from

Shiv Sainiks after reports from the police.[64] Raj appeared at Shivaji Park only after the procession arrived there and was at Uddhav's side with Jaidev when the last rites were being performed with the who's who of the country in attendance. As his uncle's pyre was lit, Raj broke into tears.

As frenzied crowds shouted slogans like '*Parat ya, parat ya, Balasaheb parat ya* (Balasaheb come back)', Thackeray, one of the most controversial politicians in India, was given a state funeral with a twenty-one-gun salute. Soon after the cremation, there were demands from Shiv Sena leaders that a memorial for the departed party chief be constructed at the spot where his last rites were conducted.

Manohar Joshi was among the first to set the cat among pigeons by demanding that the memorial be constructed at Shivaji Park.[65] Not to be outdone, Sanjay Raut told reporters: '*Mandir wahin banayenge* (The temple will be built there itself)', echoing a slogan popularized by the Sangh Parivar demanding the construction of the Ram Temple at Ayodhya.[66]

As pressure to remove the temporary funeral platform mounted, the Shiv Sena dug its heels in, with Sainiks from Mumbai and neighbouring areas keeping a vigil to prevent any action by the civic body and police. The platform became a place of pilgrimage for Shiv Sainiks and party supporters who flocked to pay their respects.

As the stand-off escalated, Uddhav urged restraint and said that 'the will of Shiv Sainiks on the memorial would prevail', in what was a tacit approval of the stance taken by the party hawks.[67]

The BMC, which was ironically controlled by the Sena–BJP alliance, wrote to the police pointing out that though the permission was granted for a day, the structure continued to exist well beyond that.[68] However, the state machinery was mindful of the consequences on law and order if the platform was dismantled by force.

The Shiv Sena finally blinked after a month-long deadlock, removing the plinth that had been barricaded with bamboo poles and had the party's saffron flags and posters of Thackeray. At around 1 a.m. on 18 December 2012, the Shiv Sena began the dismantling.

'This was a partial victory for both, the government and the Sena. While the platform was removed, the Shiv Sena got a small landscaped garden at the site. This was a climbdown from their earlier position of a memorial and statue. However, the détente came after days of negotiations between the Shiv Sena and the police. The Shiv Sena may have taken legal advice and also realized that the police were in no mood to relent,' the former Congress minister explained. Milind Narvekar, Uddhav's private secretary, is said to have negotiated with the state government for a détente.[69]

In January 2019, at the height of speculation about whether the Shiv Sena would ally with the BJP for the Lok Sabha elections, the Maharashtra cabinet approved a Rs 100-crore grant for the late Sena chief's memorial.[70] The Balasaheb Thackeray National Memorial is scheduled to come up on the 11,551-square-metre site of the sea-facing mayor's bungalow opposite Shivaji Park at Dadar, metres away from where the Shiv Sena chief was cremated. The public trust formed for administering the memorial has Sena president Uddhav Thackeray and his son and Yuva Sena chief, Aaditya, as life members. The BMC handed over the heritage structure to the trust on lease with nominal rent and Mayor Vishwanath Mahadeshwar moved to a bungalow on the Byculla Zoo premises.[71] A committee appointed by the state government had selected the mayor's bungalow as the site for the memorial.[72] However, in 2015, Raj made a sensational allegation, claiming that the choice of the site was driven by 'selfish and personal interests'.[73]

'They [Shiv Sena leaders] had been eyeing the mayor's bungalow for a long time. They only want the bungalow in the name of Balasaheb,' he said, questioning why vacant plots in the vicinity were not chosen.

Even before it was finalized as a site for the memorial, Uddhav was known to be a frequent visitor to the bungalow, where he took his evening walks on the spacious lawns, and also held party meetings.

9

The Hare and the Tortoise

Vengeance and retribution require a long time; it is the rule.

Charles Dickens, *A Tale of Two Cities*

By 2014, the slow but steady Thackeray cousin seemed to have outrun the fast yet fickle one. Like the hare in Aesop's fables who paid for being complacent and overconfident, Raj too would be outwitted by Uddhav.

In 2009, the MNS had outperformed the Shiv Sena's historic trajectory by winning thirteen seats in the legislature. Speaking with the luxury of hindsight, former MNS leaders claimed this swashbuckling performance may have laid the ground for the party's subsequent downfall.[1]

According to Shishir Shinde, the first flush of victory affected Raj. 'There were times when MNS workers from far-flung districts like Amravati and Akola would come to meet him. Raj would make them wait for hours, shake hands and ask them to come later. His link with the people was broken,' Shinde claimed. 'Though political parties impart a certain stature to their workers, it is also the other way around.'[2]

'The MNS took a lift, went to the top floor, and jumped down. Its rise and fall was so dramatic,' said Haji Arafat Shaikh.[3]

Another MNS legislator, who subsequently switched loyalties to the BJP, claimed that Raj rarely met his own MLAs, barring a couple of them from his clique.[4]

Though Raj had quit the Shiv Sena due to a coterie around his uncle, his associates charged he was surrounded by a similar set of people.[5]

A matter of organization

One of the reasons for the downslide in the fortunes of the MNS after its initial success was the absence of a grassroots-based organization. Unlike the Shiv Sena, which had a legacy to fall back on, the MNS was a largely greenfield project. Like the Shiv Sena, which remained tied to its chief's image even after his death, the MNS too was an extension of its supreme leader's persona. However, it lacked something that the Shiv Sena had—a strong second rung which had produced leaders like Chhagan Bhujbal, Manohar Joshi and Narayan Rane in the past.

The MNS's Achilles heel was its inability to replicate the Shiv Sena's network of shakhas. Authors like Mary Fainsod Katzenstein have already documented the importance of these shakhas, which organized activities that provided 'concrete material incentives' to party members.[6] The shakhas also serve as a vital link between the Sena and local communities, especially in slums and lower-income areas, providing a support system to residents and lubricating their interactions with the various arms of government like the police and civic authorities.

Chhagan Bhujbal said the Shiv Sena's initial shakha structure was changed by Datta Pradhan, who had a background in the RSS and was the 'Sanghatana Pramukh' (chief of organization) of the Sena for a brief while. Earlier, the shakhas covered a huge geographical expanse. For instance, when Bhujbal took charge in the first batch of Shiv Sena shakha pramukhs, his jurisdiction was from Dongri to Lalbag.

Pradhan ensured that every shakha covered a municipal ward and a vibhag comprised one Lok Sabha constituency, ensuring that it had a formidable organization at the grass roots.[7] Pradhan, quit the Shiv Sena in 1977, reportedly after being cut to size.

MNS leaders often complained how the party was run in a top-down manner with little authority being devolved to local leaders. This shortfall was accentuated by Raj's supposedly laid-back leadership and hit-and-run brand of politics, which saw the party make a volte-face on several issues like the toll agitation, which in turn affected its credibility.

For instance, in August 2012, Ameya Khopkar, who leads the MNS's film workers wing, trained his guns on singer Asha Bhosle and two entertainment channels for a singing reality show featuring artistes and judges from Pakistan. Khopkar warned that if the show was not withdrawn, they would not allow the channel to shoot anywhere in Maharashtra.

When Bhosle, who was a judge on the show, stressed on the *atithidevo bhava* (treat your guest as a god) maxim,[8] Raj questioned whether it was *paisadevo bhava* (treat money as god).[9] However, a week later, the MNS withdrew its protest after the top brass from these channels met Raj. In a volte-face, Khopkar said they would not oppose the show because fifteen weeks of it had been shot and that they had been given an assurance that the channels would not have any more programmes featuring Pakistani artistes.[10]

Such blow-hot-blow-cold tactics seemed to affect the MNS's credibility among the masses, as party leaders admitted in private.

The MNS did not have something that was critical to its survival—the 'reward economy' as the analyst Dr Deepak Pawar calls it,[11] that the Shiv Sena had built up through its control over the BMC. The Shiv Sena has a strong network of workers who survive on the spoils of this politics that emanates through the civic body. As the former BVS-worker-turned-journalist noted, many Shiv Sena leaders were toying with the idea of joining the MNS after its launch but pulled back for this very reason.[12]

'The Shiv Sena has a parallel economy working for them. It serves as a source of income for Shiv Sainiks. Raj did not have this advantage. The communists and socialists too faltered in their approach as their workers had no such support system. Their leadership felt that parties could be run on ideologies,' said journalist Nikhil Wagle.[13]

'There were many expectations from Raj, but they were not fulfilled. His ideas of development were as clear as that of the Shiv Sena—building gardens and beautifying lakes, with no larger focus,' Wagle added. 'The MNS had little to demonstrate in terms of performance. Did they ensure any show-piece scheme even at the municipal ward level?'[14]

Shiv Sena insiders state that between 2008 and 2014, when the chips seemed to be down for the party with even the media and a section of the cadre having a soft corner for Raj who had pitched himself as his uncle's natural heir, Uddhav worked hard to strengthen the organization. He would consult his father on political strategies and oratorical style and also tapped into agrarian distress by mobilizing the cadre on the issue.

In December 2012, a month after Bal Thackeray's death, Uddhav embarked upon a statewide tour. He refused to be anointed 'Shiv Sena pramukh' after his father and was instead appointed as the party's president.

Sachin Parab said that Balasaheb's and Raj's charisma was a double-edged sword. 'They chose to rely more on this to take their message across rather than build a strong party organization beyond Greater Mumbai. On the contrary, Uddhav, whose personality stands in contradiction to them, tried to overcome this lack of charisma by strengthening the Shiv Sena in areas outside its traditional zones of influence.'[15]

The Modi effect

In 2011, Raj committed one of his many tactical errors.

According to a senior Congress leader, some BJP leaders from Maharashtra, in an attempt to rile the Shiv Sena, had been working on Raj, asking him to reach out to Narendra Modi, who was then the chief minister of Gujarat.[16] Modi and Raj had something in common—fascination with an authoritarian model of development.[17]

In 2007, when the MNS was yet to make a mark, Shishir Shinde said he visited Gujarat as Raj's emissary to meet Modi and hand him a letter offering good wishes from his leader.[18]

In August 2011, Raj toured Gujarat for nine days with a team of experts as a state guest, wherein he visited various projects like the Tata Nano plant and sat through marathon presentations. Lauding Modi's development model, Raj claimed the people of Gujarat were 'fortunate' to have Modi as their leader.

More importantly, Raj was the first to endorse the Gujarat chief minister as prime minister material.[19] A senior BJP leader noted that Raj had floated Modi's name for prime minister even before there was a formal demand from the BJP itself.[20] This, according to Sanjay Nirupam, had led to a section of Maharashtrians in Mumbai, which was already uneasy at the increasing assertion of Gujaratis, slipping away from the MNS.[21]

After it became evident that the BJP's upper-middle-class vote that had gravitated to the MNS, had returned to it, Raj began to attack Narendra Modi, by then the prime minister, for failing to deliver on his promises and being biased towards Gujarat.

Raj also criticized demonetization and the plans for an over 500 kilometre high-speed rail corridor between Mumbai and Ahmedabad, which would be the first in India, and alleged this 'bullet train' was part of a 'conspiracy' to vivisect Mumbai from Maharashtra by allowing people from Gujarat to travel easily.[22]

The Shiv Sena may be loath to admit this, but it was the Narendra Modi wave that helped the party hold its own in the 2014 Lok Sabha elections. The Shiv Sena had uneasy vibes with Narendra Modi even when he was the chief minister of Gujarat. Like the Sena, Modi too espoused an aggressive form of Hindutva.

The BJP's old guard like L.K. Advani and Atal Bihari Vajpayee, and even younger leaders like Pramod Mahajan, shared a personal rapport with Bal Thackeray and would acknowledge him as the leader of the saffron alliance in Maharashtra. Thackeray too would assert himself as the BJP's senior ally in the state. Modi did not share a similar equation with the Sena leadership.

Bal Thackeray would claim that when then deputy prime minister L.K. Advani consulted him on whether they should sack Modi after the 2002 post-Godhra riots, he had warned him: '*Modi gaya to Gujarat gaya* (You will lose Gujarat if you remove Modi),' ensuring the Gujarat chief minister lived to fight another day.[23] In 2012, before Modi had been anointed the BJP's prime ministerial nominee, Bal Thackeray backed then leader of Opposition Sushma Swaraj as his choice.[24]

The new, aggressive BJP under Modi and party president Amit Shah was in no mood to ego-massage the Sena and play second fiddle. Before the 2014 Lok Sabha elections, as the BJP girded its loins to take on the Congress, the BJP high command tried to reach out to Raj to prevent a division of votes that could ruin the plot like in 2009. The saffron alliance had already managed to rope in smaller players like farmer leader Raju Shetti, Vinayak Mete, who had some base in the Marathas, *dhangar* (shepherd) leader Mahadeo Jankar and Dalit leader Ramdas Athavale, who had their own boroughs of influence.

A senior BJP minister said they had wanted the warring cousins to unite politically. 'However, somewhere deep down, we were sceptical as we knew that the personal bitterness ran deep. While Gopinath Munde wanted this reconciliation to come through, the real Gopinath [Lord Krishna], was unable to prevent the battle of Kurukshetra, that was the result of such fratricidal disagreements.'[25]

Before the Lok Sabha elections, former BJP president Nitin Gadkari asked Raj not to field candidates against the saffron alliance. The two also met at a five-star hotel in Mumbai in March 2014. Vasant Gite, then a party general secretary and MLA, said the BJP offered Raj an attractive trade-off: The MNS could get thirty assembly seats and two Rajya Sabha nominations.[26]

Uddhav opposed the inclusion of the MNS and warned that any support by the BJP to either Raj or Sharad Pawar would affect the alliance.[27]

'In retrospect, we should have taken the offer as being a regional party we had no stakes at the national level. The MNS could have kept away from contesting the Lok Sabha elections. However, a section of our leaders, who had an equation with the Congress–NCP alliance, thought otherwise, and their opinion prevailed,' said Gite.

The MNS eventually put up nine candidates, mostly against the Shiv Sena. Though Raj was supporting Modi's prime ministerial run, he fielded nominees from two seats (Pune and Bhiwandi) from where the BJP was contesting.

'Flirting with Modi was Raj Thackeray's blunder. Perhaps he felt that the BJP would form an equation with him if they wanted to ditch the Shiv Sena,' said political analyst Dr Deepak Pawar. He added that a section of BJP voters and Sangh Parivar supporters had gravitated towards the MNS as they felt a sense of fatigue with the BJP, but could not side with the Congress–NCP alliance.[28]

This was evident from the success of the MNS in cities like Pune and Kalyan-Dombivli, where upper castes like Brahmins, seen as the BJP's electoral catchment, have sizeable numbers. 'However, after Modi's rise on the national stage, these people reverted to the BJP,' Pawar noted.[29]

Shishir Shinde admitted that the Marathi manoos was upset with Raj's support to Narendra Modi as prime ministerial nominee while putting up candidates against the Shiv Sena and BJP in the Lok Sabha elections.[30]

The results were a huge disaster for the MNS as its candidates bit the dust. The Shiv Sena won eighteen of the twenty seats it contested, up from eleven in 2009, and the BJP won twenty-three. Raju Shetti, leader of Swabhimani Paksha who was then an ally of the BJP- Shiv Sena, held on to his Hatkanangale seat in Western Maharashtra. Ashok Chavan, who had to quit as chief minister in 2010 due to the Adarsh society scam controversy, and Rajeev Satav, the Youth Congress president, were the only face-savers for the Congress, winning from Nanded and Hingoli respectively.

The NCP too scraped through in four seats, with party chief Sharad Pawar's daughter Supriya Sule retaining their traditional family stronghold of Baramati by less than 70,000 votes against the Rashtriya Samaj Party's (RSP) Mahadeo Jankar. Even NCP supporters admitted that Jankar, a little-known face in the constituency, could have scored an upset had he contested as a BJP nominee.

An NCP leader, who was then a minister in Maharashtra, later admitted that the Modi wave had begun as a subterranean movement, gradually picking up pace, and turned into a giant tsunami, sweeping everything in its path.[31] It also created unlikely victors.

For instance, a BJP nominee from a constituency in western Maharashtra, who was pitted against a Congress heavyweight. 'This man felt he was fighting a lost battle. He would campaign till lunch, complain of body ache and go home for a beer and siesta. But, to his amazement, he was elected. That is how the Modi wave worked. While those who lost felt the outcome was unexpected, so did the winners!'[32]

For the first time since Rajiv Gandhi's runaway victory in 1984, Narendra Modi and the BJP secured a clear majority in the Lok Sabha with 282 seats. The Congress could get just forty-four seats.

For the Shiv Sena, which was fighting its first elections after the death of its party supremo, the results came as manna from heaven. It won all three constituencies in Mumbai where the MNS had put up candidates against it, including film-maker Mahesh Manjrekar from Mumbai North-west.

In the cosmopolitan Mumbai South constituency, said to have the highest per capita income in India, the Shiv Sena's Arvind Sawant defied all predictions to defeat the Congress heavyweight and Union minister of state, Milind Deora, by a margin of over 1 lakh votes. Bala Nandgaonkar of the MNS who had beaten the Shiv Sena to the runner-up position in 2009 against Deora with almost 1.60 lakh votes, had to be content with just over 84,000 this time round.

It seemed the tortoise was gradually catching up with the hare.

A Shiv Sena leader, who is now with the BJP, claimed that Uddhav's changed style of working and focus on strengthening the organization were now yielding results.[33]

'The Congress and NCP created institutions in the cooperatives sector that helped it control the rural areas. Likewise, the Shiv Sena helped build families by ensuring that the Marathi manoos secured jobs in public sector banks, insurance companies, five-star hotels and Central government units. Luckily, for the Shiv Sena, the workers at the grass roots are emotionally driven and committed, which the MNS could not replicate. This is not something that can be done overnight, it is organic and takes time,' the leader noted, adding that the Shiv Sena worked hard to overcome the voter fatigue that had cost it dearly in 2009, while the MNS became complacent with its initial success.[34]

According to Sandeep Pradhan, the rise of Narendra Modi on the national stage affected the fortunes of the MNS because it led to the elite and the middle- and upper-class Marathi votes gravitating back to the BJP.

'The younger generation, which forms the catchment of the MNS, is impatient. They want speedy results and are not prepared to spend ten years shouting slogans of *zindabad* and *murdabad*. They felt that despite showing some promise initially, the MNS had been unable to deliver. Unlike the MNS, the Shiv Sena controlled the BMC, enabling it to dole out patronage to its followers,' said Pradhan.[35]

MNS leaders claimed that Raj would see a shift in loyalties by Shiv Sena cadre and voters in the post–Bal Thackeray era but the MNS plans had clearly begun to unravel. 'We got twenty-eight corporators elected to the BMC in 2012. However, our people got used to the perks of power too fast. This led to disillusionment within the cadre and voters,' admitted a former MNS MLA.[36]

According to a former Congress minister, Uddhav's success in the 2014 assembly elections could be attributed to a plethora of factors. For one, Raj's charisma was on the wane. Second, the Shiv Sena, which had faced a setback at the hands of the MNS in 2009, was able to ensure that its enviable organization at the grass roots was in fine fettle, something that the MNS, which relied more on Raj's individual charisma for votes, lacked. 'People liked Raj's aggression and oratory. But he was unable to convert the crowds to votes,' he explained.[37]

'One of Uddhav's endearing attributes is consistency, something that Raj lacks due to his short attention span. This makes Uddhav the proverbial *lambi race ka ghoda* [a horse who can run longer],' beamed a Shiv Sena source.[38]

By 2012, when Thackeray Senior passed away, the MNS bubble had begun to burst according to Congress leader Kripashankar Singh, ensuring that the party could not capture the political space occupied by the Shiv Sena.[39] 'It was Balasaheb's talismanic hold over the party faithful that prevailed even after his death,' exclaimed a former Shiv Sena leader.[40]

As an afterthought, Raj admitted that the decision to contest the Lok Sabha elections was a blunder. 'Sometimes, you have to take some decisions though you do not agree with them. I was not surprised about the results, as I had an inkling,' he said, adding this downslide would serve as a springboard for the party's resurgence.[41]

Shifting power equations

Despite its avowed antipathy to Pakistanis on Indian soil, the Shiv Sena had a guarded reaction to Modi's invitation to his Pakistani counterpart, Nawaz Sharif, to his swearing-in as India's prime minister. Uddhav said in a statement that it was 'difficult to trust Pakistan'.[42]

'Modi wanted educated ministers in his cabinet and was hence rooting for Suresh Prabhu from the Shiv Sena's quota,' claimed Prem Shukla.[43] Prabhu, a chartered accountant, who with his urbane image was the antithesis of an archetypal Shiv Sainik, was the Union power minister and chairman of the task force on interlinking of rivers during the Atal Bihari Vajpayee regime. In 2009, Prabhu lost his Ratnagiri–Sindhudurg seat to Narayan Rane's elder son, Nilesh (Congress), and was not nominated by the party in 2014.

'However, the Shiv Sena chose Anant Geete [who belongs to the powerful Kunbi community in the Konkan region], and a miffed Modi gave him the lacklustre heavy industries portfolio. This was a clear snub as the Shiv Sena with eighteen MPs was the second-largest constituent of the NDA. Smaller parties like the Telugu Desam Party (TDP) and Lok Janshakti Party (LJP) were given more lucrative ministries,' added Shukla.[44]

In November 2014, Prabhu joined the BJP and was appointed railway minister.

The Sena's relationship with Prime Minister Modi was off to a rocky start.

In July 2014, after an Indian Army soldier was killed in shelling by Pakistan along the Line of Control (LoC), Sanjay Raut slammed India's 'saree and shawl' diplomacy with Pakistan.[45] This was a jibe at Nawaz Sharif sending a saree for Modi's mother. Modi had earlier gifted a shawl to Sharif's mother when he had visited India for his swearing-in. Modi was 'quite angry' at his mother being dragged into a political issue and is said to have conveyed this to Uddhav.[46]

While Uddhav expected the BJP to give him the same kind of respect as it had accorded to his father, the BJP often held back, claimed a senior BJP minister.[47]

Earlier, on 1 May 2014, which is Maharashtra Day, the BJP was incensed at an editorial in *Saamna* where the Shiv Sena attacked the Gujaratis who had rallied behind Modi.[48] 'The Gujarati and other *bepari* [mercantile] communities in Maharastra, who united with pride as Gujaratis for Modi, must now come together for Shivray's [Chhatrapati Shivaji Maharaj] Maharashtra and join the celebrations on Maharashtra's foundation day,' said the editorial, which was published after the conclusion of voting in Maharashtra but before the declaration of results.[49]

The editorial charged these communities of having 'exploited Mumbai' and calling the shots in the country's power politics because of this wealth. It added that the beparis who otherwise claimed to have no relation with politics, had united to ensure a prime minister from their state and community.

Seen as Sanjay Raut's handiwork, the editorial caused consternation even within the Sena as it came soon after polling where the beparis had turned out in huge numbers to vote for the Shiv Sena, and consequently Modi, handing the party its best performance in the Lok Sabha.

After the Modi wave helped the saffron alliance pull off a runaway victory in Maharashtra, the Shiv Sena felt it had a chance of getting its chief minister in the state as a senior partner in the alliance.

Uddhav's elder son, Aaditya, who led the Yuva Sena, spoke about his party's 'Mission 150', which in effect meant that the Shiv Sena was aiming at the halfway mark in the assembly.

Buoyed by its success in the Lok Sabha polls, the BJP began flexing its muscle against the Sena. In July, its leader Madhu Chavan set the ball rolling for what would eventually lead to the party's divorce with the Shiv Sena. Speaking at a party convention in July 2014, Chavan sought that the BJP snap ties with the Sena before the assembly elections to avoid being dragged into a 'three-legged race'.[50]

A section of BJP leaders felt that the Narendra Modi wave was intact in Maharashtra, and riding on it, the Shiv Sena, being the bigger partner, would be able to get its man as the chief minister.[51]

In Mumbai, a senior NCP leader informally told reporters that a BJP heavyweight from the central leadership had spoken about the need to 'finish the Shiv Sena'. 'The BJP leader claimed that the word "lumpen" in the English dictionary was coined just for this party,' the NCP man said, predicting that the BJP would choose to ditch the Sena before the assembly elections.[52]

While the BJP wanted to fight from 130 seats, the Sena offered the BJP the same number of seats (119) it contested in 2009. As various seat-sharing formulas, including those where the Sena would contest 155 of 288 seats, leaving 125 for BJP and the rest for smaller allies,[53] were thrown around, the alliance seemed to dangle by a thread. Aaditya was dispatched to meet BJP's election in-charge, Om Prakash Mathur, to break the ice. However, some in the BJP interpreted sending a young leader to deal with the veteran Mathur as an affront.[54]

Finally, on 25 September, just two days before the nominations were to end, the BJP did the unthinkable—it called off its twenty-five-year old alliance with the Shiv Sena, with then leader of the Opposition Eknath Khadse making the announcement.

As if on cue, NCP leaders Praful Patel, Deputy Chief Minister Ajit Pawar and state unit chief Sunil Tatkare too announced they were ending ties with the Congress. The NCP blamed Chief Minister Prithviraj Chavan, a known Pawar baiter, for the decision. The NCP was demanding 50 per cent of Maharashtra's assembly seats from the Congress, up from the previous figure of 114. The Congress, which refused to heed the demand, had after weeks of talks, announced its first list of 118 candidates in a take-it-or-leave-it move. The Congress had been belligerent on its stand of not parting with over 128 seats for the NCP.[55]

BJP sources admitted that the decision to snap ties with the Shiv Sena was driven by the central leadership. Some BJP leaders wanted an alliance to prevent a split in anti-incumbency votes, but there was anger at the Shiv Sena for 'humiliating' them. In a meeting, some state leaders objected when Amit Shah asked if they should snap ties with the Sena. However, Shah said they could ditch the Shiv Sena and take their four smaller allies along to carry the day on the Modi wave.[56]

The twenty-five-year-old alliance had hobbled the growth of these parties in seats contested by their allies. The Shiv Sena was caught on the wrong foot with the announcement, with party leaders admitting that they had to scurry to find candidates at the last minute in constituencies where the BJP had traditionally contested.

A Congress leader claimed that the NCP and BJP were in cahoots regarding the decision to split from their respective allies as was evident from the timing of the announcements.[57] A senior NCP functionary admitted that the leaders of the two parties were in touch. 'This was being considered for some time. It was a question of who would move first. Hence, when the BJP bit the bait, we followed suit,' he said.[58]

On the very day that the alliance broke, Uddhav called Raj with the mediation of Thackeray family friend Bajirao Dangat, and offered a negotiation. Rajya Sabha MP Anil Desai was the Shiv Sena's negotiator while Bala Nandgaonkar and Nitin Sardesai represented the MNS.

Raj stopped the distribution of party nominations but finally went ahead after there was no response from the Shiv Sena the next day. 'I knew this was going to happen,' said Raj, while adding that such back and forth and lack of a firm decision was the Sena's hallmark.[59]

Despite the overtures, another stream of thought within the Shiv Sena felt that any truck with the MNS would help revive it. The MNS was seen to be losing popular support, and an alliance with the Shiv Sena would inject fresh blood into it. The two nativist parties were competing for the same electoral catchment. There was another contentious issue—seats where the Shiv Sena and MNS were direct rivals. The MNS had won assembly segments like Mahim and Shivdi, and the Sena would have to accommodate their incumbent MLAs at the cost of its own men.[60]

Before the state assembly elections, Raj unveiled his much-awaited 'blueprint' for the development of Maharashtra. It sought more autonomy for Maharashtra, compulsory and high-quality education in English while Marathi would be the main medium of instruction, direct benefit transfers and a special police force for universities and industrial organizations.[61]

During the assembly election campaign, Uddhav launched the Sena's most blistering attack on Modi and the BJP, likening them to the army of Afzal Khan, the Adilshahi general who had ravaged Maharashtra and its temples, before being killed by Shivaji Maharaj in the Battle of Pratapgad (1659).[62] In an attempt to spite the BJP, the Sena also put up banners of Modi standing before the late Bal Thackeray with folded hands.

Prem Shukla lashed out at Modi through *Dopahar ka Saamna*, claiming that: 'Modi had not secured a mandate in the BJP's name alone. Had the Sena acted like the BJP before the Lok Sabha elections, even Modi's father Damodardas could not have helped the BJP secure a majority in 2014.'[63]

Shukla claimed Uddhav, who was in the loop about these writings, distanced himself from it later. Shukla, who called himself a 'de facto member of the Shiv Sena, who was among the list of star campaigners',[64] resigned as the executive editor of the newspaper on 31 December 2015 to join the BJP.

The BJP overcame its status as a minnow in the state and emerged as the single-largest party with 122 of 288 seats in the legislative assembly with ally RSP picking up one. The Shiv Sena was a distant second with sixty-three seats, losing its strongholds like Goregaon and Thane to the BJP. The Congress and NCP fared much worse, with forty-two and forty-one wins.

In the 122 seats that the BJP won, the Shiv Sena was number two at thirty-two, a notch below the Congress at forty-five.

The worst shock was reserved for the MNS—it lost all the thirteen seats that it had won in 2009. It scored just one win with Sharad Sonawane being elected from Junnar in Pune (Sonawane switched to the Shiv Sena in March 2019). The All India Majlis-e-Ittehad-ul-Muslimeen (AIMIM) led by the Owaisi brothers performed better than the MNS, picking up two seats, while Azmi held on to his Mankhurd–Shivajinagar constituency as the sole SP MLA in the legislature.

The BJP's 260 candidates cornered 1,47,09,276 or 31.15 per cent votes, followed by the Shiv Sena's 282 at 1,02,35,970 or 19.80 per cent. The MNS, which contested 209 seats got just 16,65,033 (4.18 per cent) votes.[65] Like in 2009, the MNS had entered into an understanding with Raj's friend and former minister Vinay Kore-Savkar, who had his own party, Jana Surajya Shakti. Kore lost from his Panhala–Shahuwadi seat in Kolhapur to the Sena.

After its Lok Sabha success, the BJP had adopted the 'outsourcing model' of the Congress and NCP, wherein leaders with elective merit handled the party's interests in their constituency or areas, with the favour being returned at the state and national levels.[66] This helped shore up numbers in the assembly.

The silver lining for the Shiv Sena was that it had managed to wrest seats won by the MNS earlier like Mahim, Shivdi, Vikhroli, Bhandup, Kalyan Rural and Magathane.

The polarization of the political space between the BJP and the Shiv Sena ensured that the latter cornered the Marathi vote at the cost of the MNS, which was already on the decline. 'As the number of Marathi speakers in Mumbai dwindles, Marathi voters are developing a minority complex, which makes it easy for the Shiv Sena to polarize them,' said the veteran journalist on the Shiv Sena beat.[67]

The Sena also had its sweet revenge when Narayan Rane was trounced by its candidate Vaibhav Naik from the Kudal assembly constituency in Sindhudurg. Earlier, the Sena's Vinayak Raut had defeated Rane's son Nilesh from the Ratnagiri–Sindhudurg Lok Sabha seat. The Shiv Sena rubbed it in the next year by handing Rane Senior his second consecutive defeat in the by-election to the Bandra East seat.

Though the Shiv Sena had the tables turned on it by the BJP, even his political foes admitted that Uddhav held his own at a time when regional satraps were biting the dust in the wake of the Modi wave. The Sena's successes in 2009 and the BMC elections in 2007 and 2012 were attributed to Bal Thackeray. Now, with his father no more, this was entirely Uddhav show.

Even veteran politicians like Chhagan Bhujbal are nonplussed while speaking about 'the stunning decline of the MNS'. 'This may be because of their back and forth on several issues,' he opined.[68]

'Hat's off,' said Bhujbal, when asked about how Uddhav had managed to lead the Shiv Sena through the crisis. 'One cannot help but appreciate Uddhav for steering the Shiv Sena in turbulent times. Uddhav is a good planner who can delegate power well. Even when others claimed it was facing an existential crisis, I always said that the Sena could never be finished off as its roots were subterranean.'[69]

'This was the first election after Balasaheb's death and Uddhav fought it single-handedly to generate a performance better than in Balasaheb's times,' said Sandeep Pradhan.[70]

Prakash Mahajan, the younger brother of slain BJP leader Pramod Mahajan, joined the MNS after it was launched, and then shifted to the Shiv Sena after differences. 'During the Kurukshetra war,' says Mahajan, 'Arjun shot an arrow at Karna. Such was its force, that Karna's chariot moved back by five *yojan*s [a unit for measuring distance]. Gifted archer that he was, Karna shot a similar missile at Arjuna, which threw his chariot back by two yojanas. At this, Krishna, who was Arjuna's charioteer, started praising Karna. Arjuna was confused—why was Krishna praising Karna when his [Arjuna's] arrow had greater impact? To this, Krishna replied that Karna's achievement was greater because of the odds against him. Arjuna's chariot had been given to him by Indra, had the god of strength Hanuman on the flagstaff and the Godhead himself as the charioteer.'[71]

Before the Lok Sabha elections, Raj claimed his uncle was fed oily *batata vada*s (potato fritters) which were detrimental to his health. Speaking at a rally at Dombivli in April 2014, Raj claimed he would send chicken soup to Bal Thackeray from his home in his last days. 'All this time he never felt that I had backstabbed him,' said Raj, who was responding to Uddhav's allegation that his younger cousin had stabbed the late Sena chief in the back.[72]

'This statement was not received well among Maharashtrians as it seemed Raj was trying to derive political capital by misusing his late uncle's name. One does not speak about what they did for those who are no more. Plus, this was the first election to be held after Balasaheb's death,' said one of Raj's supporters.[73]

After the Lok Sabha debacle, Raj, in an attempt to boost the morale of his party, announced he would contest the assembly polls. The MNS also projected Raj as its chief ministerial candidate and hoped that the enthusiasm about its party chief being the first from the Thackeray family to seek public office would generate support for it.

Raj was considering contesting from Mahim but backed off after he realized that the MNS was on the wane.[74] Vageesh Saraswat said the 'vada and chicken soup' statement had caused anger among Maharashtrians. 'I moved around in Dadar speaking to people without disclosing I was an MNS leader. They were incensed at what they felt, that is, Raj trying to show he had done Balasaheb a favour,' he explained.[75]

A senior MNS leader admitted that while the 'vada and chicken soup' statement had hurt them, Raj going back on his decision to contest the assembly elections made things worse. 'Our surveys revealed that if Raj contested from Mahim, he would win hands down. However, some party leaders felt he should not limit himself to one constituency and instead focus on the entire state. We also could not afford to let our star campaigner be bogged down in just one seat'[76]

Saraswat admitted another critical flaw in the politics of the MNS: barring some like Bala Nandgaonkar, none of its leaders had experience of electoral politics.

The Shiv Sena had also stemmed the erosion of youth support to the MNS by launching the Yuva Sena under Aaditya in 2010. This provided politically ambitious Marathi youth a platform for upward mobility within the party.[77]

The MNS was unable to balance the contradiction of attacking the incumbent Congress–NCP government and yet eating into the Opposition Shiv Sena–BJP's votes by its presence in the arena. The Shiv Sena was able to send across a message to its electorate that the MNS was a Trojan Horse of the government of the day, admitted insiders from both parties.

However, an MNS leader bristles at the charge. 'The anti-migrant cases saw police cases being lodged against us. Many MNS leaders and workers are fighting them in court even today and some were even externed. There was a time when the government had withdrawn security to Raj saheb. MNS workers from across Mumbai took turns to guard him while the inner ring of his protection was made up of retired army men with licensed weapons,' he added.[78]

Shishir Shinde claimed Raj's opposition to the state government's plan for a memorial for Dr Babasaheb Ambedkar, on the lands of the now-defunct Indu Mills at Dadar, had rankled Dalits.[79]

On 11 August 2012, Muslim groups organized a protest at Azad Maidan in south Mumbai to condemn violence against their community in Myanmar and Assam. At the rally, the crowds numbering thousands, were incensed after incendiary speeches.

The mob attacked media crews and policemen. Two people were killed in police firing and over fifty, most of them policemen, were injured.[80] Women police constables were molested.[81]

Raj announced a morcha from Girgaum Chowpatty to Azad Maidan to protest the police inaction against those responsible for the mayhem. He also sought the resignations of Home Minister R.R. Patil and Commissioner of Police Arup Patnaik.

Though a senior police official admitted to an 'intelligence failure' leading to the riots, he said any heavy-handed action on the spot would have caused a communal flare-up. The official, now retired, claimed the MNS morcha had blessings of some elements in the NCP, who were 'willing accomplices in a transactional relationship' to ease out Patnaik, who had reportedly fallen foul of the NCP leadership. He however conceded that the protest had worked as a 'safety valve' to prevent a larger conflagration between the police and the minority community.[82]

Raj's 21 August protest march and rally saw a massive response, including from non-Maharashtrians and the family members of policemen.

At his public meeting at Azad Maidan, Raj criticized Muslims from Uttar Pradesh and Bihar, but denied the rally had undertones of Hindutva. He added that his only religion was 'Maharashtra dharma'. Raj also theatrically produced a Bangladeshi passport, which he claimed had been found on the grounds after the riots and alleged that the violence had links to elements from Bangladesh.

Though his protest ticked most of the right boxes for his target vote base, Raj, who sought that any memorials for icons must be useful for the society, rather than be just brick-and-mortar structures, slammed politicians for their obsession with statues and memorials.

He ridiculed Dalit leaders seeking a memorial for the maker of India's Constitution at Indu Mills on the Dadar seashore. 'Where is Mayawati? Where is that Ramdas Athavale? Where is R.S. Gavai? Where is Prakash Ambedkar? Why are they all silent? All they're obsessed with, as if possessed by a ghost, is Indu Mills Indu Mills Indu Mills Indu Mills. Don't they have anything else to do? What do they want to build in Indu Mills, a bungalow?' he asked.[83]

Though the morcha led to Patnaik being transferred just two days later Shishir Shinde said these statements, which were made sans any provocation, led to a backlash from the Dalits in the 2014 elections.

That the upper-class Maharashtrian elite in Dadar, including MNS supporters, crinkled their noses at lakhs of 'Bhim Sainiks' (followers of Ambedkar) who turned up to pay their respects to

Ambedkar at nearby Chaityabhoomi (his final resting place) on his birth and death anniversaries did not help matters.

Forming the government

While the Shiv Sena was trying to reconcile itself to the possibility of the BJP emerging as the single-largest political party in the assembly and working on the power-sharing terms, the NCP played spoilsport. Even as the counting was under way, senior NCP leader Praful Patel, who was a minister in the Manmohan Singh government, offered outside support to BJP 'in the interest of stability and development'.[84]

Later, journalist-turned-Congress MP Kumar Ketkar described the NCP as the BJP's 'reserve force' which was 'meant to add ballast to the party in case its numbers fell short' of a majority.[85]

By sending a message that the NCP, which incidentally Modi had referred to as a 'naturally corrupt party', during the Maharashtra assembly campaign,[86] was waiting in the wings if the Shiv Sena dithered on supporting the BJP, the statement took away most of the Sena's bargaining power.

'Some NCP leaders were worried at their decisions during their ministerial tenures in the Union government and the Maharashtra government being probed. For a while after the assembly elections, the BJP was also planning to tie up with the NCP in Maharashtra,' said a senior Congress leader, pointing to Prime Minister Modi's frequent visits to Pawar's Baramati and fulsome praise for the Maratha strongman.[87]

Till mid-2018, BJP leaders claimed the NCP was willing to join hands with them, eloping from the marriage pandal 'like Kareena Kapoor in the film *3 Idiots*!'[88]

BJP's Maharashtra president, Devendra Fadnavis, an MLA from Nagpur, upstaged other leaders from his party including Nitin Gadkari and Eknath Khadse to become chief minister of Maharashtra. Uddhav shared the dais with Modi and Shah during Fadnavis's swearing-in on 31 October. This came after a last-minute call by Shah after Uddhav complained of 'constant humiliation' by the BJP during government formation talks.[89]

In the assembly, the motion of confidence for the Fadnavis government was carried in a voice vote, despite the party's strength being short of the halfway mark. As Shiv Sena and Congress legislators protested seeking a division of votes, NCP legislators remained silent.[90]

The Shiv Sena claimed democracy had been 'strangled' and the Congress, whose five legislators were suspended for heckling Governor C. Vidyasagar Rao, called it 'a black day'.[91]

The Shiv Sena's Eknath Shinde became the leader of Opposition. However, Uddhav was forced to capitulate a month later and the Shiv Sena joined the Fadnavis government in December 2014, albeit in a truncated role. Sena sources admitted this decision was prompted by fears that the BJP, with its access to power and resources, would poach on its flock.[92] For the BJP, drafting the Sena into the government lent it greater stability than depending on the NCP for support.[93]

The NCP's unconditional offer of support had left the Sena with little bargaining power. Though the Shiv Sena eventually secured six cabinet berths and seven for minister of state, it had to give up its demand for the deputy chief minister's post and powerful portfolios like home. Fadnavis drove the agenda in some departments handed over to the Sena's cabinet ministers, like industries and public works (public undertakings), leaving it with truncated authority.

Despite joining the government, the Shiv Sena continued a balancing act—being in power yet play-acting the role of an Opposition party. *Saamna* continued to attack BJP, Modi, Shah and Fadnavis. Sanjay Raut also praised Rahul Gandhi, then vice-president of the Congress party, as having outgrown his image as a 'Pappu' (loser) after the Congress put up a good show in the state assembly elections in Madhya Pradesh, Rajasthan and Gujarat.

Even veteran Shiv Sena leaders admitted there were contradictions galore in this stance. While a section of the party, largely the cadre, had wanted to brazen it out in the Opposition, others, mostly legislators, had been in favour of joining the government. Within the legislature party, there was resentment at four of the five cabinet ministers being members of the Upper House. In June 2019, two more cabinet ministers were inducted from the Shiv Sena's quota: NCP leader Jaydutt Kshirsagar, who had joined the Sena days ago, and another NCP-man-turned-Sainik, Tanaji Sawant. Health minister Deepak Sawant, who had apparently fallen foul of the leadership, had to step down earlier that year after he was not renominated to the Upper House. The only showpiece policy decision that the Shiv Sena could boast of was an ill-executed ban in 2018 on the use of disposable, single-use plastic.[94]

The Shiv Sena initially opposed Fadnavis's dream project, the 700-kilometre Mumbai-Nagpur Samruddhi super-communication expressway. The over Rs 46,000-crore road aimed at bringing down travel time between the two cities to just eight hours from the present eighteen and was billed as a regional development project that would connect ten districts, twenty-six talukas and 392 villages.[95]

The Shiv Sena joined voices with farmers opposing the acquisition of land but incidentally, the minister in charge of the project was the Shiv Sena's Eknath Shinde, who held the portfolio of public works (public undertakings). In November 2018, the Sena demanded that the road be named after their late party chief.[96]

'The Shiv Sena has the character of an Opposition party. We flourish in the Opposition. Now, we are in power, but not in authority. We are unable to go the whole hog against the Modi and Fadnavis regimes as we have some stakes in them. This contradiction is not lost on the people,' complained a former MLA.[97]

On the record, Shiv Sena leaders claimed their role in the government was that of a mahout reigning in an elephant.

The battle for BMC

The Shiv Sena felt it had a chance to turn the tables on the BJP in the 2017 BMC elections that it contested on its own, spurning overtures for an alliance from the BJP. The party hoped the Marathi versus non-Marathi consolidation would work in its favour in Mumbai, helping it win over 100 seats.

Before the polling, the BJP did something unthinkable—it made allegations of corruption against Uddhav. Without directly naming Uddhav, Kirit Somaiya, BJP MP from Mumbai Northeast, charged that the BMC was in the grip of a 'powerful mafia' being controlled by a 'sahib from Bandra and his PA'.[98] He also dared Uddhav to make his financial transactions public.[99] Though the Shiv Sena and BJP tied up for the Lok Sabha elections later, Somaiya was the only incumbent MP from Mumbai to be dropped. One reason for this was attributed to the Shiv Sena's tooth-and-nail opposition to his renomination.

When the BMC election results were announced, the Shiv Sena realized it had won a pyrrhic victory. While its seats increased from seventy-five to eighty-four, the BJP, which campaigned on the plank of 'transparency' in the BMC whose budget outmatches those of several smaller states, saw the number of its corporators jump from thirty-one to eighty-two, just two short of the Sena's numbers in the 227-member house.

The tally of the Congress and NCP dipped to thirty-one and nine seats respectively. The MNS, whose Bala Nandgaonkar had reached out to the Sena for a pre-poll alliance to stem the party's electoral erosion,[100] too was unable to repeat its swashbuckling performance of 2012 and won just seven seats. Leaders from the Sena and BJP admitted they had gained from linguistic polarization, with other players like the Congress, NCP and MNS falling by the roadside. However, apart from gaining the votes of non-Maharashtrians, the BJP had walked off with seats in areas dominated by the Maharashtrian elite like Girgaon.

Speaking at his party's foundation day in 2017, Raj charged that the people had rejected his party despite their hard work and added that these voters would have to repent for wrong choices. 'I will replicate the methods used by these parties to win . . . This is your last defeat,' he said, asking his cadre to keep their chin up after successive reverses in the Lok Sabha, assembly and civic elections.[101]

Sandeep Deshpande, the general secretary and spokesperson of the MNS, who was the party's group leader in the BMC, said the debacle was not a reflection on their performance in the civic house. 'From exposing a scam in the construction of roads to taking errant civic engineers to task and . . . ensuring good-quality roads and the creation of a selfie point at Shivaji Park, we almost functioned like the principal Opposition in the BMC.'[102]

Deshpande said the delimitation of constituencies, which saw the wards of many MNS corporators being reserved for categories like women and other backwards, ensured they could not contest again. Raj's presence in the campaign was also affected by the illness of his son Amit.

A former Maharashtra minister, who is close to both the Sena and the BJP, claimed that BJP Mumbai unit chief, Ashish Shelar, who later became a minister in the Fadnavis government, had almost pieced together the numbers to get the BJP its first mayor in Mumbai. However, despite the BJP's best-ever showing, Shelar was asked to back off by the party leadership at the last moment to prevent upsetting the Sena further.[103]

The Shiv Sena finally roped in independent corporators to retain power. The BJP extended unconditional support to the Sena.[104]

In October 2017, the Shiv Sena sprang a surprise by poaching six of the seven MNS corporators. The defections were led by MNS group leader, Dilip Lande, who was said to be miffed after being slighted in civic politics by Sandeep Deshpande despite being a veteran. The six corporators formally joined the Shiv Sena in Uddhav's presence at Matoshree. Ironically, no one in the MNS leadership got a whiff of 'Mama's' (as Lande is called) moves to wean away its flock in the civic house. Lande blamed a clique around Raj for his defection. This happened after the BJP won a civic by-election, raising its numbers to eighty-three, and renewing fears that it could wrest control of the BMC from the Sena.

A miffed Raj, who had just days before organized a huge morcha at the Western Railway Office at Churchgate to protest the 29 September 2017 stampede at the Elphinstone Road railway station that claimed twenty-three lives, lashed out at Uddhav and the Shiv Sena.

'I quit the Shiv Sena after telling Balasaheb about my decision . . . I was tired of such low-level politics by Uddhav and others,' said Raj, claiming he had not encouraged Shiv Sena MLAs to join the MNS while it was being formed, as he did not believe in such politics. 'Henceforth, the clap (will not be on the hand but) on the cheek,' Raj warned the Shiv Sena when asked if he would respond to any overtures from them.[105]

The chips may have been down for him, but despite his party's electoral washout and desertions from the ranks (almost all MNS MLAs elected in 2009 have gradually quit the party), Raj continued to remain in the public eye, sharpening his attack on Modi and the BJP, even joining hands with the Opposition, to enforce a 'Bharat bandh' in Maharashtra in September 2018.

In September 2017, Raj made a sensational claim that fugitive underworld don Dawood Ibrahim was in talks with the Modi government to return to India and surrender. This, he said, would be claimed as an achievement by the BJP and Modi for winning the Lok Sabha polls.[106]

Over a year later at Vikhroli, where he had launched his tirade against Amitabh Bachchan in 2008, Raj also claimed that the BJP was in talks with AIMIM chief Asaduddin Owaisi to stage riots on the Ram Temple issue.[107]

That Raj retained his spunk and appeal was evident in 2017 when some Shiv Sainiks returning home after hearing Uddhav speak in the Dussehra rally at Shivaji Park shouted slogans outside his house located next door for a glimpse of him![108]

To ally or not

On the evening of 18 February 2019, Uddhav Thackeray, Amit Shah and Devendra Fadnavis met a media contingent where they announced that the Shiv Sena and BJP would tie-up for the Lok Sabha and state assembly elections. It was an anticlimactic moment and put to rest the Sena's stillborn idea to contest all future polls sans an alliance with the BJP.

The Shiv Sena, which was forced to play the role of a junior partner in Maharashtra, believed the BJP's success was temporary and would subside once the Modi wave abated. A stream of thought within the leadership advocated that the Sena needed to strike out on its own and emerge as a pan-Maharashtra regional force.

On 23 January 2018, a motion was moved at the Shiv Sena national executive by Sanjay Raut for the party to contest future elections on its own. The cadre felt they could capture the anti-incumbency vote that could have gone to the Congress–NCP combine, though some Sena Lok Sabha MPs were cagey about the impact of the decision on their fortunes.

Time and again, the Shiv Sena had threatened to pull out of the Fadnavis government, with Sanjay Raut saying that

Uddhav would take a decision at the right time.[109] A BJP minister claimed that despite this bravado, Shiv Sena ministers and elected representatives would meet him in person to seek that the two parties mended fences.[110]

Those toeing the 'go-it-alone' line claimed that if the Shiv Sena and BJP fought alone, the elections would be polarized between the two parties. For instance, in the by-polls to the Palghar Lok Sabha seat abutting Mumbai, which was the semi-final for a larger BJP versus Sena face-off, the BJP edged out the latter by just over 29,000 votes.

In an apparent face-saver for the Sena, while announcing the alliance, its share of Lok Sabha seats had been hiked from the earlier twenty-two to twenty-three. The Shiv Sena took Palghar and the BJP's MP Rajendra Gavit into its kitty.

A senior Shiv Sena MP, who was running for office again, admitted there was trepidation within the Sena Lok Sabha corps on whether their chances of re-election would be marred if they broke off with the BJP. 'Actually, the BJP needed us equally in a crucial state like Maharashtra. Hence, there was an eventual meeting of minds,' he added.[111]

Despite the Shiv Sena's flip-flop, the BJP was insistent on an alliance, with Amit Shah (June 2018) and election strategist and Janata Dal (United) vice-president Prashant Kishor (February 2019) meeting Uddhav to press for it. The reasons were not tough to discern: a good performance in Maharashtra with its forty-eight seats was crucial for the BJP to return to power at the Centre. The Shiv Sena's turnaround is said to have come after several backchannel attempts by the BJP, which also involved RSS functionaries.

However, Sanjay Raut had continued to claim that reports of a Sena–BJP tie-up were 'rumours' and even accused the BJP of stalking it like a 'frustrated road Romeo'.[112] The Shiv Sena kept up pressure on the BJP, by attacking it over the Rafale deal,[113] repeating Congress president Rahul Gandhi's *'chowkidar chor hai'* (the watchman is a thief) jibe,[114] and seeking the construction of a Ram temple at Ayodhya with Uddhav visiting the town in Uttar Pradesh to catch the BJP in a bind on its poll promise.

When it became evident that the Sena and BJP would finally break bread, the Sena cadre was incensed. A Shiv Sainik claimed that months of relentless attacks by the Shiv Sena against the BJP had led to estrangement between workers and second-rung functionaries of the two parties, which would affect the transfer of votes. Moreover, Sena candidates who had been given a green signal by the leadership to prepare for a contest in seats represented by the BJP, also found themselves left in the lurch.

Though Fadnavis claimed their alliance had been formalized on grounds like Hindutva, the Ram temple, streamlining welfare schemes for farmers, and an equal sharing of seats in the state assembly elections, it seemed that the Shiv Sena had capitulated. While Sena leaders claimed they would get the chief minister's post after the assembly elections, BJP leaders said otherwise.

Many in the Shiv Sena believed that their party would have to pay the price for this 'misadventure'. A senior Sena leader admitted that their internal reports suggested the party was likely to win just eight to ten Lok Sabha segments.[115]

On the other hand, though the MNS leadership denied this on record, the party was eager to strike an understanding with the NCP for at least one Lok Sabha seat in Mumbai, Thane or Nashik. Former Maharashtra chief minister Ashok Chavan, who was the state Congress chief at the time of the elections, said during the seat-sharing talks, the NCP indicated it was eager to accommodate the MNS. 'However, this was opposed by Congress leaders from Mumbai due to the MNS opposition to north Indians . . . this was out of sync with our ideology and credo.'[116]

Though Raj's party eventually did not contest, he launched a surrogate campaign for the Congress and NCP, with blistering attacks on Modi, Shah and the BJP through audio-visual tools in his rallies. These public meetings which saw Raj use videos, which he claimed exposed Modi's double speak on issues like his changing opinions about NCP chief Sharad Pawar, became a talking point for their unique style. Raj's sentence '*Ae laav re to video*' (play that video) asking his team to play these videos, trended on social media.

However, when the results were announced, it was clear that the BJP and Shiv Sena's charge had paid off. The saffron combine swept Maharashtra again, with forty-one of forty-eight seats. Though the Shiv Sena's old warhorses Anant Geete (Raigad), Chandrakant Khaire (Aurangabad), Anandrao Adsul (Amravati) and Shivajirao Adhalrao Patil (Shirur), lost, the party held on to its tally of eighteen.

However, Adsul and Khaire who lost to NCP-backed independent Navneet Kaur Rana (whose husband and independent MLA Ravi Rana is close to Chief Minister Fadnavis) and the AIMIM's Imtiaz Jaleel respectively, blamed BJP leaders for their defeat.[117]

Like the MNS which hurt the saffron alliance in 2009, the newly formed Vanchit Bahujan Aghadi (VBA), which was led by Prakash Ambedkar, the grandson of Dr Babasaheb Ambedkar, played spoilsport for the Congress–NCP combine. The VBA, which fought in an alliance with the AIMIM, is blamed for the defeat of the Opposition in at least eight seats, in addition to Jaleel's victory from Aurangabad.

Though Raj Thackeray campaigned against Narendra Modi and the BJP, Chavan admitted it was tough to gauge if this had been converted into votes for the Congress and NCP. 'It doesn't seem so,' said Ashok Chavan, who faced a shock defeat in his stronghold of Nanded.

10

The Snake That Ate Its Own Tail

The people follow their leaders.
The actions of these leaders set a precedent for others.

Saint Dnyaneshwar, 'Dnyaneshwari'

Give them bread and circuses.

Juvenal, Roman poet

In January 1984, Bal Thackeray, who was then flirting with socialism, organized a statewide convention of the Shiv Sena at Dadar and invited S.A. Dange, who by then had been expelled by the CPI, to address the cadre. During his speech (a Shiv Sena leader told the author they were mesmerized by Dange's oratory),[1] the stalwart of the communist movement in India put his finger on the Shiv Sena's Achilles heel which was that the organization did not have a theory and that it was impossible for an organization to survive sans one, he said.[2]

'The Shiv Sena is clearly devoted to action, and, it could be argued at first sight, to action alone. The party had no programme at all during the sixties and seventies. It still does not have serious economic proposals,' said political scientist Gerard Heuze.[3]

According to Heuze, action was the catalysing factor of the Sena's work. 'In the Shiv Sena, you are always ready to react. The enemy builds you, in a sense. It does not matter much who the enemy is,' said Heuze, adding that the 'enemies' could range from non-Maharashtrians to communists, Bhaiyas, Udupis, Muslims to pavement dwellers.[4]

Jayant Lele, professor emeritus in the departments of political studies, sociology and global development studies at Queen's University at Kingston in Canada, says that even before the Shiv Sena's formation, during its first five years, *Marmik* had shown few signs of a clear ideological position except its anti-communism. This sentiment was further inflamed by the India–China war of 1962 and the reluctance of Indian communists to condemn China.[5]

Lele says conspiratorially or not, the Shiv Sena fought hard to divert popular attention away from the dominance of capital over Bombay, even describing some big capitalists as *annadata*s (food givers) of Maharashtrians. Though hard evidence is impossible to come by, there are clear indications that it is involved in fostering and being fostered by this form of capitalism. It gains handsomely by protecting some and punishing others at will. Hindutva has become a convenient ideology in sustaining this posture in many ways, he added.[6]

Indeed, Heuze noted that while the Shiv Sena has led successive movements, it has never solved any problems as such, with its mix of demagogy and militancy seemingly unable to replace a programme.[7]

Heuze also points to common features between the Sena and the fascist and Nazi movements in pre-war Europe such as the petit bourgeois and urban recruitment, relation between unemployment and identity, cult of violence and weapons, martial spirit and hatred expressed towards minorities viewed as foreign and corrupting.[8]

Limited appeal

Liberalism, as a lived ideology, has its existential limitations, which leads to the birth of nativist movements seeking a better deal for the sons of the soil, whose grievances they claim to articulate. Such political groups appeal to communities or sections who feel deprived and left out in the process of development.

The Shiv Sena and MNS have rarely gone beyond emotional, existential issues to advocate a wider discourse. Even today, they are unable to take a forward-looking, rational stand on gender justice, environmentalism or even basic, rule-of-thumb economic policy, led as they are by political expediency.

This has resulted in the Shiv Sena and MNS developing their greatest drawback—the lack of an aspirational agenda at a time when the urban youth, including those from the Maharashtrian working class, is becoming more cosmopolitan, upwardly mobile and politically independent sans ideological commitments or underpinnings.

Though the Shiv Sena claims to be a Hindutva force, its weather-vane brand of politics has seen it respond to issues in a knee-jerk manner as per the need of the moment. In comparison, the Sangh Parivar cadre is grounded in its ideology.

'The basic limitation of Bal Thackeray was that he did not understand the spectrum of linguistic and identity politics around Marathi. Language is like a side dish and not the main course, it is just one element in a larger grid of culture, economics and society. It has to be linked to the economic life of its speakers for their financial prosperity,' said academician-analyst Dr Deepak Pawar.[9]

Bal Thackeray was a good organizer, though, who could make up for any lack of depth in his content through charisma and organizational skills.

'Raj can analyse things better, but like Balasaheb, was anti-south Indian in his earlier days. He frames his political discourse in the construct of the other, like his anti–north Indian protests. He is hence unable to touch issues like the agrarian crisis and the poor law-and-order situation,' said Pawar.[10]

A leader of Raj's BVS, who is now with the MNS, recalls his moment of epiphany in the mid-1990s.[11] He was at a missionary-run school in a Mumbai suburb to seek admissions for some children in his constituency, when he got into an argument with a nun. 'I complained that the school preferred to admit Christians. The nun retorted yes, they were partial towards their own flock as the church had created these institutions. The clincher came when she asked me why those who claimed to be the leaders of the Marathi manoos in Mumbai had failed to do likewise. This made me think about the limitations of the cause I was espousing.'

Unlike the Congress and NCP, whose leaders control a strong network of cooperatives and educational institutions, allowing them to exercise power and dole out patronage at the local level, the Shiv Sena and MNS are non-starters.

'Creating institutions helps empower people. However, this process needs great effort, at least till a break-even,' said Dr Deepak Pawar. The brand of politics by the Shiv Sena and MNS was centred around events. 'They cannot go beyond this. The Shiv Sena has been ruling the BMC for over two decades but can it point to a single Marathi school that has been run properly? There is an absence of vision.'[12]

Non-availability of quality education led to enrolment in BMC-run Marathi schools declining, as a 23 January 2017 report in the *Times of India* noted.[13]

But, even critics of the Shiv Sena and MNS point out that while the liberal intelligentsia is quick on its feet to denounce these nativist organizations, they often ignore similar regional and linguistic chauvinism and sub-nationalism in their own states. It often fails to acknowledge that opportunities are often secured through networks linked to caste, linguistic and regional identities with merit per se taking a back seat.[14]

However, the appeal of the pro-Marathi stance taken by the Shiv Sena and MNS is restricted only to urban centres like Mumbai, Pune, Thane and Nashik. Chhagan Bhujbal pointed out that despite being a regional force, the Shiv Sena had been hobbled electorally by the fact that it failed to create a larger Marathi identity, unlike regional parties in the south. 'After south Indians and the communists, the Sena alienated sections of Dalits and Muslims,' he said.[15]

Bhujbal said if the Sena had built a larger social coalition of these forces, it would have been able to rule Maharashtra. The constant 'othering' of Muslims by the Sangh Parivar and the Shiv Sena led them to counter-mobilize and become more hard-line and inward-looking even in rural areas, where the Hindus and Muslims have greater integration when it came to language, dress and culture.[16]

Anti-intellectualism

Maharashtra, which was once the cradle of reformist movements, has seen a steady decline in these social forces, in what has been attributed to the dumbing down and de-intellectualization of society.

The Shiv Sena and later the MNS, have been blamed for lumpenizing the Marathi youth, with their focus on 'thokshahi' (use of physical force) instead of 'lokshahi' (democracy) and 'direct action', which often encroaches into the realm of vigilantism (Gerard Heuze refers to this as the legitimization of the *dada* [goon] culture[17]). Julia M. Eckert describes the Shiv Sena as a 'party, movement and gang at once'[18] and the conduct of the MNS has shown it might attract similar charges.

For instance, an undercover investigation by *India Today* detected how MNS men were willing to start protests for a hefty sum.[19]

Though Raj is known to be close to the Marathi cultural and literary elite, the two parties are known for their anti-intellectualism. As scholar and editor the late Aroon Tikekar notes, in the nineteenth century Maharashtrians were preferred for employment even by Parsi and Gujarati employers as they were reputed to be hard-working, god-fearing, honest and sincere and had respect for scholarship. Tikekar laments that though Bal Thackeray united them, he made them insincere, dishonest, defiant, apathetic towards intellectual challenges and dismissive of scholarship.[20]

Despite claiming to uphold the cause of the Marathi manoos, the two Senas watched as the organized working class of Mumbai, which was predominantly Maharashtrian, was gradually run into the ground, beginning with textile mill workers.

Architect-cum-activist Neera Adarkar says a 'complex set of factors' beyond the 1982 strike led to the decline of the industry and the defeat of the workers. 'The workers were let down by Shiv Sena leader Bal Thackeray who, at the last minute, withdrew a strike he was to lead and announced his faith in the Congress government. This led the workers to *gherao* Dr [Datta] Samant to lead the strike who himself admitted that he was not familiar with the industry,' added Adarkar.[21]

P.N. 'Dada' Samant, the younger brother of Dr Datta Samant, and a trade unionist himself, notes that the ruling Congress deliberately allowed the mill strike to fester and fail. 'Otherwise, Dr Samant would have become the uncrowned king of Mumbai,' he said, admitting that another reason for the strike being unsuccessful could be his brother's decision to 'fight it as a political issue, rather than an economic one'.[22]

In 1991, the state government allowed around 600 acres of land belonging to the mills to be opened for redevelopment, with the mill owners retaining a third, and the remaining one-third each going to the BMC and Maharashtra Housing and Area Development Authority (MHADA) for developing open spaces and affordable housing, particularly for mill workers. In 2001, the state government controversially amended the formula under which the owners would have to surrender two-thirds of only the vacant land (non-built-up land) to these two bodies, thus keeping bulk of the prime land with themselves.[23] This was however upheld by the Supreme Court in 2006.[24]

'Mill owners had realized it was easy to sell mill lands (due to the profits involved) rather than running the mills,' said Dada Samant. 'The Shiv Sena did not oppose this (change in the use of mill lands) despite being in power in the BMC. All political parties were involved in breaking the textile mill workers movement,' he charged.[25]

In his memoirs, senior Communist Party of India (CPI) leader Gangadhar Chitnis details how the erstwhile Shiv Sena–BJP government dragged its feet on ensuring that mill workers got their pending salaries.[26]

Chitnis, who was associated with the 'Girni Kamgar Union' (the CPI union for mill hands), said when the protesting workers organized a morcha to the state administrative headquarters, the Mantralaya, then labour minister, late Sabir Shaikh (who belonged to the Shiv Sena), made promises to them. 'Not even one of the assurances given by Sabir Shaikh was implemented. (The workers) did not get salaries for work done, nor were attempts made to run the mills,' said Chitnis, who has detailed how the strike uprooted mill workers and their families.[27]

'The Shiv Sena and MNS claim to represent the Marathi manoos, but have betrayed them. They are confidence tricksters,' charged trade unionist Rajan Raje of the Dharmarajya Kamgar Karmachari Mahasangh, who fought the 2014 Lok Sabha and assembly elections from Thane as a MNS nominee. 'Today, most blue-collar jobs are on contractual basis and the terms of employment are exploitative. Politicians across party lines are into labour contracting and flourish by looting workers.'[28]

The gradual sense of loyalty of the organization to the people and vice versa, which saw Sainiks act against black marketing and other malpractices, was eroded as a policy of maintaining the status quo set in. Senior journalist and executive editor of *EPW*, Lina Mathias, who covered the labour movement in Mumbai, notes that the communist polymath S.A. Dange was popular among the mill workers as he made knowledge accessible to them. Dange, through his public speeches peppered with references from religious texts and the basics of Marxism, had brought the workers into the Left movement. 'Workers were given a focus beyond usual economic demands due to the political and ideological education imparted by these Leftist labour unions. However, as the Shiv Sena emerged, economic demands and those centred around regional identity started taking precedence. This struck a chord as people were desperate due to the dismal job and economic scene. Gradually, communalization and regional identity took over,' explained Mathias.[29]

The situation was compounded by the rise of the militant leadership of Dr Datta Samant, who had no ideological underpinnings and was completely focused on ensuring better wages and bonus for his workers. The labour unions gradually went into a terminal decline in the post-globalization era.[30]

Despite claiming to stand up for Marathi speakers, the Shiv Sena and MNS failed to redeem their promises as is evident from the retreat and decline of the Marathi manoos in Mumbai. From 1966 to 2019, some of the demands of the two parties have remained the same—be it jobs for sons of the soil or Marathi signboards!

Girish Kuber, editor, *Loksatta*, said the Shiv Sena was perhaps the only political party which allowed its core vote base to diminish under its watch like during the textile mill workers' strike. The increasing numbers of non-Maharashtrians in Mumbai and surrounding areas translated into support for national parties like the BJP. 'For instance, if someone from Mumbai moves to Chennai, he will not vote for (regional parties like) the Dravida Munnetra Kazhagam (DMK) or All India Anna Dravida Munnetra Kazhagam (AIADMK), but for (national parties like) the BJP or Congress. So, the seeds of the BJP's rise are embedded in the Sena's decline,' he noted.[31]

The Shiv Sena did little to showcase Maharashtra's rich culture, heritage and cuisine. Despite controlling the BMC, which has a Rs 30,692.59 crore budget,[32] which surpasses that of states like Goa (Rs 19,548 crore),[33] most builders and civil contractors working in Mumbai are from Rajasthan.[34] The Sena also has little to boast of in terms of the quality of its governance in Mumbai.

The former BMC official, 'Demolition Man' G.R. Khairnar, who became the civic body's deputy commissioner later, added that the Shiv Sena had presided over the decline of the institution. 'Be it civic-run hospitals or schools, their deterioration has been gradual,' he noted.[35]

An MNS leader admitted the politics of the two Senas was hobbled by the fact that by and large, Maharashtrians, especially those from the educated and middle class, lack a strong sense of native and regional pride and identity, unlike those in the south.

'Some of my shakha functionaries supply milk to households and hotels, including those owned by the Shettys, who hail from Karnataka. They started getting inquiries if a particular brand of milk could be supplied. We put two and two together and realized that these Shetty restaurant owners wanted that brand as it was from their home state. Their sense of identity and pull for their roots is so strong,' he exclaimed.[36]

Lack of results

Despite his charismatic authority, Bal Thackeray, whom Gyan Prakash refers to as the original 'angry young man',[37] undoubtedly had several chinks in his armour. But, the masses, mesmerized by his personality, were unable to see them. As Kumar Ketkar notes, Bal Thackeray was never a planner or a strategist, was not well read in history or politics and had little understanding of economics. Ketkar added that during the Shiv Sena–BJP regime, Bal Thackeray could have launched projects to enrich Marathi literature, culture, historical research, cinema and language, but did not.[38]

Senior journalist Rakshit Sonawane links this lack of a larger ideology with the meteoric rise and fall of the MNS in Nashik between 2012 and 2017. The party lost its base in the opportunistic floating constituency that had gravitated towards it after the initial success, only to revert to other political options later.[39]

Sonawane stated that two of the Shiv Sena's pet schemes—'Shiv vada' (with plans of centralized kitchen, standardized ingredients and professionally managed supply chain) where Marathi youth were promised carts to sell vada paav, the snack that the Sena is credited for popularizing, and *zhunka bhakar* (unleavened jowar bread with besan curry) for Rs 1 (floated during the erstwhile Sena–BJP regime) had gone to seed. Similarly, the Shiv Udyog Sena (SUS), Raj's dream project to provide employment for local youth, has also floundered.

'The Shiv Sena and MNS emotionally mesmerize their cadre and use them as their foot soldiers. This leads to lumpen elements joining them for recognition, status and protection. The working classes in slums and chawls, which form the backbone of the Shiv Sena, need help to solve their day-to-day problems involving local government officials, and in turn provides electoral support.'[40]

Sonawane noted that the Thackeray cousins lacked consistency. They did not advocate structural changes on issues like agrarian distress, which include a change in crop patterns, remunerative pricing, urban outlets for farmers to eliminate middlemen, and the need to supplement incomes through sources like the dairy business. 'Raj, who loves PowerPoint presentations, had initiated a novel procedure in 2012 to select candidates for the civic elections through an examination process where their knowledge of subjects was tested. However, it was wound up.'

Sonawane pointed to a critical lacuna in the anti-migrant politics of the two parties—they opposed migrants who stayed in low-income housing like slums and not those who were well-off and lived in skyscrapers, thereby clearly indicating that they were concerned only with their vote-bank politics.[41] As Gerard Heuze notes, the right of the Gujarati sheth (trader or bourgeoisie) to be a citizen of Mumbai has never been seriously questioned by the organization. This sets it apart from similar nativist movements like that of the tribals of Jharkhand in eastern India. It is the migrant especially the poor migrant, who is threatened with expulsion.[42]

The Senas have also failed to respond to a serious crisis that has gripped the working and middle class in Mumbai—lack of affordable housing that has led to many habitating slums or migrating from the city to the suburbs and beyond. It was the socialists under the late Mrinal Gore and P.B. (Baburao) Samant who led a protest since 1981 that culminated in land for over 6000 tenements being given to their 'Nagari Nivara Parishad' at Goregaon in 1992.[43]

Unlike the BJP, which had the RSS, and the socialists, who had the Rashtra Seva Dal, the Shiv Sena has no 'conscience keepers' or 'guiding lights'.

The Shiv Sena, despite its wide social base, did not embrace Prabodhankar's *Bahujanwad* (espousal of the cause of the Bahujan

Samaj), said journalist-researcher Sachin Parab.[44] 'Perhaps Balasaheb saw how Prabodhankar suffered for his convictions,' said Parab, who has documented Prabodhankar's life and works. The co-option of castes like the CKPs, Shenvis (Saraswats) and Sonars (goldsmiths) by the Brahmanical order may have dulled some of this anger, Parab feels.

While he sees Prabodhankar's influence on the Shiv Sena through its social profile and representation given to castes traditionally out of the power matrix, this was missing in case of the MNS. 'Prabodhankar, whose knowledge of the caste system was impeccable, was associated with stalwarts like Acharya P.K. Atre, Gadge Maharaj and Karmaveer Bhaurao Patil. Hence, Balasaheb was aware of these social realities. However, Raj is surrounded largely by upper-class and upper-caste Hindus. Many leaders from Bahujan communities have deserted him. Though the nature of politics in and around Mumbai is polarized on linguistic lines, caste undercurrents cannot be ignored.'[45]

The irony is stark when Prabodhankar's legacy is compared with the Shiv Sena's political trajectory, wherein it has exhibited social and cultural rigidity.

For instance, the Shiv Sena opposed the erstwhile Congress–NCP government's bill to ban black magic and practices like human sacrifices. A diluted version of the law was approved in 2013 after it claimed a martyr—rationalist Dr Narendra Dabholkar—who was championing the cause, and was killed on 20 August 2013 by masterminds still at large.

Some Shiv Sena leaders had 'misled' members of the influential *varkari* (bhakti) sect, and said they would not be allowed to continue with their pilgrimage to the temple of Lord Vithoba at Pandharpur if the law was passed.[46]

The Shiv Sena also opposed works of expression like Vijay Tendulkar's acclaimed play *Ghashiram Kotwal* for depicting Peshwa statesman Nana Fadnavis, who is hailed as the Peshwa-era Niccolò Machiavelli, as a debauch. Similarly, Tendulkar's *Sakharam Binder* and Deepa Mehta's 1996 movie *Fire*, which was among the first in mainstream Hindi cinema to explore the theme of lesbian love, ran into rough weather with the party.

The Shiv Sena opposed the renaming of Marathwada University after Dr Babasaheb Ambedkar, which caused large-scale violence against Buddhist Dalits and even Hindu Dalits in Marathwada. The Shiv Sena's opposition to this 'Namantar' (renaming) movement (1978–94), polarized upper-caste Hindus against Buddhist Dalits, and helped its spread into Maharashtra's dust bowl of Marathwada, beyond its traditional base in Mumbai–Thane.

Despite having a strong base among the OBCs, the Sena opposed then prime minister V.P. Singh's decision to implement the Mandal Commission report that granted quotas in jobs and education to these intermediate classes.

However, a former Maharashtra minister appreciated the MNS chief for going against the current and becoming the lone dissenting voice on issues like quotas for the Maratha community, unlike Uddhav, who fell in line.[47] Raj had pointed to how morchas by the Marathas, which were organized in 2016 and 2017 for demands like quotas, had led to caste divisions growing in society, and sought reservations based on economic criteria.[48] In 2018, the Maharashtra government approved 16 per cent quotas for the dominant community, which the Bombay High Court brought down to 12 and 13 per cent in education and jobs respectively.[49]

'Raj and Uddhav can react to the issues of the day to elicit a response from the masses but cannot think for the long term. It is easy to blame non-Maharashtrians for taking jobs meant for Maharashtrians, but did either of the Senas bother to train local youth in trades dominated by migrants like construction and plumbing? Why didn't they launch skill development programmes and use their influence to ensure that these trained youth secured employment?' said a former Shiv Sena MLA.[50]

He noted that neither the Shiv Sena nor the MNS had taken up issues like the plight of unorganized workers, farmers, farm labourers and the tribals and nomadic tribes as 'this [mobilization at the grassroots level for these exploited sections] needed years of hard work and did not result in cheap publicity'.

The former MLA, who has a grounding in left-of-centre politics, said emotional politics and violent protests 'had destroyed generations'.[51] He added that a section of the press, especially the Marathi print and electronic media deliberately built up Raj's image. Like his rise, his fall was also led by the media, which found a new hero, who generated TRPs on a much larger scale—Narendra Modi.

However, Chhagan Bhujbal said the Shiv Sena, with its deep roots in local communities would survive, regardless of political reverses.[52]

A senior BJP leader, who began his career with the ABVP at the same time when Raj was launched as the chief of BVS, noted that despite electoral setbacks, it was wrong to write off Raj or his party. 'After all, he has charismatic authority. Such leaders can latch on to any issue and convert it into political capital as he did in case of the 2008 anti-migrant protests.'[53]

Afterword:
The Men behind the Image

They may be first cousins twice over, but their personalities are poles apart.

One is abrasive, a fire-breathing demagogue, who is blunt to the point of being arrogant but remains one of the most popular crowd-puller in Maharashtra despite a string of electoral reverses. The other is introvert, soft-spoken, an enigma for many associates, and with his penchant for boardroom strategies, seems to be out of character with his rough-and-tumble party, which dominates the streets of India's financial capital, thanks to its muscle.

This, in a nutshell, is a description of the personalities of the two warring Thackerays, Shiv Sena president Uddhav Thackeray and MNS chief Raj Thackeray.

A Shiv Sena loyalist attributes these differing styles to their starting points in politics. For instance, Raj cut his teeth in student politics, which was violent and rough in those days, while Uddhav's springboard was the party newspaper *Saamna*. Hence, Raj gradually imbibed Balasaheb's behavioural style realizing it would be his USP, thus fitting the stereotype of an archetypal Shiv Sainik, whereas Uddhav is more comfortable as a back-room manipulator, diplomat and strategist.[1]

'Raj is streetwise compared to Uddhav, who is a late bloomer in politics,' explained the Sena source, who has worked with both brothers. 'Uddhav was coming of age when the Shiv Sena was launched. Hence, he was seen as the party chief's son and led a protected life,' he said.[2]

While Raj connected to his cadre via his aura and charisma, Uddhav had a strong party organization to back him. However, both lacked the ability Bal Thackeray possessed—going beyond one's immediate circle and connecting with the workers at the grass roots. Being based out of Mumbai, where society is more cosmopolitan, they do not understand the finer points about caste politics that holds the key for any political mobilization in rural areas. This restricts their ability to launch any social engineering projects.

The Sena source said the cousins were also unable to hold on to influential leaders, choosing to rely instead on their close advisers with no real mass base. Uddhav is said to have a healthy distrust for mass leaders within his party. This may be because many of them like Chhagan Bhujbal, Ganesh Naik and Narayan Rane had grown beyond a point and then split from the Shiv Sena. Instead, he relies on people who are more comfortable with office-level politics.

A close associate of Raj Thackeray, who has since fallen out with him explained that the 'interference' of some of his advisers and personal friends in the party's internal affairs, had led to influential party leaders deserting it in cities like Nashik, where the MNS had a strong presence.

'These people would paratroop from Mumbai and dictate terms to local leaders with a mass following. The inevitable happened with them finally quitting the party,' he said, adding that a sore point for many in the MNS was that many of Raj's personal friends, who were not 'professional politicians' were calling the shots.[3] Ironically, Raj had blamed the Shiv Sena's coterie politics for his decision to quit the party.

A former Uddhav loyalist said he liked to listen to devotional songs in Marathi sung by Bhimsen Joshi and others. In his autobiography, Shrikant noted that Raj had an ear for music, even pointing to how a top-notch singer had faltered in a song.[4]

Raj is said to be enamoured with tinsel town, which is natural considering his love for films. He also likes the music of Bach, Beethoven, Hans Zimmer, John Williams and R.D. Burman. 'Raj generally has a do not disturb sign on his face while interacting with cadre, but lights up when he meets film personalities,' said one of Raj's associates from his student days.[5] Another associate recalled how Raj provided technical inputs for films including a voice-over for Marathi movie *Jatra* (2005) by Kedar Shinde. He added that the MNS chief would also help financially distressed yet promising film-makers and music directors.[6]

Those familiar with both cousins note that while Raj has a vast circle of friends across sectors like cinema, media and politics, Uddhav is choosy with people.[7] While Raj is a great drawing room conversationalist, Uddhav is said to have a hampered ability for small talk.

'Raj is a *yaaron ka yaar* [someone who stands by his friends through thick and thin],' said a former business associate. In contrast, Uddhav is an intensely private man, an introvert, with a limited circle of friends.'[8]

While Raj has friends ranging from cricketer Sachin Tendulkar, actor Salman Khan, film personalities Sajid Khan, Sajid Nadiadwala and Marathi actor Vinay Yedekar, the introvert yet well-spoken Uddhav is said to have just a handful of close friends, all of them non-political. This includes actor Milind Gunaji, J.J. Institute alumnus Bhupal Ramnathkar, Sanjay Sure and Ravi Jasra, who heads a digital production firm.[9] Ramnathkar and Sure have helped design the Shiv Sena's campaigns.[10]

Uddhav is a shutterbug with a love for aerial photography and has clicked Maharashtra's forts spread across hill ranges, including

Dhodap, which is linked to the Thackeray family's history, and the procession of varkaris to the temple of Lord Vithoba at Pandharpur.

Milind Gunaji, who accompanied Uddhav on his helicopter sorties during his aerial photography tours, recalled how Uddhav would undertake this venture with the attendant risks, like the safety belt coming apart in the open chopper.[11] Gunaji has written about how Uddhav and he waited at Raigad Fort to take a photograph of the statue of Shivaji Maharaj with the sun forming a halo around it, believing they would get the desired effect at sunset. However, they realized that the sun would be at the desired position only in the morning and were forced to camp overnight at the fort.[12]

Uddhav and his family also make an annual visit to the temple of Goddess Ekvira located at Karla near the hill station of Lonavala.[13]

A Shiv Sena leader said Uddhav had not imbibed his father's oratory and mannerisms, which led people to infer that Raj was the better leader of the two. He added that Uddhav preferred to stick to what he was, rather than use borrowed feathers.[14] However, Uddhav would consult his father on improving his public speaking.

Compared to Raj, who smokes and loves his drink, Uddhav does not like the taste of alcohol. 'On 22 January 1992 midnight, *Saamna*'s anniversary was celebrated. Later, some of us including Balasaheb, Uddhavji and myself, went to Hotel Sea Princess at Juhu. Balasaheb opened a bottle of champagne and asked Uddhavji to take a sip. We too asked him to drink. Uddhavji, whose unease was apparent, must have taken a small sip when he broke into a cough,' said Shishir Shinde.[15]

Unlike Raj, who is known to be blunt to a fault, Uddhav, who is described as a gentleman even by his political adversaries, has his own way of dealing with people who get on to his wrong side, said a former Shiv Sena leader who is now with the NCP. 'Whenever he was angry, Balasaheb would never mince his words. But he had great love for his cadre. For instance, when I once bent down to touch his feet, he told me I was gradually losing hair, something that neither me nor my father, whose feet I touched similarly, had ever noticed. Uddhav will never insult someone if he is angry, but will put him down in a cloaked, yet venal manner that is worse,' he says.[16]

While most Shiv Sena dissidents blame Uddhav's controversial personal assistant Milind Narvekar for controlling access to his boss, the former Sena leader said Narvekar often carried out Uddhav's instructions.

A former Shiv Sena MP describes Uddhav as a good human being, but a better manipulator than the outspoken Raj. However, while Uddhav is a good listener, Raj reportedly has a shorter attention span.[17]

Agreed a Shiv Sena legislator close to the seat of power at Matoshree. 'If I say something that Uddhav does not like, he will never tell me on my face. He will just block access. Milind may be acting at Uddhav's behest when he spurns people or rubs them in the wrong way,' he admits.[18]

A former Shiv Sena legislator recalls how Uddhav put a high-profile defector in place. 'This leader who had quit the Shiv Sena after bitter acrimony was looking at returning to its fold as he was feeling stifled in his new party. A controversial godman, who is no more, and I negotiated with Sena leaders. A breakthrough seemed imminent as Uddhav was supposed to meet him at a hotel near the Mumbai airport. But, on the chosen day, Uddhav did not turn up at the meeting. The leader realized he had been snubbed.'[19]

His friends claim Raj is one of the most aesthetically gifted politicians across the country and a great host who will surprise guests with their favourite food and drink.[20] Both Raj and Uddhav are foodies with the elder cousin partial towards seafood like crabs and lobsters. Uddhav, a frugal eater, now takes special care of his diet after his heart ailment. Raj loves non-vegetarian food and based on his whims, can also whip up a dish or two like 'warhadi bhaat' that is a speciality of western Vidarbha cuisine.[21]

Milind Gunaji says Uddhav plays good cricket. He added that both Uddhav and Raj play badminton well and can give a tough time to their opponents in these games.[22]

Unlike Uddhav, Raj is a man who revels in his own image. During public events and election campaigns, Raj is tailed by a team from friend Milind Sabnis's Zen Video. The feed is provided to television channels and serves as a force multiplier for the hero-worshiping party, whose existence is inextricably linked to its chief.[23]

Uddhav has a select bunch of advisers like Milind Narvekar, Sanjay Raut, Subhash Desai and Anil Desai, but is said to know his own mind. 'Uddhav's opinions may also be shaped by wife Rashmi as she has a good understanding of politics,' said a Sena source. In contrast, Raj's circle of advisers is like a revolving door.[24]

According to a close associate of Raj's, in the early 1990s, Raj had launched a restaurant named 'Flying Saucer' at Dadar in partnership with some friends. The restaurant was inaugurated by Bal Thackeray, who had also christened it. However, it was shut down later and the space has been leased out to an outlet selling Bengali sweets. Raj is said to have exited his stake in Matoshree Infrastructure Private Limited. He claimed that both Raj and Uddhav had stakes in a unit launched by a former cricketer which manufactured sports goods and garments, but they quit it later.[25]

In June 2017, *DNA* reported that Raj's wife, Sharmila, was constructing a seventeen-storey building named 'Madhuwanti' opposite their Shivaji Park residence.[26]

'There is one critical gap in the functioning of both the cousins. They do not follow up on issues and ensure checks and balances within the organization. This ensures that some of their plans fall through. They are also unable to make new allies, especially among smaller, subregional players who can tilt the scales,' said the Sena source quoted earlier.[27]

Though Raj's cartooning abilities are well known, few know that Uddhav is a gifted artist too.[28] While Raj is famous for his ability to mimic political opponents ranging from Chhagan Bhujbal to Ramdas Athavale and Ajit Pawar, Milind Gunaji says that even Uddhav can imitate people.[29]

Uddhav is described by his men as a typical family man attached to his wife and two sons, often speaking to Aaditya and Tejas when he sees them passing by even during party meetings at Matoshree. Aaditya, who shot into the public glare after making the University of Mumbai drop Rohinton Mistry's *Such a Long Journey* from its curriculum, is also a poet who launched his first book, *My Thoughts in White and Black*, in 2007.

In 2008, he released an album, *Ummeed*, in the presence of his grandfather and Amitabh Bachchan. The soft-spoken Aaditya, who is active on social media, heads the Mumbai District Football Association (MDFA) and was appointed the Yuva Sena chief in 2010. Ironically, while the Shiv Sena stresses on Marathi, the 1990-born Aaditya passed out from the elite Bombay Scottish School and St Xavier's College. He was promoted as a leader of the Shiv Sena in 2018.

His younger brother, Tejas, loves animals and wildlife and has a menagerie in Matoshree's backyard. He discovered three new species of freshwater crabs endemic to the Western Ghats, one of which was named after his family. This included *Ghatiana atropurpurea*, *Ghatiana splendida* and *Gubernatoriana thackerayi*. In a 2010 rally, Tejas was praised by his grandfather for being aggressive like him.

In January 2018, Tejas was also permitted by the Maharashtra State Board for Wildlife to collect live crabs (belonging to genera *Ghatiana*, *Gubernatoriana*, *Ingletelphusa* and *Barytelphusa*) for research purposes from the Chandoli National Park in the Sahyadris.

Raj's son, Amit, is being groomed for politics. A commerce graduate, Amit was described by his teachers from Manik Vidya Mandir at Bandra as a 'good, if not model student' who lacked airs.[30] Like his father, Amit is said to be a fine artist.[31] His younger sister, Urvashi, is a fashion designer. Amit married his fashion designer girlfriend, Mitali Borude, in 2019. Mitali is a close friend of Urvashi and the two have a clothes label called 'The Rack'.[32]

Ironic as it may sound, Raj, who, like his uncle, has never hidden his admiration for Adolf Hitler, is inspired by Mahatma Gandhi and has watched Sir Richard Attenborough's *Gandhi* at least 150 times, sometimes sitting through two shows a day![33]

However, Raj also planned to create a storm-trooper force of MNS cadre who would be the party's vanguard in attempts to enforce its writ. The force was also meant to greet Raj using a Nazi salute (the hand extended with a clenched fist). This was to be launched in a programme at Thane before the 2009 state assembly polls, but the plan was dropped after a consensus that it would result in bad optics.[34]

Raj also tries to watch a film daily. He has a collection of 2,000 to 3,000 DVDs apart from around 7,000 to 8,000 movies in a Drobo device.[35] The film buff also has a fascination for black-and-white films like Steven Spielberg's *Schindler's List*.[36]

Raj is also bringing out a book which will have a collection of songs written by Lata Mangeshkar during her music recordings in her own hand. When Mangeshkar began her career, many lyricists and poets would pen their works in Urdu. Hence, she wrote these songs with their notations in her own handwriting before singing them.[37]

The MNS chief also plans to make a film on two personalities—Chhatrapati Shivaji Maharaj and Indira Gandhi. 'I am thinking about this,' he said, adding that however, 'one cannot stand on two stones. If I want to make a film, I will have to take a sabbatical from politics for some time. It is not possible at least now.'[38]

Acknowledgements

चंद्र भारल्या जीवाला, नाही कशाचीच चाड
मला कशाला मोजता, मी तो भारलेले झाड

Chandra bharlya jiwala, naahi kashyachich chada,
Mala kashyala mojata, mee to bharlele zhaad

(One who is mesmerized by the beauty of moonlight, does not bother about anything else
Why do you take me into account? I am like that laden tree)

Ga.Di Madgulkar

I would like to express my gratitude to those without whom this book would not have been completed. These people are responsible for the good things in the book, any errors and omissions are entirely mine:

My wife Kadambari and daughter Ananya, who are my best friends, for suffering my long absences, both physical and emotional, from their lives when I plunged into writing this book, trying to fill the unforgiving minute with sixty seconds worth of distance run. I promise to make up for everything.

My parents, Supriya and Shamsunder Kulkarni, for bearing my long absences and silences. And Hemi Pacchi, Shyamal Amma and Keya.

Bhavika Jain—the true friend in need who rescued me from the horns of the beast called dilemma and encouraged me to write. Thanks for the doses of bitter medicine.

Lina Mathias, mentor, hand-holder and sounding board, who made a world of difference by reading my drafts and suggesting changes wherever needed.

Rakshit Sonawane for giving me a much-needed perspective. A true mentor, guide and moral compass, who imbibed in me the spirit of inquiry.

Prof. Gopal Guru, a man whose intellect sits lightly on his shoulders. Thank you, Guru sir, for your valuable intellectual inputs.

Sachin Parab, a good journalist, researcher and a great human being, provided me much-needed references, suggestions and perspectives.

Kapil Kelkar and Alex Fernandes who went through my early drafts and suggested changes. Kapil's fine-toothed reading and suggestions on my draft helped improve my writing.

Dnyanesh Maharao for the wealth of his knowledge.

Swapnil Savarkar and Sandeep Acharya aka Bhai for helping open many doors.

Jatin Gandhi for everything . . .

My in-laws, Padmaja and Vikas Vithalker.

Aruna for the endless cups of coffee.

Special thanks to Surendra P. Gangan, Dr Tejas Garge, Urvi and Rahul Mahajani, Anurag Tripathi, Manish Pachouly, Rajendra Hunje, Kaustubh Kulkarni, Virat A. Singh, Kirti Pandey Tai and Sanjay Jog. And to the leaders and cadre from the Shiv Sena, MNS, Congress and NCP, beat colleagues, bureaucrats and police officials (both serving and retired), who opened up to me for the book, but cannot be acknowledged for obvious reasons. The staff at the Yashwantrao Chavan Pratishthan and Dadar Sarvajanik Vachanalay libraries for smooth access to the books and references.

Swati Chopra, my commissioning editor, and Trisha Bora, for pushing me to do better, and the editorial, design and legal team at Penguin Random House India.

Notes

Chapter 1: The History of the Thackeray Family and 'Prabodhankar' Thackeray

1. 'Prospice' by Robert Browning, https://www.poetryfoundation.org/poems/43773/prospice
2. 'Prabodhankar' Keshav Sitaram Thackeray, *Majhi Jeevangatha* (The Story of My Life), *Collected Works of Prabodhankar Thackeray*, Vol. I, Maharashtra Rajya Sahitya Aani Sanskruti Mandal, Mumbai, 1997, ebook, p. 45.
3. Milind Gunaji (writer), Uddhav Thackeray (photos), *Havai Mulukhgiri* (Aerial Tours), Riya Publications, Kolhapur, 2018, pp. 52, 54.
4. 'Prabodhankar' Keshav Sitaram Thackeray, *Majhi Jeevangatha* (The Story of My Life), *Collected Works of Prabodhankar Thackeray*, Vol. I, Maharashtra Rajya Sahitya Aani Sanskruti Mandal, Mumbai, 1997, ebook, p. 45.
5. Ibid., p. 45.
6. Ibid., p 49.
7. Ibid., p 44.
8. 'Prabodhankar' Thackeray, *Gramnyancha Sadyanta Itihas Arthat Nokarshahiche Banda* (A History of Village Disputes or Rebellion of the Bureaucracy), *Collected Works of Prabodhankar Thackeray*, Vol. V, Maharashtra Rajya Sahitya Aani Sanskruti Mandal, Mumbai, 2007, ebook, p. 40.
9. 'Prabodhankar' Keshav Sitaram Thackeray, *Majhi Jeevangatha* (The Story of My Life), *Collected Works of Prabodhankar*

Thackeray, Vol. I, Maharashtra Rajya Sahitya Aani Sanskruti Mandal, Mumbai, 1997, ebook, pp. 131–34.
10. Interview with Prabodhankar's daughter, Sanjeevani Karandikar, on 23 March 2019.
11. 'Prabodhankar' Keshav Sitaram Thackeray, *Majhi Jeevangatha* (The Story of My Life), '*Collected Works of Prabodhankar Thackeray*, Vol. I, Maharashtra Rajya Sahitya Aani Sanskruti Mandal, Mumbai, 1997, ebook, pp. 174, 178
12. Ibid., p. 222.
13. Ibid., pp. 130–131, 188, 247.
14. Shrikant Thackeray, *Jasa Ghadla* Tasa, *Chinar* Publishers, Pune, 2002, p. 47.
15. Dnyanesh Maharao (ed.), *Prabodhankaranche Jwalanta Hindutva* (The Fiery Hindutva of Prabodhankar), Navata Book World, Mumbai, 2011, p. 7.
16. 'Prabodhankar' Keshav Sitaram Thackeray, *Majhi Jeevangatha*, *Collected Works of Prabodhankar Thackeray*, Vol. I, Maharashtra Rajya Sahitya Aani Sanskruti Mandal, Mumbai, 1997, ebook, p. 324.
17. Neera Adarkar and Meena Menon, *Katha Mumbaichya Girangaonchi: Girni Kamgarancha Maukhik Itihas*, (An Oral History of Girangaon), Mauj Prakashan, Mumbai, 2009, p. 201.
18. Dnyanesh Maharao (ed.), *Prabodhankaranche Jwalanta Hindutva* (The Fiery Hindutva of Prabodhankar), Navata Book World, Mumbai, 2011, p. 20.
19. Ibid., p. 22,
20. Ibid., p. 27.
21. Ibid., p. 44.
22. Shrikant Thackeray, *Jasa Ghadla Tasa* (As it Happened), Chinar Publishers, Pune, 2002, p. 46.
23. Ibid., pp. 46–47.
24. Walter K. Anderson and Shridhar D. Damle, *The RSS: A View to the Inside*, Penguin Random House India, Gurgaon, 2018, p. xii.
25. G.K. Karanth, 'Caste in Contemporary Rural India', *Caste: Its Twentieth Century Avatar,* (ed.) M.N. Srinivas, Penguin Books India, Delhi, 1996, p. 107.
26. Ibid., pp. 107–08.
27. Author's interview with Sachin Parab on 23 January 2019.

28. 'Prabodhankar' Keshav Sitaram Thackeray, *Majhi Jeevangatha*, Collected Works of Prabodhankar Thackeray, Vol. I, Maharashtra Rajya Sahitya Aani Sanskruti Mandal, Mumbai, 1997, ebook, pp. 345–51.
29. Ibid., p. 348.
30. Interview with author on 23 January 2019.
31. 'Prabodhankar' Keshav Sitaram Thackeray, *Majhi Jeevangatha*, Collected Works of Prabodhankar Thackeray, Vol. I, Maharashtra Rajya Sahitya Aani Sanskruti Mandal, Mumbai, 1997, ebook, pp. 247–48.
32. Interview with author on 23 March 2019.
33. Rayat Shikshan Sanstha website, http://rayatshikshan.edu/Content.aspx?ID=890&PID=1
34. 'Prabodhankar' Keshav Sitaram Thackeray, *Majhi Jeevangatha*, Collected Works of Prabodhankar Thackeray, Vol. I, Maharashtra Rajya Sahitya Aani Sanskruti Mandal, Mumbai, 1997, ebook, pp. 364–67.
35. Ibid., p. 262.
36. Ibid., p. 263.
37. Dnyanesh Maharao, *Thackeray: Life and Style*, Pushpa Prakashan, Pune, 2001, p. 53.
38. Interview with author on 18 April 2019.
39. Dnyanesh Maharao, *Thackeray: Life and Style*, Pushpa Prakashan, Pune, 2001, p. 53.
40. Ibid., p. 53.
41. Ibid., p. 57.
42. Ibid., p. 57.
43. 'Prabodhankar' Keshav Sitaram Thackeray, *Majhi Jeevangatha*, Collected Works of Prabodhankar Thackeray, Vol. I, Maharashtra Rajya Sahitya Aani Sanskruti Mandal, Mumbai, 1997, ebook, p.240.
44. Ibid., p. 240.
45. Ibid., p. 241.
46. Ibid., p. 242.
47. Dinoo Randive, *Aatwani Maharashtra Janmachya* (Memories of the Birth of Maharashtra), Prabhat Prakashan, Bhayender, Thane, 2007, p. 112.
48. Ibid., p. 113.

49. Bal Keshav Thackeray, *Fatkare*, Prabodhan Prakashan, Mumbai, 2012.
50. Shrikant Thackeray, *Jasa Ghadla Tasa*, Chinar Publishers, Pune, 2002, pp. 56–57.
51. Raj Thackeray, *Bal Keshav Thackeray: A Photobiography*, UBS Publishers' Distributors, New Delhi/ Mumbai, 2005, p. 26.
52. Bal Keshav Thackeray, *Fatkare*, Prabodhan Prakashan, Mumbai, 2012.
53. Dinoo Randive, *Aatwani Maharashtra Janmachya* (Memories of the Birth of Maharashtra), Prabhat Prakashan, Bhayender, Thane, 2007, p. 113.
54. Dnyanesh Maharao, *Thackeray: Life and Style*, Pushpa Prakashan, Pune, 2001, pp. 62–63.

Chapter 2: Quest for a Marathi Identity

1. Lalji Pendse, *Maharashtrache Mahamanthan* (The Great Churn for Maharashtra), Lokvadmay Gruha, Mumbai, 2010, p. 70.
2. *Lokrajya*, Director General of Information and Public Relations (DGIPR), Government of Maharashtra, Mumbai, May 2019, p. 9.
3. Arun Sadhu, 'Samyukta Maharashtra: Swapnapurti ki Swapnabhanga?' (Samyukta Maharashtra: Dreams fulfilled or shattered?), *Badalta Maharashtra: Sathottar Parivartanacha Magova (Changing Maharashtra)*, (eds) Bhaskar Lakshman Bhole and Kishor Bedkihal, Dr Babasaheb Ambedkar Academy, Satara, 2003, p. 12.
4. Shankarrao Kharat, *Maharashtratil Maharancha Itihas*, The History of the Mahars of Maharashtra) (Dr Shakuntala Kharat, Pune, 2003, pp. 7–9.
5. 'Maharashtra: Land and Its People', Government of Maharashtra, Gazetteers Department, 2009, p. 15.
6. Dr Madhukar Keshav Dhavalikar, *Maharashtrachi Kulakatha* (The Saga of Maharashtra), Rajhans Prakashan, Pune, 2016, pp. 29–42, 60–61.
7. Dr Madhukar Keshav Dhavalikar, *Bharatachi Kulakatha* (The Saga of India), Rajhans Prakashan, Pune, 2018, p. 291.
8. Govind Pansare, *Shivaji Kon Hota*, Lokvadmay Gruha, Mumbai, December 2010.

9. Prabodhankar's speech at the Shiv Sena's first public meeting in October 1966. Quoted in *Prabodhankaranche Jwalanta Hindutva* (The Fiery Hindutva of Prabodhankar), Dnyanesh Maharao (ed), Navata Book World, Mumbai, 2011, p. 17.
10. The Committee Appointed by The All Parties' Conference 1928: The Nehru Report: An anti-separatist manifesto. Michiko and Panjathan, New Delhi, 1975 https://www.indiaofthepast.org/images/pdf/1920s/nehrureport1928part1.pdf
11. Ramachandra Guha, *India After Gandhi: The History of the World's Largest Democracy*, Picador, London, 2008, p. 180.
12. Ibid., p. 181.
13. Ibid.
14. Ibid., pp. 182–83.
15. Ibid., p. 183.
16. Ibid., pp. 183–84.
17. Ibid., pp. 185–89.
18. Ibid., p. 189.
19. Ibid.
20. Ibid.
21. Manohar Kadam, *Mumbaichya Ubharnit Telugu Samajache Yogdan* (The Contribution of the Telugu Community in Mumbai's History), Akshar Prakashan, Mumbai, 1999, p. 19.
22. Bapurao Naik (ed.), *Mumbaicha Vruttant: Balkrishna Bapu Acharya and Moro Vinayak Shingane* (A Report of Mumbai), Maharashtra Rajya Sahitya aani Sanskrutik Mandal, Mumbai, 2011, p. 23.
23. Manohar Kadam, *Mumbaichya Ubharnit Telugu Samajache Yogdan* (The Contribution of the Telugu Community in Mumbai's History), Akshar Prakashan, Mumbai, 1999, p. 17.
24. Ibid., p. 17.
25. *J.R.B. Jeejeebhoy's Bombay Vignettes: Explorations in the History of Bombay*, Murali Ranganathan (ed.), Asiatic Society of Mumbai, Mumbai, 2018, p. 350.
26. Ibid., p. 351.
27. Ibid., p. 358.
28. Manohar Kadam, *Mumbaichya Ubharnit Telugu Samajache Yogdan* (The Contribution of the Telugu Community in Mumbai's History), Akshar Prakashan, Mumbai, 1999, pp. 17–18.

29. Gyan Prakash, *Mumbai Fables*, HarperCollins Publishers India, Noida, 2011, p. 35.
30. Ibid., pp. 36–37.
31. Darryl D'Monte, *Ripping the Fabric: The Decline of Mumbai and Its Mills*, Oxford University Press, New Delhi, 2005, p. 72.
32. Ibid., pp. 73–74.
33. Shashi Bhushan Upadhyay, 'Cotton Mill Workers in Bombay, 1875 to 1918: Conditions of Work and Life', *EPW*, Mumbai, 28 July 1990.
34. Vaibhav Purandare, *Bal Thackeray and the Rise of the Shiv Sena*, Roli Books, New Delhi, 2012, p. 17.
35. Meera Kosambi, 'British Bombay and Marathi Mumbai: Some Nineteenth Century Perceptions', *Bombay: Mosaic of Modern Culture*, Sujata Patel and Alice Thorner (eds), Oxford University Press, New Delhi, 2007, pp. 7–8.
36. Ibid., p. 7.
37. Ramachandra Guha, *India After Gandhi: The History of the World's Largest Democracy*, Picador, London, 2008, p. 191.
38. Ibid., p. 192.
39. Ibid.
40. Ibid., pp. 192–93.
41. Manohar Kadam, *Mumbaichya Ubharnit Telugu Samajache Yogdan* (The Contribution of the Telugu Community in Mumbai's History), Akshar Prakashan, Mumbai, 1999, p. 109.
42. Ibid., pp. 109–10.
43. Dr Babasaheb Ambedkar, 'Maharashtra as a Linguistic Province', *Dr Babasaheb Ambedkar: Writings and Speeches*, Vol. I, Dr Babasaheb Ambedkar Source Material Publication Committee, Education Department, Government of Maharashtra, 2016, pp. 113–14.
44. Ibid., p. 119.
45. Ramachandra Guha, *India After Gandhi: The History of the World's Largest Democracy*, Picador an imprint of Pan Macmillan Ltd, London, 2008, p. 194.
46. Gyan Prakash, *Mumbai Fables*, HarperCollins Publishers India, Noida, 2011, pp. 222–23.
47. Lalji Pendse, *Maharashtrache Mahamanthan* (The Great Churn for Maharashtra), Lokvadmay Gruha, Mumbai, 2010, pp. 178–79.

48. Ibid., pp. 198–99.
49. Gyan Prakash, *Mumbai Fables*, HarperCollins Publishers India, Noida, 2011, pp. 224–25.
50. Neera Adarkar and Meena Menon, *Katha Mumbaichya Girangaonchi: Girni Kamgarancha Maukhik Itihas*, Mauj Prakashan, Mumbai, 2009, p. 156.
51. Gyan Prakash, *Mumbai Fables*, HarperCollins Publishers India, Noida, 2011, p. 225.
52. Neera Adarkar and Meena Menon, *Katha Mumbaichya Girangaonchi: Girni Kamgarancha Maukhik Itihas*, Mauj Prakashan, Mumbai, 2009, p. 162.
53. Lalji Pendse, *Maharashtrache Mahamanthan*, Lokvadmay Gruha, Mumbai, 2010, p. 362.
54. Sanjay Raut, *Ekavachani-II*, Mehta Publishing House, Pune, 2017, pp. 371–72.
55. Vaibhav Purandare, *Bal Thackeray and the Rise of the Shiv Sena*, Roli Books, New Delhi, 2012, p. 12.
56. Dinoo Randive, *Aatwani Maharashtra Janmachya* (Memories of the Birth of Maharashtra), Prabhat Prakashan, Bhayender, Thane, 2007, pp. 113–15, 167–68.
57. Ibid., pp. 114–15.
58. Ibid., p. 114.
59. Prakash Akolkar, *Jai Maharashtra: Ha Shiv Sena Navacha Itihas Aahe* (Jai Maharashtra: This Is History Called the Shiv Sena), Manovikas Prakashan, Pune, 2013, p. 41.
60. Gyan Prakash, *Mumbai Fables*, Harper Collins Publishers India, Noida, 2011, p. 225.
61. Prakash Akolkar, *Jai Maharashtra: Ha Shiv Sena Navacha Itihas Aahe* (Jai Maharashtra: This Is History Called the Shiv Sena), Manovikas Prakashan, Pune, 2013, p. 41.

Chapter 3: The Tiger Comes to Life

1. Sujata Patel and Alice Thorner (eds), *Bombay: Mosaic of Modern Culture*, Oxford University Press, New Delhi, 2007, p. 148.
2. Interview with author on 3 January 2019.
3. Dipankar Gupta, *Nativism in a Metropolis: The Shiv Sena in Bombay*, Manohar Publications, New Delhi, 1982, pp. 60–61.

4. Ibid., p. 61.
5. Neera Adarkar and Meena Menon, *Katha Mumbaichya Girangaonchi: Girni Kamgarancha Maukhik Itihas*, Mauj Prakashan, Mumbai, 2009, pp. 198–99.
6. Ibid., p. 202.
7. Ibid., p. 204.
8. Interview with author on 27 January 2019.
9. Interview with author on 27 January 2019.
10. Neera Adarkar and Meena Menon, *Katha Mumbaichya Girangaonchi: Girni Kamgarancha Maukhik Itihas*, Mauj Prakashan, Mumbai, 2009, pp. 214.
11. Vaibhav Purandare, *The Sena Story*, Business Publications Inc, Mumbai, 1999, p. 32.
12. Neera Adarkar and Meena Menon, *Katha Mumbaichya Girangaonchi: Girni Kamgarancha Maukhik Itihas*, Mauj Prakashan, Mumbai, 2009, p. 200.
13. Sudha Gogate, *The Emergence of Regionalism in Mumbai: History of the Shiv Sena*, Popular Prakashan Pvt Ltd, Mumbai, 2014, pp. iii, v.
14. Ibid., p. 1.
15. Ibid., pp. 1–2.
16. Ibid., p. 7.
17. Vaibhav Purandare, *The Sena Story*, Business Publications Inc, 1999, p. 33.
18. Mary Fainsod Katzenstein, *Ethnicity and Equality: The Shiv Sena Party and Preferential Policies in Bombay*, Cornell University Press, Ithaca and London, 1979, p. 48.
19. Ibid., p. 76.
20. Vaibhav Purandare, *The Sena Story*, Business Publications Inc, Mumbai, 1999, p. 33.
21. Mary Fainsod Katzenstein, *Ethnicity and Equality: The Shiv Sena Party and Preferential Policies in Bombay*, Cornell University Press, Ithaca and London, 1979, p. 66.
22. Ibid., p. 66–67.
23. Interview with author on 27 January 2019.
24. Mary Fainsod Katzenstein, *Ethnicity and Equality: The Shiv Sena Party and Preferential Policies in Bombay*, Cornell University Press, Ithaca and London, 1979, p. 69.

25. 'I Never Gave Speeches', *Mumbai Mirror*, 29 August 2009, https://mumbaimirror.indiatimes.com/mumbai/other/i-never-gave-speeches/articleshow/15950335.cms
26. Shrikant Thackeray, *Jasa Ghadla Tasa*, Chinar Publishers, Pune, 2002, p. 58.
27. Neera Adarkar and Meena Menon, *Katha Mumbaichya Girangaonchi: Girni Kamgarancha Maukhik Itihas*, Mauj Prakashan, Mumbai, 2009, p. 198.
28. Ibid., p. 198.
29. Interview with author on 4 January 2019.
30. Interview with author on 4 January 2019.
31. Vaibhav Purandare, *The Sena Story*, Business Publications Inc, Mumbai, 1999, p. 22.
32. Interview with author on 27 January 2019.
33. Manohar Joshi, *Shiv Sena: Kaal-Aaj-Udya*, Prabodhan Goregaon, Mumbai, 2008, pp. 4–5.
34. Interview with author on 27 January 2019.
35. Sudha Gogate, *The Emergence of Regionalism in Mumbai: History of the Shiv Sena*, Popular Prakashan Pvt Ltd, Mumbai, 2014, pp. 36–37.
36. V.S. Naipaul, *India: A Million Mutinies Now*, Picador an imprint of Pan Macmillan, London, 2010, p. 51.
37. Mary Fainsod Katzenstein, *Ethnicity and Equality: The Shiv Sena Party and Preferential Policies in Bombay*, Cornell University Press, Ithaca and London, 1979, p. 79.
38. Gyan Prakash, *Mumbai Fables*, HarperCollins Publishers India, Noida, 2011, p. 234.
39. Mary Fainsod Katzenstein, *Ethnicity and Equality: The Shiv Sena Party and Preferential Policies in Bombay*, Cornell University Press, Ithaca and London, 1979, pp. 79–80.
40. Manohar Joshi, *Shiv Sena: Kaal-Aaj-Udya*, Prabodhan Goregaon, Mumbai, 2008, p. 21.
41. Vaibhav Purandare, *The Sena Story*, Business Publications Inc, Mumbai, 1999, p. 36.
42. Sudha Gogate, *The Emergence of Regionalism in Mumbai: History of the Shiv Sena*, Popular Prakashan Pvt Ltd, Mumbai, 2014, pp. 34–35, 385.
43. Vaibhav Purandare, *The Sena Story*, Business Publications Inc, Mumbai, 1999, pp. 36–37.

44. Ibid., p. 37.
45. Ibid. p. 39.
46. Neera Adarkar and Meena Menon, *Katha Mumbaichya Girangaonchi: Girni Kamgarancha Maukhik Itihas*, Mauj Prakashan, Mumbai, 2009, p. 203.
47. Ibid., p. 255.
48. Vaibhav Purandare, *The Sena Story*, Business Publications Inc, Mumbai, 1999, p. 40.
49. Neera Adarkar and Meena Menon, *Katha Mumbaichya Girangaonchi: Girni Kamgarancha Maukhik Itihas*, Mauj Prakashan, Mumbai, 2009, pp. 214–15.
50. Vaibhav Purandare, *The Sena Story*, Business Publications Inc, Mumbai, 1999, pp. 40–41.
51. Prabodhankar Thackeray speech at the Shiv Sena's first public meeting, https://www.youtube.com/watch?v=pobBqr0E7tM&t=202s
52. Manohar Joshi, *Shiv Sena: Kaal-Aaj-Udya*, Prabodhan Goregaon, Mumbai, 2008, p. 22.
53. Ibid.
54. Kumar Ketkar, 'Bal Thackeray: A Legacy of Pride and Identity', *DNA*, 18 November 2012, https://www.dnaindia.com/mumbai/report-bal-thackeray-a-legacy-of-pride-and-identity-1765933

Chapter 4: Raj and Uddhav: The Early Years

1. Interview with a college friend of Raj Thackeray in November 2018. A family friend also recalled this anecdote during an interview in December 2018 and in multiple conversations later.
2. Interview with Sanjeevani Karandikar in March 2019 and on 28 June 2019.
3. Dnyanesh Maharao, *Thackeray: Life and Style*, Pushpa Prakashan, Pune, 2001, pp. 72–73; Shrikant Thackeray, *Jasa Ghadla Tasa*, Chinar Publishers, Pune, 2002, p. 66.
4. Shrikant Thackeray, *Jasa Ghadla Tasa*, Chinar Publishers, Pune, 2002, p. 57.
5. Raj Thackeray, *Bal Keshav Thackeray: A Photobiography*, UBS Publishers' Distributors Pvt Ltd, New Delhi/ Mumbai, 2005, p. 146.

6. '. . . And Balasaheb re-christened Raj', *Lokmat*, 23 January 2019, http://www.lokmat.com/maharashtra/balasaheb-thackeray-changed-my-name-swararaj-thackeray-says-mns-chief-raj-thackeray/
7. Interview with family friend in December 2018 and with a college friend of Raj Thackeray in November 2018.
8. Shrikant Thackeray, *Jasa Ghadla Tasa*, Chinar Publishers, Pune, 2002, p. 114; Dnyanesh Maharao, *Thackeray Family: Life and Style*, Pushpa Prakashan, Pune, 2001, p. 73.
9. Dnyanesh Maharao, *Thackeray: Life and Style*, Pushpa Prakashan, Pune, 2001, p. 81.
10. Shrikant Thackeray, *Jasa Ghadla Tasa*, Chinar Publishers, Pune, 2002, pp. 13–14.
11. Ibid., pp. 14–15.
12. Ibid., pp. 17–18; Dnyanesh Maharao, *Thackeray: Life and Style*, Pushpa Prakashan, Pune, 2001, p. 52.
13. Yogendra Thakur, *Shiv Sena: Samaj Gairsamaj*, Gaurav Thakur, Aamod Prakashan, Mumbai, April 2012, p. 358.
14. Shrikant Thackeray, *Jasa Ghadla Tasa*, Chinar Publishers, Pune, 2002, p. 26.
15. Dnyanesh Maharao, *Thackeray: Life and Style*, Pushpa Prakashan, Pune, 2001, p. 69.
16. 'Raj ki Baat', Zee Marathi, Diwali issue, 2018.
17. Ibid.
18. Raj Thackeray, *Bal Keshav Thackeray: A Photobiography*, UBS Publishers' Distributors Pvt Ltd, New Delhi, 2005, p. 390.
19. Author's interview on 19 April 2019 with senior journalist who has covered the Shiv Sena for over three decades.
20. Interview with author on 18 April 2019.
21. Interview with author on 18 April 2019.
22. Uttara Kelkar, 'Shrikantji ek manasvi kalawanta (Shrikantji, an intense artiste)', *Loksatta*, 14 June 2016, https://www.loksatta.com/uttarrang-news/uttara-kelkar-sharing-his-experiences-with-her-guru-shrikant-thackeray-1251292/
23. Interview with author on 23 March 2019.
24. Raj Thackeray, *Bal Keshav Thackeray: A Photobiography*, UBS Publishers' Distributors Pvt Ltd, New Delhi, 2005, p. 390.

25. Ibid.
26. Interview with author in December 2018.
27. Dilip Thakur, 'Shrikant Thackeray: An Independent University', *Lokprabha,* 4 January 2017, https://www.marathisrushti.com/articles/shrikant-thakarey-an-university/
28. Ibid.
29. Interview with a college friend of Raj Thackeray in November 2018.
30. Shrikant Thackeray, *Jasa Ghadla Tasa,* Chinar Publishers, Pune, 2002, p. 115.
31. Dilip Thakur's interview with author on 17 December 2018.
32. Bal Thackeray, *Gajaadil Diwas*, Parchure Prakashan Mandir, Mumbai, 2009, p. 103.
33. Dnyanesh Maharao, *Thackeray: Life and Style*, Pushpa Prakashan, Pune, 2001, p. 72.
34. Ibid., p. 75.
35. Ibid., pp. 73–74.
36. '*Lahanpani shalet na janyasathi Uddhav Thackeray hi shakkal ladhwayche* (Uddhav Thackeray used this trick to miss school)', *Loksatta*, 18 January 2019, https://www.loksatta.com/maharashtra-news/uddhav-thackeray-talks-about-childhood-memories-with-balasaheb-in-manacha-mujara-of-colors-marathi-1825411/
37. Dnyanesh Maharao, *Thackeray: Life and Style*, Pushpa Prakashan, Pune, 2001, p. 74.
38. 'Jaidev Thackeray Withdraws Case Challenging Father Bal Thackeray's Will', PTI, 2 November 2018, https://www.ndtv.com/india-news/jaidev-thackeray-withdraws-case-challenging-father-bal-thackerays-will-1941907
39. Dnyanesh Maharao, *Thackeray: Life and Style*, Pushpa Prakashan, Pune, 2001, pp. 83, 85.
40. Interview with author on 28 December 2018.
41. Interview with author on 22 March 2019.
42. Interview with author on 22 March 2019.
43. '*Aamcha Dingudada* (Our Dingudada)', Kirti Pathak, as told to Rupali Waghmare, *Runanubandha* Diwali Issue 2016, and interviews with author on 22 and 23 March 2019.
44. Interview with author in March 2019.
45. Interview with author on 22 May 2019.

46. Interview with author on 20 May 2019.
47. Interviews with author on 14 April and 4 May 2019.
48. Interview with author on 27 January 2019.
49. 'Raj ki baat', Zee Marathi, Diwali issue, 2018.
50. Dnyanesh Maharao, *Thackeray: Life and Style*, Pushpa Prakashan, Pune, 2001, pp. 82–83.
51. Ibid.
52. Ibid., p. 75.
53. Ibid., p. 83.
54. Unmesh Gujarathi (ed.), *Hinduhriday Samrat*, Navchaitanya Prakashan, Mumbai, 2012, pp. 19–20.
55. Bal Thackeray's interview with Nikhil Wagle, IBN Lokmat, 14 February 2012, https://www.youtube.com/watch?v=72wJ5e8i0mo, accessed in December 2018.
56. Interview with one of Raj's old-time friends in December 2018.
57. Interview with author on 10 March 2019.
58. Interview with author on 22 March 2019.
59. Interview with author on 13 March 2019.
60. Interviews with Kirti Pathak on 22 March 2019, Sanjeevani Karandikar on 23 March 2019 and one of Raj's old-time friends in December 2018.
61. Interview with author on 16 April 2019.
62. Dilip Thakur, 'Shrikant Thackeray: An Independent University', *Lokprabha*, 4 January 2017, https://www.marathisrushti.com/articles/shrikant-thakarey-an-university/.
63. Interview with author on 22 March 2019.
64. Dnyanesh Maharao, *Thackeray: Life and Style*, Pushpa Prakashan, Pune, 2001, p. 86.
65. Interview with author on 23 April 2019.
66. Interview with author on 23 April 2019.
67. Interview with author on 23 April 2019.
68. Musab Qazi, '64 stab wounds, fingers chopped off: The murder that spurred Maharashtra to end campus polls', *Hindustan Times*, 31 October 2018, https://www.hindustantimes.com/mumbai-news/64-stab-wounds-fingers-chopped-off-the-murder-that-spurred-maharashtra-to-end-campus-polls/story-eLqcdtFZxeHKeSzQ4KrtsN.html
69. Interview with author on 18 January 2019.

70. Interview with author on 23 March 2019.
71. Interview with author on 23 March 2019.
72. Interview with author on 20 October 2018.
73. Interview with author on 20 October 2018.
74. Interview with author in December 2018.
75. Interview with author in December 2018.
76. Dnyanesh Maharao, *Thackeray: Life and Style*, Pushpa Prakashan, Pune, 2001, p. 87.
77. Author's interview with one of Raj's friends on 4 May 2019.
78. Interview with author on 14 January 2019.
79. Dnyanesh Maharao, *Thackeray: Life and Style*, Pushpa Prakashan, Pune, 2001, p. 88.
80. Interview with author on 18 April 2019.
81. Interview with author on 4 January 2019.
82. Interview with author on 4 January 2019.
83. Interview with author on 19 April 2019.
84. Interview with author on 4 January 2019.
85. Interview with author on 6 December 2018. This was corroborated by one of his former business associates and friends in an interview on 8 January 2019 and by another friend on 4 May 2019.
86. Interview with author on 6 December 2018.
87. Dnyanesh Maharao, *Thackeray: Life and Style*, Pushpa Prakashan, Pune, 2001, p. 89.
88. Interview with author on 6 December 2018.
89. Interview with author on 10 March 2019.
90. Interview with author in December 2018 and January 2019.
91. Interview with author on 19 April 2019.
92. Interview with a former Shiv Sena leader on 21 December 2019.
93. Manohar Joshi, *Shiv Sena: Kaal-Aaj-Udya*, Prabodhan Goregaon, Mumbai, 2008, pp. 489–90.
94. Sanjay Raut, *Ekavachani*, Part I, Mehta Publishing House, Pune, 2017, p. 33.
95. Dnyanesh Maharao, *Thackeray: Life and Style*, Pushpa Prakashan, Pune, 2001, pp. 104–05.
96. Sanjay Raut, *Ekavachani*, Part I, Mehta Publishing House, Pune, 2017, p. 66.
97. Manohar Joshi, *Shiv Sena: Kaal-Aaj-Udya*, Prabodhan Goregaon, Mumbai, 2008, pp. 347–48.

98. Ibid., p. 362.
99. Vaibhav Purandare, *The Sena Story*, Business Publications Inc, Mumbai, 1999, p. 256.
100. Ibid., p. 257.
101. Manohar Joshi, *Shiv Sena: Kaal-Aaj-Udya*, Prabodhan Goregaon, Mumbai, 2008, p. 362.
102. Ibid.
103. Dnyanesh Maharao, *Thackeray: Life and Style*, Pushpa Prakashan, Pune, 2001, pp. 75–76; Author's interview with a Raj Thackeray associate on 6 December 2018.
104. Manohar Joshi, *Shiv Sena: Kaal-Aaj-Udya*, Prabodhan Goregaon, Mumbai, 2008, p. 363.
105. Interview with author on 3 May 2019; G.R. Khairnar, *Ekaki Zhunja: Go Ra Khairnar Hyanche Atmacharitra* (A Lonely Fight: An Autobiography of G.R. Khairnar), Pushpa Prakashan Limited, Pune, August 1999, pp. 102–10.
106. Pinky Virani, *Once Was Bombay*, Penguin Books, Gurgaon, 2001, pp. 124–25.
107. Interview with author on 27 January 2019.
108. Shrikant Thackeray, *Jasa Ghadla Tasa*, Chinar Publishers, Pune, 2002, p. 86.
109. Suhas Palshikar, *Jaat va Maharashtratil Sattakaran* (Caste and Power Politics in Maharashtra), Sugava Prakashan, Pune, 2003, p. 13.
110. Author's interview with former Raj Thackeray associate in December 2018.
111. Manohar Joshi, *Shiv Sena: Kaal-Aaj-Udya*, Prabodhan Goregaon, Mumbai, 2008, p. 435.
112. Sanjay Raut, *Ekavachani*, Part II, Mehta Publishing House, Pune, 2017, p. 28.
113. Vaibhav Purandare, *The Sena Story*, Business Publications Inc, Mumbai, 1999, p. 348.
114. Ibid., pp. 348–49.
115. Pinky Virani, *Once Was Bombay* (Penguin Books, Gurgaon, 2001), p. 129.
116. Conversation with author in November 2012.
117. Interview with author on 25 January 2019.
118. Manohar Joshi, *Shiv Sena: Kaal-Aaj-Udya*, Prabodhan Goregaon, Mumbai, 2008, pp. 485–86.

119. Ibid., pp. 486–87.
120. Vaibhav Purandare, *Bal Thackeray and the Rise of the Shiv Sena*, Roli Books, New Delhi, 2012, p. 189.
121. Manohar Joshi, *Shiv Sena: Kaal-Aaj-Udya*, Prabodhan Goregaon, Mumbai, 2008, p. 487.
122. Prakash Akolkar, *Jai Maharashtra: Ha Shiv Sena Navacha Itihas Aahe* (Jai Maharashtra: This Is History Called the Shiv Sena), Prabhat Prakashan, Mumbai, 1998, p. 229.
123. Vaibhav Purandare, *The Sena Story*, Business Publications Inc, Mumbai, 1999, pp. 356–57.
124. Manohar Joshi, *Shiv Sena: Kaal-Aaj-Udya*, Prabodhan Goregaon, Mumbai, 2008, p. 487.
125. Ibid., p. 488.
126. Ibid., pp. 488–92.
127. Vaibhav Purandare, *The Sena Story*, Business Publications Inc, Mumbai, 1999, p. 358; Prakash Akolkar, *Jai Maharashtra: Ha Shiv Sena Navacha Itihas Aahe* (Jai Maharashtra: This Is History Called the Shiv Sena), Manovikas Prakashan, Pune, 2013, pp. 346–47.
128. Prakash Akolkar, *Jai Maharashtra: Ha Shiv Sena Navacha Itihas Aahe*, Jai Maharashtra: This is History Called the Shiv Sena), Manovikas Prakashan, Pune, 2013, p. 347.
129. Manohar Joshi, *Shiv Sena: Kaal-Aaj-Udya*, Prabodhan Goregaon, Mumbai, 2008, p. 493.
130. Interview with author in December 2018.
131. Interview with Shishir Shinde on 8 February 2019.
132. Interview with author on 21 January 2019.
133. Interview with author on 21 January 2019.
134. Interview with author on 4 January 2019.
135. Interview with author on 4 May 2019.
136. Interview with author on 6 May 2019.
137. Interview with author on 6 May 2019.
138. Manoj Awale, *Marathi Manacha Raja*, S.M. Awale, Pune, 2014, p. 13.
139. Manohar Joshi, *Shiv Sena: Kaal-Aaj-Udya*, Prabodhan Goregaon, Mumbai, 2008, p. 547.
140. Interview with author on 16 January 2019.
141. Interview with author on 3 January 2019.

142. Interview with author on 4 May 2019.
143. Interview with author on 4 January 2019.
144. Interview with author on 4 January 2019.
145. Interview with author on 3 January 2019.
146. Interview with author on 8 January 2019.
147. Interview with Raj Thackeray's former business associate on 25 June 2019.
148. Website of Matoshree Infrastructure Pvt. Ltd, http://www.matoshreeinfra.com/group.php
149. Interview with author in December 2018.
150. Interview with author on 8 January 2019.
151. Manohar Joshi, *Shiv Sena: Kaal-Aaj-Udya*, Prabodhan Goregaon, Mumbai, 2008, p. 586.
152. Interview with author in December 2018.
153. Interview with author in December 2018.
154. Interview with author on 21 December 2018.
155. Manohar Joshi, *Shiv Sena: Kaal-Aaj-Udya*, Prabodhan Goregaon, Mumbai, 2008, p. 541.
156. Prakash Akolkar, Jai Maharashtra: *Ha Shiv Sena Navacha Itihas Aahe (Jai Maharashtra: This is History called the Shiv Sena)*, Manovikas Prakashan, Pune, 2013, pp. 156–60.
157. Interview with author on 21 January 2019.
158. Lekha Rattanani, 'The Tiger Cub', *Outlook*, 13 March 1996, https://www.outlookindia.com/magazine/story/the-tiger-cub/200994
159. Ibid.

Chapter 5: Cracks in the Edifice

1. Interview with author on 27 January 2019.
2. Interview with author on 27 January 2019.
3. Manohar Joshi, *Shiv Sena: Kaal-Aaj-Udya*, Prabodhan Goregaon, Mumbai, 2008), p. 621; Vaibhav Purandare, *The Sena Story*, Business Publications Inc, Mumbai, 1999, p. 417; *Sheela Ramesh Kini And Anr vs Union of India (Uoi) And Ors.*, on 20 September 1996: Criminal Writ Petition No. 853 with Cri.W.P. No. 854 of 1996, https://indiankanoon.org/doc/1670444/ and https://www.legalcrystal.com/case/354421/sheela-ramesh-kini-vs-union-india

4. Neeta Kolhatkar, 'Sheela Kini: A Forgotten Voice of Mumbai', 4 February 2014, https://www.rediff.com/news/column/sheela-kini-a-forgotten-voice-of-mumbai/20140206.htm
5. Interview with author on 27 January 2019.
6. *Sheela Ramesh Kini And Anr vs Union of India (Uoi) And Ors.*, on 20 September 1996: Criminal Writ Petition No. 853 with Cri.W.P. No. 854 of 1996, https://indiankanoon.org/doc/1670444/) and, https://www.legalcrystal.com/case/354421/sheela-ramesh-kini-vs-union-india
7. Manohar Joshi, *Shiv Sena: Kaal-Aaj-Udya*, Prabodhan Goregaon, Mumbai, 2008), p. 621.
8. *Sheela Ramesh Kini And Anr vs Union of India (Uoi) And Ors.*, on 20 September 1996: Criminal Writ Petition No. 853 with Cri.W.P. No. 854 of 1996, https://indiankanoon.org/doc/1670444/) and, https://www.legalcrystal.com/case/354421/sheela-ramesh-kini-vs-union-india.
9. Ibid.
10. Yogesh Naik and Pandurang Mhaske, 'Matunga building, Raj's' 90s political nightmare, razed', *Mumbai Mirror*, https://mumbaimirror.indiatimes.com/mumbai/cover-story/matunga-building-rajs-90s-political-nightmare-razed/articleshow/29172482.cms
11. Vaibhav Purandare, *The Sena Story*, Business Publications Inc, Mumbai, 1999, pp. 140–41, 145.
12. Ibid., *p.* 147.
13. Dipankar Gupta, *Nativism in a Metropolis: The Shiv Sena in Bombay*, Manohar Publications, New Delhi, 1982, p. 159.
14. Gyan Prakash, *Mumbai Fables*, HarperCollins Publishers India, Noida, 2011, p. 242.
15. Dipankar Gupta, *Nativism in a Metropolis: The Shiv Sena in Bombay*, Manohar Publications, New Delhi, 1982, pp. 82–83.
16. Prakash Akolkar, Jai Maharashtra: Ha Shiv Sena Navacha Itihas Aahe *(Jai Maharashtra: This is History Called the Shiv Sena)*, Manovikas Prakashan, Pune, 2013, p. 168.
17. Ibid., pp. 106–07; *State of Maharashtra Vs. Anand Chintaman Dighe*, 2 May 1991: Supreme Court of India, Criminal Appeal no. 336 of 1991, Ranganath Misra, CJ, Kuldip Singh, and P.B Sawant, JJ, https://indiankanoon.org/doc/1069704/, https://

www.legalcrystal.com/case/655724/state-maharashtra-vs-anand-chintaman-dighe
18. Prakash Akolkar, *Jai Maharashtra: Ha Shiv Sena Navacha Itihas Aahe*, Manovikas Prakashan, Pune, 2013, p. 107.
19. Praveen Swami, '"The General" in His Labyrinth', *Frontline*, 29 August 29 to 11 September 1998, https://frontline.thehindu.com/static/html/fl1518/15180200.htm
20. Sanjay Jog, 'Nilesh Rane levels serious charges against Bal Thackeray', *DNA*, 16 January 2019, https://www.dnaindia.com/india/report-nilesh-rane-levels-serious-charges-against-bal-thackeray-2708431
21. 'I believe in some Gandhian principles. Violence and non-violence have their own place in society. It all depends on the situation': The Rediff Interview, Arun Gawli: Syed Firdaus Ashraf, https://m.rediff.com/news/aug/13gawli.htm
22. Manohar Joshi, *Shiv Sena: Kaal-Aaj-Udya*, Prabodhan Goregaon, Mumbai, 2008, p. 621.
23. Ibid.
24. Pritish Nandy, 'When people are lined up and killed in Bihar, V.P. Singh does not go there but he comes here to meet Sheila Kini!', Rediff.com, http://m.rediff.com/news/sep/05nandy.htm
25. Vaibhav Purandare, *The Sena Story*, Business Publications Inc, Mumbai, 1999, p. 418.
26. https://indiankanoon.org/doc/1670444/
27. Interview with author on 22 March 2019.
28. Vaibhav Purandare, *The Sena Story*, Business Publications Inc, Mumbai, 1999, p. 418.
29. Manohar Joshi, *Shiv Sena: Kaal-Aaj-Udya*, Prabodhan Goregaon, Mumbai, 2008, p. 622.
30. Interview with author on 15 January 2019.
31. Interview with author on 14 January 2019; Saira Menezes, 'Kapil Patil: A defiant editor takes on the mighty Sena by launching his daily *Saanj Dinank*', *Outlook*, 20 November 1996, https://www.outlookindia.com/magazine/story/kapil-patil/202567
32. Interview with author on 14 January 2019; Saira Menezes, 'Kapil Patil: A defiant editor takes on the mighty Sena by launching his daily *Saanj Dinank*', *Outlook*, 20 November 1996, https://www.outlookindia.com/magazine/story/kapil-patil/202567

33. Vaibhav Purandare, *The Sena Story*, Business Publications Inc, Mumbai, 1999, p. 417.
34. Ibid., pp. 417–18.
35. Interview with author on 6 December 2018.
36. Manohar Joshi, *Shiv Sena: Kaal-Aaj-Udya*, Prabodhan Goregaon, Mumbai, 2008, p. 621–22.
37. Ibid., p. 622.
38. Interview with author on 4 January 2019.
39. Manohar Joshi, *Shiv Sena: Kaal-Aaj-Udya*, Prabodhan Goregaon, Mumbai, 2008, p. 622.
40. Sanjay Raut, *Ekavachani*, Part I, Mehta Publishing House, Pune, 2017, pp. 140, 163.
41. Ibid., p. 142.
42. Ibid., p. 143.
43. Manohar Joshi, *Shiv Sena: Kaal-Aaj-Udya*, Prabodhan Goregaon, Mumbai, 2008, p. 622.
44. Vaibhav Purandare, *The Sena Story*, Business Publications Inc, Mumbai, 1999, p. 418; Yogesh Naik and Pandurang Mhaske, 'Matunga building, Raj's '90s political nightmare, razed', *Mumbai Mirror*, 22 January 2014, https://mumbaimirror.indiatimes.com/mumbai/cover-story/matunga-building-rajs-90s-politicalnightmare-razed/articleshow/29172482.cms; Case no. 1194 of 1997 in the court of Additional Sessions Judge S.P. Nikam.
45. Interview with author on 15 January 2019.
46. Sujata Anandan, 'The wise man this Christmas', *Hindustan Times*, 24 December 2013, https://www.hindustantimes.com/columns/thewise-man-this-christmas/story-mC9InE3ecKAJagRRa1QDdK.html
47. Ibid.
48. Interview with author on 25 January 2019.
49. Sanjay Raut, *Ekavachani*, Part I, Mehta Publishing House, Pune, 2017, pp. 196–97.
50. 'Uddhav launches fresh offensive against Raj', *Mumbai Mirror*, 24 May 2009, https://mumbaimirror.indiatimes.com/mumbai/other/uddhav-launches-fresh-offensive-against-raj/articleshow/15926505.cms
51. 'Bhujbal rakes up Kini murder case in a bid to corner Raj', *Indian Express*, https://indianexpress.com/article/cities/mumbai/bhujbalrakes-up-kini-murder-case-in-a-bid-to-corner-raj/

52. Interviews with multiple people for the book between November 2018 and May 2019.
53. Interview with author on 27 March 2019.
54. Naresh Kamath, 'Raj's firm will redevelop bldg where Kini lived', https://www.hindustantimes.com/mumbai/raj-s-firm-will-redevelop-bldg-where-kini-lived/story-wXXBRL1KfoMvUf0xhZV9ZJ.html
55. Yogesh Naik and Pandurang Mhaske, 'Matunga building, Raj's '90s political nightmare, razed', *Mumbai Mirror*, https://mumbaimirror.indiatimes.com/mumbai/cover-story/matunga-building-rajs-90spolitical-nightmare-razed/articleshow/29172482.cms
56. Manohar Joshi, *Shiv Sena: Kaal-Aaj-Udya*, Prabodhan Goregaon, Mumbai, 2008, pp. 599–600.
57. Interview with author on 8 January 2019.
58. Interview with author in November 2018.
59. Interview with author on 28 December 2018.
60. Interview with author on 28 December 2018.
61. Interview with author on 7 January 2019.
62. Interview with author on 21 December 2018.
63. Interview with author on 19 December 2018 and 7 January 2019.
64. Interview with author on 28 December 2018.
65. Interview with author on 28 December 2018.
66. Interview with author on 7 January 2019.
67. Multiple interviews with former BVS leaders and former MNS MLAs.
68. Interview with author in December 2018.
69. Interview with author on 7 January 2019.
70. Interview with author on 18 January 2019.
71. Interview with author on 3 January 2019.
72. Interview with author on 4 January 2019.
73. Manohar Joshi, *Shiv Sena: Kaal-Aaj-Udya*, Prabodhan Goregaon, Mumbai, 2008, p. 625.
74. Interview with author on 4 January 2019.
75. Manohar Joshi, *Shiv Sena: Kaal-Aaj-Udya*, Prabodhan Goregaon, Mumbai, 2008, p. 644.
76. V. Shankar Aiyar, 'Raj Thackeray refuses to be shaken by controversies he has stirred', *India Today*, 15 May 1997, https://www.indiatoday.in/magazine/profile/story/19970430-

raj-thackeray-refuses-to-be-shaken-by-controversies-he-has-stirred-831313-1997-05-15

77. Manohar Joshi, *Shiv Sena: Kaal-Aaj-Udya*, Prabodhan Goregaon, Mumbai, 2008, p. 645.
78. Raj Thackeray, 'I was Jacko's fan', https://timesofindia.indiatimes.com/entertainment/hindi/bollywood/news/I-was-Jackos-fan-Raj-Thackeray/articleshow/4709158.cms
79. Shekhar Gupta, 'I asked Balasaheb Thackeray, "Are you a mafioso?"—and lived to tell the tale', *The Print*, https://theprint.in/opinion/i-asked-balasaheb-thackeray-are-you-a-mafioso-and-lived/31131/
80. Vaibhav Purandare, *Bal Thackeray and the Rise of the Shiv Sena*, Roli Books, New Delhi, 2012, pp. 230–31.
81. Raj Thackeray, 'I was Jacko's fan', https://timesofindia.indiatimes.com/entertainment/hindi/bollywood/news/I-was-Jackos-fan-Raj-Thackeray/articleshow/4709158.cms
82. Vaibhav Purandare, *Bal Thackeray and the Rise of the Shiv Sena*, Roli Books, New Delhi, 2012, p. 231.
83. Julia M. Eckert, *The Charisma of Direct Action: Power, Politics and the Shiv Sena*, Oxford University Press, New Delhi, 2003, p. 20–21.
84. Vaibhav Purandare, *Bal Thackeray and the Rise of the Shiv Sena*, Roli Books, New Delhi, 2012, p. 231.
85. Sanjay Raut, *Ekavachani*, Part I, Mehta Publishing House, Pune, 2017, pp. 217, 260.
86. Vaibhav Purandare, *The Sena Story*, Business Publications Inc, Mumbai, 1999, p. 423.
87. Manohar Joshi, *Shiv Sena: Kaal-Aaj-Udya*, Prabodhan Goregaon, Mumbai, 2008, p. 630.
88. Interview with author on 30 January 2018.
89. Interview with author on 28 December 2018.
90. Interview with author on 28 December 2018.
91. Interview with author on 28 December 2018.
92. 'Thackeray had tumultuous "bond" with estranged son Jaidev', TNN, https://timesofindia.indiatimes.com/india/Thackeray-had-tumultuous-bond-with-estranged-son-Jaidev/articleshow/29131050.cms.
93. Ibid.
94. Ibid.

95. Ibid.
96. Multiple interviews with author between December 2018 and February 2019.
97. Nauzer Bharucha, 'Raj Thackeray's firm made Rs 300 cr by selling stake in mill', TNN, 15 November 2009, https://economictimes.indiatimes.com/news/politics-and-nation/raj-thackerays-firm-made-rs-300-cr-by-selling-stake-in-mill/articleshow/5231751.cms
98. Makarand Gadgil, 'Ex-CM's son loses Dadar twin towers after defaulting on loans worth Rs 900 crore', *Mumbai Mirror*, 5 January 2019, https://mumbaimirror.indiatimes.com/mumbai/cover-story/ex-cms-son-loses-dadar-twin-towers-after-defaulting-on-loans-worth-900-cr/articleshow/67390441.cms
99. 'From receptionist to powerful socialite, Smita Thackeray has come a long way', *India Today*, https://www.indiatoday.in/magazine/profile/story/19990712-from-receptionist-to-powerful-socialite-smita-thackeray-has-come-a-long-way-824557-1999-11-30
100. Vaibhav Purandare, *The Sena Story*, Business Publications Inc, Mumbai, 1999, pp. 409–12.
101. Ibid., p. 420.
102. Narayan Rane with Priyam Gandhi-Mody, *No Holds Barred: My Years in Politics*, HarperCollins Publishers India, Noida, 2019, pp. 27–28.
103. Interview with author on 21 December 2018.
104. 'Supreme Court indicts Manohar Joshi over land misuse case', https://www.ndtv.com/india-news/supreme-court-indicts-manohar-joshi-over-land-misuse-case-565500; *Manohar Joshi vs State of Maharashtra and others*, Civil appeals nos 2102- 103 with nos 2120, 198–99, 2450, 2105–106 and 196–97 of 2000: Supreme Court, R.V. Raveendran and H.L Gokhale, JJ.
105. Vaibhav Purandare, *The Sena Story*, Business Publications Inc, Mumbai, 1999, pp. 421–22, 427–30.
106. Author's interview with former Shiv Sena leader on 21 December 2018.
107. Julia M. Eckert, *The Charisma of Direct Action: Power, Politics and the Shiv Sena*, Oxford University Press, New Delhi, 2003, p. 21.
108. Multiple interviews with author during reporting career.
109. Interview with author on 21 December 2018.
110. Vaibhav Purandare, *The Sena Story*, Business Publications Inc, Mumbai, 1999, p. 414.

111. Interview with author on 21 December 2018.
112. Interview with author on 14 April 2019.
113. Interview with author on 21 December 2018.
114. Interview with author on 25 January 2019.
115. Manohar Joshi, *Shiv Sena: Kaal-Aaj-Udya*, Prabodhan Goregaon, Mumbai, 2008, p. 638; Author's interview with former Sena leader on 21 December 2018.
116. Interview with author on 4 January 2019.
117. Narayan Rane with Priyam Gandhi-Mody, *No Holds Barred: My Years in Politics*, HarperCollins Publishers India, Noida, 2019, p. 53.
118. Manohar Joshi, *Shiv Sena: Kaal-Aaj-Udya*, Prabodhan Goregaon, Mumbai, 2008, p. 638.
119. Narayan Rane with Priyam Gandhi-Mody, *No Holds Barred: My Years in Politics*, HarperCollins Publishers India, Noida, 2019, pp. 54–55.
120. Interview with author on 21 December 2018.
121. Narayan Rane with Priyam Gandhi-Mody, *No Holds Barred: My Years in Politics*, HarperCollins Publishers India, Noida, 2019, pp. 55–56.
122. P.C. Alexander, *Through the Corridors of Power: An Insider's Story*, HarperCollins Publishers India, New Delhi, 2004, p. 452.
123. *Ibid.*, pp. 452–53.
124. 'I don't believe in alliance politics, says Raj Thackeray', *Loksatta*, 10 October 2014, https://www.youtube.com/watch?v=EXn87f1VHso&ts=82s, accessed on 13 February 2019.
125. Multiple interviews with Shiv Sena and MNS leaders between January and March 2019.
126. Manohar Joshi, *Shiv Sena: Kaal-Aaj-Udya*, Prabodhan Goregaon, Mumbai, 2008, p. 638.
127. Ibid.
128. Interview with author on 19 November 2016.
129. Interview with former BVS leader on 7 January 2019.
130. 'Mob torches former CM's home', Our Correspondent, *The Telegraph*, 23 November 2002, https://www.telegraphindia.com/india/mob-torches-former-cm-s-home/cid/855638
131. Prakash Akolkar, *Jai Maharashtra: Ha Shiv Sena Navacha Itihas Aahe*, Manovikas Prakashan, Pune, 2013, p. 330.

132. Interview with author on 15 January 2019.
133. Kiran Tare, 'Farmers' Leader Comes Under Scanner for Massive Wealth', *Sunday Standard*, 15 November 2015, http://www.newindianexpress.com/thesundaystandard/2015/nov/15/Farmers-Leader-Comes-Under-Scanner-for-Massive-Wealth-843256.html
134. 'PWP a party of goondas: Tatkare', TNN, 27 March 2002, https://timesofindia.indiatimes.com/city/mumbai/PWP-a-party-of-goondas-Tatkare/articleshow/5004010.cms
135. Sheela Raval, 'Maharashtra: Cong-NCP tries hard to stem tide of defections, Sena-BJP eyes power', *India Today*, 17 June 2002, https://www.indiatoday.in/magazine/states/story/20020617-maharashtra-cong-ncp-tries-hard-to-stem-tide-of-defections-sena-bjp-eyes-power-795096-2002-06-17
136. Ibid.
137. Ibid.; Narayan Rane with Priyam Gandhi-Mody, *No Holds Barred: My Years in Politics*, HarperCollins Publishers India, Noida, 2019, p. 66.
138. Manohar Joshi, *Shiv Sena: Kaal-Aaj-Udya*, *Prabodhan Goregaon*, Mumbai, 2008, p. 707.
139. Interview with author on 28 January 2019.
140. Interview with author on 28 January 2019.
141. Interview with author on 27 January 2019.
142. Interview with author on 29 December 2018.
143. Sheela Raval, 'Maharashtra: Cong-NCP tries hard to stem tide of defections, Sena-BJP eyes power', *India Today*, 17 June 2002, https://www.indiatoday.in/magazine/states/story/20020617-maharashtra-cong-ncp-tries-hard-to-stem-tide-of-defections-sena-bjp-eyes-power-795096-2002-06-17); Manohar Joshi, *Shiv Sena: Kaal-Aaj-Udya* (*Prabodhan Goregaon*, Mumbai, 2008, p. 707.
144. Narayan Rane with Priyam Gandhi-Mody, *No Holds Barred: My Years in Politics*, HarperCollins Publishers India, Noida, 2019, p. 66.
145. Ibid.
146. 'I was detained by Sena: Valvi', TNN, 12 June 2002, https://timesofindia.indiatimes.com/city/mumbai/I-was-detained-by-Sena-Valvi/articleshow/12799609.cms
147. Interview with author on 29 December 2018.

148. Narayan Rane with Priyam Gandhi-Mody, *No Holds Barred: My Years in Politics*, HarperCollins Publishers India, Noida, 2019, p. 67.
149. 'Deshmukh bid to woo back PWP', Mumbai Bureau, *The Hindu*, 6 June 2002, https://www.thehindu.com/2002/06/06/stories/2002060602851200.htm.
150. Manohar Joshi, *Shiv Sena: Kaal-Aaj-Udya*, Prabodhan Goregaon, Mumbai, 2008, p. 708.
151. Ibid.
152. Interview with author on 21 December 2018.
153. Narayan Rane with Priyam Gandhi-Mody, *No Holds Barred: My Years in Politics*, HarperCollins Publishers India, Noida, 2019, p. 68.
154. Ibid., p. 70–71.
155. Author's interview with a senior Shiv Sena leader on 27 March 2019.
156. 'Raj Thackeray proposes Uddhav's name as working president', IBN Lokmat, 31 January 2015, https://www.youtube.com/watch?v=YDPB9FMr52w&t=10s, accessed on 13 February 2019.
157. 'Bal Thackeray says Raj appointed Uddhav as the working president sans his knowledge', IBN Lokmat, 14 February 2012, https://www.youtube.com/watch?v=5lIkNBKagHo, accessed on 13 February 2019.
158. 'Raj refutes Bal Thackeray's claims that he appointed Uddhav as the working president', ABP Majha, 26 October 2010, https://www.youtube.com/watch?v=MM-zDBbkqG4, accessed on 13 February 2019.
159. Manohar Joshi, *ShivSenechi nirmiti, vaadh, swaroop, yashapayash aani bhavitavya* (Analytical Study of the Birth, Growth Nature and Structure, Success and Failures and Future of the Shiv Sena), PhD thesis, Navchaitanya Prakashan, Mumbai, 2011, p. 41.
160. Harinder Baweja, 'E.C. Krishnamurthy clashes with CEC Gill over Shiv Sena, ends up the loser', *India Today*, 29 December 1997, https://www.indiatoday.in/magazine/nation/story/19971229-ec-krishnamurthy-clashes-with-cec-gill-over-shiv-sena-ends-up-the-loser-831170-1997-12-29.
161. Manohar Joshi, *ShivSenechi nirmiti, vaadh, swaroop, yashapayash aani bhavitavya* (Analytical Study of The Birth, Growth Nature

and Structure, Success and Failures and Future of the Shiv Sena), PhD thesis, Navchaitanya Prakashan, Mumbai, 2011, p. 51.
162. Interview with a senior Shiv Sena leader on 27 March 2019.
163. Interview with author on 21 December 2018.
164. Interview with author on 21 December 2018.
165. Interview with author on 16 April 2019.
166. 'Narayan Rane says he opposed Uddhav Thackeray's appointment as the working president', IBN Lokmat, 31 January 2015, https://www.youtube.com/watch?v=H6vP99mAhPk
167. Multiple interviews with author including on 9 February 2019.
168. Vaibhav Purandare, *Bal Thackeray and the Rise of the Shiv Sena*, Roli Books, New Delhi, 2012, p. 232.
169. Manohar Joshi, *Shiv Sena: Kaal-Aaj-Udya*, Prabodhan Goregaon, Mumbai, 2008, p. 729.
170. Multiple sources.
171. Gail Omvedt, 'Hinduism as Feudal Backwardness: The Dalit Panthers', *Dalit Visions: The Anti-caste Movement and the Construction of an Indian Identity*, Orient Longman, Hyderabad, 2006, p. 75.
172. Sachin Parab, 'Jai Shiv Bhim!', 30 January 2011, http://parabsachin.blogspot.com/2011/01/blog-post_30.html
173. Manohar Joshi, *Shiv Sena: Kaal-Aaj-Udya*, Prabodhan Goregaon, Mumbai, 2008, p. 730.
174. Interview with author on 21 January 2019.
175. Manohar Joshi, *Shiv Sena: Kaal-Aaj-Udya*, Prabodhan Goregaon, Mumbai, 2008, p. 719.
176. Interview with author on 22 January 2019.
177. Interview with author on 22 January 2019.
178. Interview with author on 22 January 2019.
179. Interview with author on 23 January 2019.
180. Interview with author on 21 January 2019.
181. Mahesh Gavaskar, 'Raj Thackeray and the Danger of Competing Regionalisms', *EPW*, 1 November 2008; 'Job bias suit on Nitish', *The Telegraph*, 27 November 2003, https://www.telegraphindia.com/india/job-bias-suit-on-nitish/cid/965608.
182. Interview with author on 4 January 2019.
183. Manohar Joshi, *Shiv Sena: Kaal-Aaj-Udya*, Prabodhan Goregaon, Mumbai, 2008, pp. 720–21.
184. Ibid., p. 721.

185. Ibid.
186. Ibid.
187. V. Venkatesan, 'Blow to a Ban, *Frontline*, Vol. 27, No. 16, 31 July to 13 August 2010, https://frontline.thehindu.com/static/html/fl2716/stories/20100813271604100.htm
188. Martha C. Nussbaum, *The Clash Within: Democracy, Religious Violence, and India's Future*, Permanent Black, Ranikhet, 2007, p. 240.
189. Interview with author on 4 January 2019.
190. 'Raj Thackeray apologises to Bahulkar', TNN, 29 December 2003, https://timesofindia.indiatimes.com/city/pune/Raj-Thackeray-apologises-to-Bahulkar/articleshow/388216.cms
191. Interview with author on 4 January 2019.
192. 'India seeks to arrest US scholar', BBC, http://news.bbc.co.uk/2/hi/south_asia/3561499.stm
193. 'Laine's book on Shivaji will not be reprinted', *Deccan Herald*, https://www.deccanherald.com/content/80961/laines-book-shivaji-not-reprinted.html
194. Sushant Kulkarni, 'Govt moves court again to withdraw case against Sena leaders', *Indian Express*, 24 October 2017, https://indianexpress.com/article/india/govt-moves-court-again-to-withdraw-case-against-sena-leaders-4903755/; Yogesh Joshi, '2010 Pune bandh: Criminal case against Sena leaders Neelam Gorhe, Milind Narvekar for inciting violence to be withdrawn', *Hindustan Times*, 26 October 2017, https://www.hindustantimes.com/pune-news/2010-pune-bandh-criminal-case-against-sena-leaders-neelam-gorhe-milind-narvekar-for-inciting-violence-to-be-withdrawn/story-PmI1qknF0z7Y5Bg53Pda5N.html.
195. Ibid.
196. 'Shiv Sena attack communally charged', TNN, 17 April 2004, https://timesofindia.indiatimes.com/city/mumbai/Shiv-Sena-attack-communally-charged/articleshow/621615.cms
197. Interview with author on 28 January 2019.
198. Interview with author on 28 January 2019.
199. Interview with author on 29 December 2018.
200. Manohar Joshi, *Shiv Sena: Kaal-Aaj-Udya*, Prabodhan Goregaon, Mumbai, 2008, p. 746.
201. Ibid., p. 747–48.

202. Ibid., p. 748.
203. Interview with author on 21 December 2018.

Chapter 6: Raj's Estrangement and the Birth of MNS

1. Interview with author on 25 January 2019.
2. Author's interview on 19 April 2019 with a senior journalist close to the Thackeray family who has covered the Shiv Sena for over three decades.
3. Interview with author on 15 June 2019.
4. Narayan Rane with Priyam Gandhi-Mody, *No Holds Barred: My Years in Politics*, HarperCollins Publishers India, Noida, 2019, p. 75.
5. Milind Narvekar vishayi (About Milind Narvekar), 4 January 2011 http://parabsachin.blogspot.com/2011/01/blog-post_04.html
6. Manohar Joshi, *Shiv Sena: Kaal-Aaj-Udya*, Prabodhan Goregaon, Mumbai, 2008, p. 761.
7. Balasaheb Thackeray, Konkan Karykarta Melawa in Mumbai, Part 01, https://www.youtube.com/watch?v=OTOaI2O-LLw, accessed on 10 February 2019.
8. Interview with author on 13 February 2019.
9. Interview with author on 9 February 2019.
10. Interview with author on 13 February 2019.
11. Narayan Rane with Priyam Gandhi-Mody, *No Holds Barred: My Years in Politics* (HarperCollins Publishers India, Noida, 2019, pp. 79–80.
12. Ibid., p. *80*.
13. Ibid., p. 81.
14. Manohar Joshi, *Shiv Sena: Kaal-Aaj-Udya*, Prabodhan Goregaon, Mumbai, 2008, p. 761.
15. Ibid.
16. Ibid.
17. Ibid.
18. Interview with author on 29 December 2018.
19. Priya Sahgal, 'Bal Thackeray expels Narayan Rane, Shiv Sena faces worst leadership crisis since inception', 18 July 2005, https://www.indiatoday.in/magazine/states/story/20050718-bal-thackeray-

expels-narayan-rane-shiv-sena-faces-worst-leadership-crisis-since-inception-787914-2005-07-18.
20. Smruti Koppikar, 'Narayan Ran . . . Tiger's capo Rane quits. Is he big enough for a split?' *Outlook*, 18 July 2005, https://www.outlookindia.com/magazine/story/narayan-ran/227984
21. Priya Sahgal, 'Bal Thackeray expels Narayan Rane, Shiv Sena faces worst leadership crisis since inception', 18 July 2005, https://www.indiatoday.in/magazine/states/story/20050718-bal-thackeray-expels-narayan-rane-shiv-sena-faces-worst-leadership-crisis-since-inception-787914-2005-07-18; 'Narayan Rane claims Raj was being sidelined in the Shiv Sena', ABP Majha, 19 September 2017, https://www.youtube.com/watch?v=nQYW8_osrHA, accessed on 13 February 2019.
22. Narayan Rane with Priyam Gandhi-Mody, *No Holds Barred: My Years in Politics*, HarperCollins Publishers India, Noida, 2019, pp. 91, 104.
23. Ibid., pp. 93–94.
24. Ibid., pp. 76–77
25. Interview with author on 19 December 2018 and 4 January 2019.
26. Interview with author on 19 December 2018 and 4 January 2019.
27. Interview with author on 19 December 2018 and 4 January 2019 and interview with Vageesh Saraswat on 25 January 2019.
28. Interview with author on 15 June 2019.
29. Vijay Samant and Harshal Pradhan, *Suvarna Mahotsavi Shiv Sena: Pannas Varshanchi Ghoddaud* (The Shiv Sena in Its Golden Jubilee: A Fifty-year Journey), Riya Publications, Kolhapur, 2019, p. 335.
30. Ibid.
31. Lyla Bavadam, 'Why Rane had to go', *Frontline*, 16–29 July 2005, https://frontline.thehindu.com/static/html/fl2215/stories/20050729004302800.htm
32. Interview with author on 28 January 2019.
33. Interview with author on 20 December 2018.
34. 'Narayan Rane speaks about how slogans in his favour were given at Sena rally', ABP Majha, 19 September 2017, https://www.youtube.com/watch?v=nQYW8_osrHA, accessed on 6 February 2019.
35. Manohar Joshi, *Shiv Sena: Kaal-Aaj-Udya, Prabodhan Goregaon*, Mumbai, 2008, p. 764.

36. Ibid., p. 770.
37. Sanjay Raut, *Ekavachani*, Part II, Mehta Publishing House, Pune, 2017, p. 219.
38. Pratibha Masand, 'Mumbai got fraction of 26/7 rain this time', *Times of India*, 27 July 2012, https://timesofindia.indiatimes.com/city/mumbai/Mumbai-got-fraction-of-26/7-rain-this-time/articleshow/15179988.cms
39. Interview with author on 25 January 2019.
40. Interview with author on 29 December 2018.
41. Manohar Joshi, *Shiv Sena: Kaal-Aaj-Udya* (*Prabodhan Goregaon*, Mumbai, 2008), p. 779.
42. Interview with author on 7 January 2019.
43. Manohar Joshi, *Shiv Sena: Kaal-Aaj-Udya*, *Prabodhan Goregaon*, Mumbai, 2008, pp. 779–80.
44. Ibid., p. 780.
45. Interview with author on 19 December 2018.
46. Interview with author in January 2019
47. http://parabsachin.blogspot.com/2011/03/blog-post_09.html
48. Manohar Joshi, *Shiv Sena: Kaal-Aaj-Udya*, *Prabodhan Goregaon*, Mumbai, 2008, pp. 766–67.
49. No police record of Sena threat to Raj: Patil, PTI, 3 November 2007, https://www.dnaindia.com/mumbai/report-no-police-record-of-sena-threat-to-raj-patil-1131376
50. Raj Thackeray's allegations unfortunate: Bal Thackeray, 31 October 2007, https://www.oneindia.com/2007/10/30/raj-thackerays-allegations-unfortunate-bal-thackeray-1193769166.html
51. 'The saga of rift in the Thackeray family', PTI, 4 November 2007, https://www.dnaindia.com/mumbai/report-the-saga-of-rift-in-the-thackeray-family-1131617
52. No police record of Sena threat to Raj: Patil, PTI, 3 November 2007, https://www.dnaindia.com/mumbai/report-no-police-record-of-sena-threat-to-raj-patil-1131376
53. Multiple interviews with author in December 2018 and January 2019.
54. Raj Thackeray announces decision to split from the Shiv Sena, https://www.youtube.com/watch?v=SIDdsZPqg4w, accessed in January 2019

55. Sandeep Unnithan, 'Raj Thackeray revolts against his cousin Uddhav, split threatens Shiv Sena future', 12 December 2005, https://www.indiatoday.in/magazine/nation/story/20051212-raj-thackeray-revolts-against-his-cousin-uddhav-split-threatens-shiv-sena-future-786457-2005-12-12
56. Interview with author on 17 April 2019.
57. Interview with author on 16 April 2019.
58. Interview with author on 13 March 2019.
59. Sandeep Unnithan, 'Raj Thackeray revolts against his cousin Uddhav, split threatens Shiv Sena future', 12 December 2005, https://www.indiatoday.in/magazine/nation/story/20051212-raj-thackeray-revolts-against-his-cousin-uddhav-split-threatens-shiv-sena-future-786457-2005-12-12.
60. http://parabsachin.blogspot.com/2011/03/blog-post_09.html
61. Interview with author on 22 January 2019.
62. Manohar Joshi, *Shiv Sena: Kaal-Aaj-Udya*, Prabodhan Goregaon, Mumbai, 2008, p. 780.
63. 'Raj ki baat', Zee Marathi, Diwali issue, 2018.
64. Interview with author on 25 January 2019.
65. Interview with author on 27 January 2019.
66. Interview with author on 27 January 2019.
67. Interview with author on 19 December 2018 and 7 January 2019.
68. Interview with author on 27 March 2019.
69. Interview with author on 8 January 2019.
70. Interview with author on 8 January 2019.
71. Sanjay Raut, *Ekavachani*, Part II, Mehta Publishing House, Pune, 2017, pp. 229, 248.
72. Interview with author on 10 March 2019.
73. Interview with author on 22 January 2019.
74. Interview with author on 22 January 2019.
75. Raj Thackeray at Loksatta Idea Exchange on 31 January 2012, https://www.youtube.com/watch?v=fycX9K2uD7M&t=1515s (accessed in January 2019
76. Interview with author on 25 January 2019.
77. Interview with author on 16 January 2019.
78. Interview with author on 4 May 2019.
79. Bal Thackeray interview with Nikhil Wagle, IBN Lokmat, 14 February 2012, https://www.youtube.com/watch?v=72wJ5e8i0mo, accessed on 20 January 2019.

80. Jaidev Thackeray interview, IBN Lokmat, 17 November 2013, https://www.youtube.com/watch?v=r1xQO5JXXF8, accessed on 2 May 2019.
81. Manohar Joshi, *Shiv Sena: Kaal-Aaj-Udya*, Prabodhan Goregaon, Mumbai, 2008, p. 780.
82. Interview with author on 4 May 2019.
83. Raj Thackeray at MNS launch rally on March 19, 2006, https://www.youtube.com/watch?v=nfRsZDjjDJg&t=381s; accessed in January 2019.
84. Ibid. also, Hee Rajbhasha ase! (This is Raj's language), Navata Book World, Mumbai, December 2011, pp. 3-14.
85. Interview with author on 3 January 2019.
86. Congress sweeps Maharashtra by-polls- Agencies, *DNA*, 24 January 2006, https://www.dnaindia.com/mumbai/report-congress-sweeps-maharashtra-by-polls-1009357
87. Sena wins Shrivardhan, Cong bags Naigaum, PTI, *DNA*, 19 February 2006, https://www.dnaindia.com/mumbai/report-sena-wins-shrivardhan-cong-bags-naigaum-1013722
88. UNI, 'Ramtek bypoll: Subodh Mohite accepts defeat', 13 April 2007, https://www.dnaindia.com/india/report-ramtek-bypoll-subodh-mohite-accepts-defeat-1090633
89. Manohar Joshi, *Shiv Sena: Kaal-Aaj-Udya*, Prabodhan Goregaon, Mumbai, 2008, p. 806.
90. Multiple interviews with the author.
91. Interview with author on 20 October 2018.
92. Interview with author on 16 January 2019.
93. Priya Sahgal, Malini Bhupta and Aditi Pai, 'Sneak peek of the shooting of the charismatic BJP leader Pramod Mahajan', *India Today*, 8 May 2006, https://www.indiatoday.in/magazine/cover-story/story/20060508-story-behind-pramod-mahajans-murder-case-785581-2006-05-08
94. Ibid.
95. Pramod Mahajan Dead, IANS, *Hindustan Times*, 7 June 2006, https://www.hindustantimes.com/india/pramod-mahajan-dead/story-45KPr3sNuZ5Qcmg0DBTUHO.html
96. Conversation with a senior Shiv Sena leader around 2015.
97. Parikshit Joshi, 'BJP sticks to Chimur claim', 6 October 2006, https://mumbaimirror.indiatimes.com/mumbai/other/bjp-sticks-to-chimur-claim/articleshow/15641469.cms

98. Manohar Joshi, *Shiv Sena: Kaal-Aaj-Udya*, Prabodhan Goregaon, Mumbai, 2008, pp. 846–48; Parikshit Joshi, 'To the victor the spoils, says Rane', 11 December 2006, https://mumbaimirror.indiatimes.com/mumbai/other/to-the-victor-the-spoils-says-rane/articleshow/15662414.cms
99. Parikshit Joshi, 'To the victor the spoils, says Rane', 11 December 2006, https://mumbaimirror.indiatimes.com/mumbai/other/to-the-victor-the-spoils-says-rane/articleshow/15662414.cms
100. Karan Thapar, 'Should Pratibha Patil be President?', *Hindustan Times*, 7 July 2007, https://www.hindustantimes.com/india/should-pratibha-patil-be-president/story-8j8WfTCSRzuzKssg6sfsoN.html
101. Tejas Mehta, 'Former President Pratibha Patil's Brother is Accused in Murder Case', NDTV, 7 July 2014, https://www.ndtv.com/india-news/former-president-pratibha-patils-brother-is-accused-in-murder-case-584875); Dhaval Kulkarni, 'Tai may become President, what about us who have been cheated?', *Indian Express*, 29 June 2007, http://archive.indianexpress.com/news/-tai-may-become-president-what-about-us-who-have-been-cheated--/203367/
102. Interview with author on 21 January 2019.
103. Interview with author on 21 January 2019.
104. Interview with author in early 2019.
105. Manohar Joshi, *Shiv Sena: Kaal-Aaj-Udya*, Prabodhan Goregaon, Mumbai, 2008, p. 881.
106. Interview with author on 29 December 2018.
107. Interview with author on 31 December 2018.
108. Author's interview on 19 April 2019 with a senior journalist close to the Thackeray family who has covered the Shiv Sena for over three decades.
109. Manohar Joshi, *Shiv Sena: Kaal-Aaj-Udya*, Prabodhan Goregaon, Mumbai, 2008, p. 887.

Chapter 7: The MNS Tastes First Blood: The Shiv Sena's Fortunes Decline

1. Raj Thackeray at Loksatta Idea Exchange: 31 January 2012, https://www.youtube.com/watch?v=fycX9K2uD7M&t=1519s, accessed on January 2019.

2. Interview with author on 4 January 2019.
3. Interview with author on 27 January 2019.
4. Interview with author on 25 January 2019.
5. Prerana Thakurdesai, 'MNS chief Raj Thackeray continues war against north Indians in Maharashtra', 26 March 2007, https://www.indiatoday.in/magazine/indiascope/story/20070326-raj-thackeray-has-launched-his-own-party2007-748960-2007-03-26
6. Ibid.
7. Interview with author on 25 January 2019.
8. Interview with author on 16 January 2019.
9. Raj Thackeray flays Amitabh for UP interests, https://www.rediff.com/news/2008/feb/02raj.htm
10. *Hee Rajbhasha Ase!* (This is Raj's language), Navata Book World, Mumbai, December 2011, p. 32; Raj Thackeray speech at Vikhroli on 2 February 2008, https://www.youtube.com/watch?v=nkCfGczGITU, accessed on 3 July 2019.
11. Ibid.
12. Ibid.
13. *Hee Rajbhasha Ase!* (This is Raj's language), Navata Book World, Mumbai, December 2011, p. 33; Raj Thackeray speech at Vikhroli on 2 February 2008, https://www.youtube.com/watch?v=nkCfGczGITU, accessed on 3 July 2019.
14. *Hee Rajbhasha Ase!* (This is Raj's language), Navata Book World, Mumbai, December 2011, p. 34; Raj Thackeray speech at Vikhroli on 2 February 2008, https://www.youtube.com/watch?v=nkCfGczGITU, accessed on 3 July 2019.
15. *Hee Rajbhasha Ase!* (This is Raj's language), Navata Book World, Mumbai, December 2011, p. 33; Raj Thackeray speech at Vikhroli on 2 February 2008, https://www.youtube.com/watch?v=nkCfGczGITU, accessed on 3 July 2019.
16. *Hee Rajbhasha Ase!* (This is Raj's language), Navata Book World, Mumbai, December 2011, p. 33–34; Raj Thackeray speech at Vikhroli on 2 February 2008, https://www.youtube.com/watch?v=nkCfGczGITU, accessed on 3 July 2019.
17. 'MNS, SP workers clash before rally', *DNA*, 4 February 2008, https://www.dnaindia.com/mumbai/report-mns-sp-workers-clash-before-rally-1149010
18. Ibid.

19. Interview with author on 7 January 2019.
20. Interview with author on 16 January 2019.
21. Dhaval Kulkarni, 'In slap spotlight, Azmi has never turned the other cheek', 11 November 2009, http://archive.indianexpress.com/news/in-slap-spotlight-azmi-has-never-turned-the-other-cheek/539970/
22. C.C No 112.PW/2005 convicted of offences punishable under sections 153, 153-A (1) (a), 153-(A) (1) (b) read with Section 34 of Indian Penal Code by Metropolitan Magistrate Court, Mazgaon on 30 April 2012, https://www.casemine.com/judgement/in/581180b12713e179479c22c6, and 'Abu Azmi convicted for hate speech', Staff Reporter, *The Hindu*, 1 May 2012, https://www.thehindu.com/news/national/abu-azmi-convicted-for-hate-speech/article3371547.ece; 'Samajwadi Party leader Abu Azmi's conviction in hate speech case suspended', PTI, 23 September 2012, https://www.dnaindia.com/india/report-samajwadi-party-leader-abu-azmi-s-conviction-in-hate-speech-case-suspended-2021055
23. Factoids gleaned by author during his reporting career.
24. Interview with author on 30 January 2019.
25. 'NCP activist withdraws case against Thackeray', UNI, *DNA*, 29 January 2008, https://www.dnaindia.com/mumbai/report-ncp-activist-withdraws-case-against-thackeray-1148079; Prem Shukla's interview with author on 30 January 2019.
26. 'Raj Thackeray arrested, released on bail', *India Today*, https://www.indiatoday.in/latest-headlines/story/raj-thackeray-arrested-released-on-bail-22856-2008-02-13
27. Interview with author on 24 and 30 January 2019.
28. Author's notes; Dhaval Kulkarni, 'To respect my brother, stop hate campaign', *Indian Express*, 15 February 2008, http://archive.indianexpress.com/news/-to-respect-my-brother--stop-hate-campaign-/273215/
29. Dhaval Kulkarni, 'To respect my brother, stop hate campaign', *Indian Express*, 15 February 2008 (http://archive.indianexpress.com/news/-to-respect-my-brother--stop-hate-campaign-/273215/)
30. *Saamna* remarks: 'Bal Thackeray distances himself', PTI, *Hindustan Times*, 5 April 2008, https://www.hindustantimes.com/india/saamna-remarks-bal-thackeray-distances-himself/story-qsfdQzIAGGwIPalfvA8WxI.html
31. Interview with author on 30 January 2019.

Notes

32. Drona music launch and Jaya Bachchan controversy, https://www.youtube.com/watch?v=8L8sgbbYZO0, accessed on 28 June 2019
33. 'Amitabh apologises for Jaya's remarks', PTI, 10 September 2008, https://economictimes.indiatimes.com/news/politics-and-nation/amitabh-apologises-for-jayas-remarks/printarticle/3468635.cms
34. 'Raj Thackeray: I accept Amitabh's apology', Rediff, 11 September 2008, https://www.rediff.com/movies/2008/sep/11raj.htm; K.L. Prasad, 'Raj accepts Amitabh apology, turns guns on "Jaya of police"', Express News Service, 11 and 12 September 2008, http://archive.indianexpress.com/news/raj-accepts-amitabh-apology-turns-guns-on--jaya-of-police--k-l-prasad/360441/
35. *Hee Raj bhasha ase*! (This is Raj's Language), Navata Book World, Mumbai, 2011, pp. 43–48; Raj Thackeray speech on 3 May 2008 rally, https://www.youtube.com/watch?v=khN8PSXmf-w, accessed on 22 June 2019
36. *Hee Raj bhasha ase*! (This is Raj's Language), Navata Book World, Mumbai, 2011, p. 46; Raj Thackeray speech on 3 May 2008 rally, https://www.youtube.com/watch?v=khN8PSXmf-w, accessed on 22 June 2019
37. Raj Thackeray speech on 3 May 2008 rally, https://www.youtube.com/watch?v=khN8PSXmf-w, accessed on 22 June 2019
38. Interview with author on 21 January 2019.
39. Marathi signboards issue: 'Is this a murder trial?', Agencies, 5 December 2008, http://archive.indianexpress.com/news/marathi-signboards-issue-is-this-a-murder/394661
40. Sanjay Raut, *Ekavachani*, Part II, Mehta Publishing House, Pune, 2017, p. 24.
41. 'MNS chief Raj Thackeray arrested', PTI, 21 October 2008, https://www.outlookindia.com/newswire/story/mns-chief-raj-thackeray-arrested/622883
42. 'Raj returns home after bail, supporters jubilant', Indo-Asian News Service, 22 October 2008, https://www.indiatoday.in/latest-headlines/story/raj-returns-home-after-bail-supporters-jubilant-32056-2008-10-22
43. 'Patna youth opens fire in Mumbai bus, shot dead', TNN, 28 October 2008, https://timesofindia.indiatimes.com/city/mumbai/Patna-youth-opens-fire-in-Mumbai-bus-shot-dead/articleshow/3645215.cms

44. 'Slain youth wanted to kill Raj: police, 30 October 2008, https://www.thehindu.com/todays-paper/tp-national/Slain-youth-wanted-to-kill-Raj-police/article15331666.ece
45. Rahul Raj cremated: PTI, 29 October 2008, https://www.outlookindia.com/newswire/story/rahul-raj-cremated/626212
46. Author's own reporting and notes.
47. Interview with author on 25 January 2019.
48. Interview with author on 3 January 2019 and 7 February 2019.
49. Interview with author on 3 January 2019 and 7 February 2019.
50. Mahesh Vijapurkar, 'How the media created the Raj Thackeray bogey', Rediff.com, 9 September 2008, https://www.rediff.com/news/2008/sep/09guest.htm
51. Ibid.
52. Ram Manohar Tripathi, *Bambai ke Uttar Bharatiya*, Savera Newspapers and Publications Limited, Mumbai, 1994, pp. 8, 47.
53. Ibid., p. 27.
54. Ibid., p. 33.
55. Chinmay Tumbe, *India Moving: A History of Migration*, Penguin Random House India, Gurgaon, 2018, p. 31.
56. Ram Manohar Tripathi, *Bambai ke Uttar Bharatiya*, Savera Newspapers and Publications Limited, Mumbai, 1994, p. 52.
57. Ibid., pp. 7, 15.
58. Interview with Congress leader Sanjay Nirupam on 18 October 2018.
59. Ram Manohar Tripathi, *Bambai ke Uttar Bharatiya*, Savera Newspapers and Publications Limited, Mumbai, 1994, pp. 24–25; https://eci.gov.in/files/file/4107-bombay-1951
60. Interview with former *Dopahar ka Saamna* executive editor, Prem Shukla, on 30 January 2019.
61. Darryl D'Monte, *Ripping the Fabric: The Decline of Mumbai and its Mills*, Oxford University Press, New Delhi, 2005, pp. 14, 80–85.
62. Gillian Tindall, *City of Gold: The Biography of Bombay*, Penguin Random House, Gurgaon, 1992, p. xvii.
63. Darryl D'Monte, *Ripping the Fabric: The Decline of Mumbai and its Mills*, Oxford University Press, New Delhi, 2005, p. 82.
64. Ibid., p. 17.
65. Interview with author on 14 January 2019.
66. Interview with author on 16 April 2019.

67. Interview with author on 16 April 2019.
68. Interview with author on 16 April 2019.
69. Interview with author on 3 January 2019.
70. Mahesh Gavaskar, 'Mumbai's Shattered Mirror', *EPW*, Mumbai, 13 February 2010.
71. Interview with author on 3 January 2019.
72. Interview with author on 3 January 2019.
73. Interview with author on 29 December 2018.
74. T.B. Hansen, 'Strangers, Neighbours, and Political Order in the South Asian City', *Interrogating India's Modernity: Democracy, Identity, and Citizenship: Essays in Honour of Dipankar Gupta*, Surinder S. Jodhka (ed.), Oxford University Press, New Delhi, 2013, p. 24.
75. Ibid.
76. Mahesh Gavaskar, 'Mumbai's Shattered Mirror', *EPW*, Mumbai, 13 February 2010.
77. Zeeshan Shaikh, 'Mumbai's growing Hindi heartland', *Indian Express*, 11 February 2019, https://indianexpress.com/article/cities/mumbai/mumbais-growing-hindi-heartland-demographic-changes-5577879/
78. Ibid.
79. Ram B. Bhagat and Gavin W. Jones, 'Population Change and Migration in Mumbai Metropolitan Region: Implications for Planning and Governance', Asia Research Institute, National University of Singapore, Working Paper Series no. 201, May 2013, pp. 10–11, http://www.ari.nus.edu.sg/wps/wps13_201.pdf
80. 'In bid to shed anti-outsider tag, MNS chief Raj Thackeray reaches out to north Indians', *DNA*, 3 December 2018, https://www.dnaindia.com/mumbai/report-in-bid-to-shed-anti-outsider-tag-mns-chief-raj-thackeray-reaches-out-to-north-indians-2691758
81. Interview with author on 30 January 2019.
82. Conversation with reporters in May 2008.
83. Interview with author on 20 October 2018.
84. Interview with author on 28 December 2018.
85. Ram Manohar Tripathi, *Bambai ke Uttar Bharatiya*, Savera Newspapers and Publications Limited, Mumbai, 1994, p. 29.
86. Interview with author on 27 January 2019.

87. Interview with author on 24 January 2019.
88. Interview with author on 8 January 2019.
89. Interview with author in 2014.
90. Interview with author in 2014.
91. Interview with author on 25 January 2019.
92. Dhaval Kulkarni and Swatee Kher, 'Get a permit to work in Maharashtra: Raj's way to get votes', *Indian Express*, 24 September 2009, http://archive.indianexpress.com/news/get-a-permit-to-work-in-maharashtra-raj-s-way-to-get-votes/520972/
93. Sanjay Raut, *Ekavachani*, Part II, Mehta Publishing House, Pune, 2017, p. 272.
94. Manu Joseph, 'Understanding Raj Thackeray', *Times of India*, 10 February 2008, https://timesofindia.indiatimes.com/Understanding-Raj-Thackeray/articleshowprint/2770251.cms
95. 'Biharis are an affliction, says Bal Thackeray', IANS, 5 March 2008, http://www.bihartimes.com/newsbihar/2008/march/newsbihar05march6.html
96. Author's notes from 2008.
97. 'Threat to Maharashtrian families in Haryana', TNN, 8 November 2008, https://timesofindia.indiatimes.com/india/Threat-to-Maharashtrian-families-in-Haryana/articleshow/3687648.cms
98. Ibid.
99. 'Marathi couple won't leave Haryana', TNN, 10 November 2008, https://timesofindia.indiatimes.com/india/Marathi-couple-wont-leave-Haryana/articleshow/3693021.cms
100. 'MNS row: Tata employee's house ransacked in Jamshedpur', PTI, 21 October 2008, https://timesofindia.indiatimes.com/india/MNS-row-Tata-employees-house-ransacked-in-Jamshedpur/articleshow/3625043.cms?referral=PM
101. 'Woman IAS officer targeted in Bihar for Thackeray surname', IANS, 1 November 2008, https://www.indiatoday.in/latest-headlines/story/woman-ias-officer-targeted-in-bihar-for-thackeray-surname-32665-2008-11-01
102. Interview with author on 28 January 2019.
103. Interview with author on 28 January 2019.
104. Interview with author on 27 January 2019.
105. Sucheta Dalal and Debashis Basu, 'I had begun to feel that I had the potential to be much more than a peon': Shivajirao Patil,

26 April 2010, https://www.moneylife.in/article/i-had-begun-to-feel-that-i-had-the-potential-to-be-much-more-than-a-peon-shivajirao-patil/4982.html
106. Vijay Dhawale, *Waghache Panje: Shivsenechi Daidipyaman Suvarnamahotsavi Vaatchal* (The Claws of the Tiger: The Glorious Golden Jubilee History of the Shiv Sena, Navchaitanya Prakashan, Mumbai, 2016, p. 363.
107. Ibid., pp. 363–64.
108. Ibid., pp. 364–65.
109. Ibid., pp. 365–66.
110. Interview with author on 8 January 2019.
111. Interview with author on 28 January 2019.
112. Interview with author on 27 January 2019.
113. 'Like politicians, govt officials should also face action for 26/11', Vilasrao Deshmukh interview with Swati Chaturvedi, Zee News, 5 December 2009, https://zeenews.india.com/exclusive/-like-politicians-govt-officials-should-also-face-action-for-26/11_2675.html
114. Author's conversations.
115. Conversation with author in 2008.
116. Interview with author on 22 January 2019.
117. Interview with author on 16 January 2019.
118. 'Raj Thackeray reaction after 2009 Lok Sabha poll result', ABP News, 20 August 2012, https://www.youtube.com/watch?v=tar8giIR3ug) (accessed on 12 February 2019
119. Interview with author on 25 January 2019.
120. Conversation with author in 2009.
121. Conversation with author in 2008–09.
122. Shiv Sena leader Diwakar Raote in V.S. Naipaul, *India: A Million Mutinies Now*, Picador an imprint of Pan Macmillan, London, 2010, p. 55.
123. Interview on 19 April 2019 with a senior journalist close to the Thackeray family who has covered the Shiv Sena for over three decades.
124. Interview with author on 29 December 2019.
125. Interview with author on 29 December 2019.
126. Interview with author on 4 January 2019.
127. 'BJP, Sena and MNS should form alliance: Munde', Rediff.com, 7 February 2011, https://www.rediff.com/news/report/bjp-sena-and-mns-should-form-alliance-munde/20110207.htm

128. Conversation with author in October 2018.
129. Raj Thackeray interview with *Loksatta*, Indian Express Online, 31 January 2012, https://www.youtube.com/watch?v=fycX9K2uD7M&t=1457s, accessed on 14 February 2019.
130. 'Hurt by Sena poll rout, Thackeray attacks Marathi manoos', PTI, 24 October 2009, https://timesofindia.indiatimes.com/india/Hurt-by-Sena-poll-rout-Thackeray-attacks-Marathi-manoos/articleshow/5156195.cms
131. 'I didn't pen the anti-Marathi manoos remark: Bal Thackeray', Agencies, *Indian Express*, 6 November 2009, https://indianexpress.com/article/india/politics/i-didnt-pen-the-antimarathi-manoos-remark-bal-thackeray

Chapter 8: The Downfall of the MNS: The Shiv Sena Holds Its Own

1. Raj Thackeray warns Abu Azmi to take oath in Marathi, 3 November 2009, https://www.youtube.com/watch?v=K1p4Jjuhpww, accessed on 10 February 2019.
2. Author's notes.
3. 'Abu Azmi slapped, Baba Siddique gets handshake', *Pune Mirror*, 11 November 2009, https://punemirror.indiatimes.com/pune/cover-story/abu-azmi-slappedbaba-siddique-gets-handshake/articleshow/32498026.cms
4. Author's notes.
5. Interview with author on 11 January 2019.
6. 'One of India's first tollways comes up in Madhya Pradesh', N.K. Singh, *India Today*, 31 March 1995, https://www.indiatoday.in/magazine/economy/story/19950331-one-of-india-first-tollways-comes-up-in-madhya-pradesh-807064-1995-03-31#ssologin=1#source=magazine
7. Author's notes.
8. Interview with author on 11 January 2019.
9. Interview with author on 27 January 2019.
10. Interview with author on 11 January 2019.
11. Sanjay Shirodkar, *Toll Ek Jhol Aani . . .* (Toll, A Scam), Chetak Books, Pune, 2018, p. 12.
12. Multiple conversations with author since 2012.

13. Report of the Comptroller and Auditor General of India on Public Sector Undertakings for the year ended 31 March 2016, Comptroller and Auditor General of India, https://cag.gov.in/sites/default/files/audit_report_files/Maharashtra_Report_No_2_of_2017_on_PSUs_1.pdf
14. Author's notes and interactions with MNS leaders.
15. MEP Infrastructure Developers Ltd, http://www.mepinfra.com/project-details/5-mumbai-entry-points.aspx
16. Kiran Tare, 'For whom the tolls sell', *India Today*, 18 December 2010, https://www.indiatoday.in/magazine/nation/story/20101227-for-whom-the-tolls-sell-745223-2010-12-18#ssologin=1#source=magazine
17. Author's notes and reporting; and conversations with Sanjay Shirodkar.
18. Author's notes and reporting; and conversations with Sanjay Shirodkar.
19. Mumbai–Pune NH4 and Mumbai–Pune Expressway Project, IRB Infrastructure Developers Ltd website, http://www.irb.co.in/home/ongoing-concessions/mumbai-pune-national-highway-4-and-mumbai-pune-expressway-project/
20. Author's notes.
21. Author's notes; 'Raj Thackeray asks people to stop paying toll tax', News 18, 25 July 2012, https://www.news18.com/news/politics/raj-thackeray-asks-people-to-stop-paying-toll-tax-490434.html
22. Interview with author on 19 January 2019.
23. Raj Thackeray interview, https://www.youtube.com/watch?v=NnVPREXpNIw&list=PL635F545536CF1997, accessed on 5 January 2019
24. 'Raj Thackeray arrested during "rasta rook" against toll collection, MNS party workers detained', PTI, *Economic Times*, 12 February 2014, https://economictimes.indiatimes.com/news/politics-and-nation/raj-thackeray-arrested-during-rasta-roko-against-toll-collection-mns-party-workers-detained/articleshow/30267975.cms
25. Interview with author on 24 and 30 January 2019.
26. 'Raj's action against toll plazas a farce: Uddhav', FPJ Bureau, *Free Press Journal*, 21 June 2012, https://www.freepressjournal.in/ujjain/rajs-action-against-toll-plazas-a-farce-uddhav/84478

27. 'Gadkari rubbishes Munde vow to make state roads toll-free', *Indian Express*, 7 February 2014, https://indianexpress.com/article/cities/mumbai/gadkari-rubbishes-munde-vow-to-make-state-roads-toll-free/
28. Dhaval Kulkarni and Ateeq Shaikh, 'Shutting toll plazas hurting government bad', 10 March 2016, https://www.dnaindia.com/mumbai/report-shutting-toll-plazas-hurting-government-bad-2187404
29. Ibid.
30. Interview with author on 4 January 2019.
31. Interview with author on 10 March 2019.
32. Kiran Tare, 'Why Raj Thackeray is the loneliest politician in Maharashtra today', 9 March 2017, https://www.dailyo.in/politics/raj-thackeray-mns-maharashtra/story/1/16060.html
33. Meena Menon, 'Sena will become irrelevant after Mumbai polls: Prithviraj Chavan', 9 February 2012, https://www.thehindu.com/news/national/other-states/sena-will-become-irrelevant-after-mumbai-polls-prithviraj-chavan/article2876210.ece
34. Pradeep Kaushal, 'Raj to Uddhav: I will drive you home . . . we'll go into the open and together', *Indian Express*, 19 July 2012, http://archive.indianexpress.com/news/raj-to-uddhav-i-will-drive-you-home . . .-well-go-into-the-open-and-together/976408/
35. Interview with author in 2012.
36. Shailesh Gaikwad, Sayli Udas Mankikar and Kunal Purohit, 'Uddhav is a misfit in politics, he lacks calibre: Raj Thackeray', 20 April 2014, https://www.hindustantimes.com/india/uddhav-is-a-misfit-in-politics-he-lacks-calibre-raj-thackeray/story-sBrKcOBKYVwgWZh47DGJ4M.html
37. Vijay Samant and Harshal Pradhan, *Suvarna Mahotsavi Shiv Sena: Pannas Varshanchi Ghoddaud* (The Shiv Sena in Its Golden Jubilee: A fifty-year journey), Riya Publications, Kolhapur, 2019, p. 384.
38. Bal Thackeray interview with Nikhil Wagle, IBN Lokmat, 14 February 2012, https://www.youtube.com/watch?v=5lIkNBKagHo&t=270s) (accessed on 12 February 2019
39. Interview with author on 25 January 2019.
40. Interview with author on 7 December 2018.
41. Interview with author on 7 December 2018.

42. Author's interview with Satish Valanju on 7 December 2018.
43. Interview with author on 7 December 2018.
44. Interview with author on 7 December 2018.
45. Interview with author on 13 January 2019.
46. Interview with author on 24 and 30 January 2019.
47. Interview with author on 24 and 30 January 2019.
48. 'Chavan proves a point to insiders & outsiders', *ET* Bureau, 11 June 2010, https://economictimes.indiatimes.com/news/politics-and-nation/chavan-proves-a-point-to-insiders-outsiders/articleshow/6035009.cms
49. Conversation with author on 28 January 2019.
50. Shantanu Nandan Sharma, '"My Name Is Khan" imbroglio gives Shiv Sena a bad name', *Economic Times*, 14 February 2010, https://economictimes.indiatimes.com/as-you-like-it/my-name-is-khan-imbroglio-gives-shiv-sena-a-bad-name/printarticle/5570525.cms
51. 'Why slam SRK and spare Big B? Raj asks Shiv Sena', News 18, 11 February 2010, https://www.news18.com/news/india/raj-on-srk-ipl-narvekar-sot-gadgil-sot-333339.html); author's notes.
52. Shantanu Nandan Sharma, '"My Name Is Khan" imbroglio gives Shiv Sena a bad name', *Economic Times*, 14 February 2010, https://economictimes.indiatimes.com/as-you-like-it/my-name-is-khan-imbroglio-gives-shiv-sena-a-bad-name/articleshow/5570525.cms
53. 'Rahul Gandhi snubs Sena, takes Mumbai local', NDTV correspondent, 6 February 2010, https://www.ndtv.com/india-news/rahul-gandhi-snubs-sena-takes-mumbai-local-410377
54. 'Rahul Gandhi arrives in Mumbai, Shiv Sena activists detained', PTI, 5 February 2010, https://www.dnaindia.com/mumbai/report-rahul-gandhi-arrives-in-mumbai-shiv-sena-activists-detained-1343560; and author's notes.
55. Interview with author on 13 January 2019.
56. Interview with author on 9 February 2019.
57. 'Raj Thackeray visits BJP office in Mumbai, irks Sena', NDTV, https://www.ndtv.com/india-news/raj-thackeray-visits-bjp-office-in-mumbai-irks-sena-442504
58. Bal Thackeray's last speech at the Shiv Sena's Dussehra rally in 2012, IBN Lokmat, https://www.youtube.com/watch?v=ITNxUt92my8&t=1043s, accessed on 10 February 2019.
59. Ibid.

60. Author's notes.
61. Author's notes.
62. Interview with author on 11 January 2019.
63. 'Bal Thackeray's funeral part of million mourners club', *Times of India*, 19 November 2012, https://timesofindia.indiatimes.com/india/Bal-Thackerays-funeral-part-of-million-mourners-club/articleshow/17274002.cms
64. 'Raj walks away, sparks rumours', *Mumbai Mirror*, 19 November 2012, https://mumbaimirror.indiatimes.com/mumbai/other/raj-walks-away-sparks-rumours/articleshow/17856923.cms?
65. Author's notes. Incidentally, Joshi was heckled off the dais by Sainiks at the Sena's Dussehra rally in 2013 after he blamed Uddhav's leadership for failing to ensure that a memorial of the late party chief was built. Manohar Joshi leaves Mumbai after humiliation at Shiv Sena rally, News 18, 14 October 2013, https://www.news18.com/news/india/manohar-joshi-leaves-mumbai-after-humiliation-at-shiv-sena-rally-645049.html
66. Author's notes.
67. 'Decision on Bal Thackeray's memorial to be taken by Shiv Sainiks, says Uddhav Thackeray', PTI, 20 November 2012, https://www.ndtv.com/mumbai-news/decision-on-bal-thackerays-memorial-to-be-taken-by-shiv-sainiks-says-uddhav-thackeray-505109
68. Chaitanya Marpakwar, 'BMC warning to cops: Shivaji Park structure law-and-order hazard', *Mumbai Mirror*, 30 November 2012, https://mumbaimirror.indiatimes.com/mumbai/cover-story/bmc-warning-to-cops-shivaji-park-structure-law-and-order-hazard/articleshow/17858023.cms
69. Interview with author on 11 January 2019.
70. 'Rs 100 cr worth Maharashtra cabinet grant for Bal Thackeray Memorial', *DNA*, 23 January 2019, https://www.dnaindia.com/mumbai/report-rs-100-cr-worth-maharashtra-cabinet-grant-for-bal-thackeray-memorial-2710980
71. Ibid.
72. Ibid.
73. 'Bal Thackeray memorial site chosen due to selfish interests: Raj Thackeray', PTI, 17 November 2015, https://www.mid-day.com/articles/bal-thackeray-memorial-site-chosen-due-to-selfish-interests-raj-thackeray/16690154

Chapter 9: The Hare and the Tortoise

1. Author's interview with a former MNS MLA in December 2018 and on 7 January 2019.
2. Interview with author on 4 January 2019.
3. Interview with author on 18 January 2019.
4. Interview with author on 4 January 2019.
5. Interview with an MNS leader on 18 January 2019.
6. Mary Fainsod Katzenstein, *Ethnicity and Equality: The Shiv Sena Party and Preferential Policies in Bombay*, Cornell University Press, Ithaca and London, 1979, p. 108.
7. Interview with author on 27 January 2019.
8. 'MNS threatens to disrupt shooting of Sur-Kshetra', IANS, *India Today*, 31 August 2012, https://www.indiatoday.in/movies/bollywood/story/mns-threatens-to-disrupt-shooting-of-sur-kshetra-114841-2012-08-31
9. 'Atithi devo bhava or Paisa devo bhava? Thackeray asks Asha Bhonsle', Zee News, 1 September 2012, https://zeenews.india.com/entertainment/idiotbox/atithi-devo-bhava-or-paisa-devo-bhava-thackeray-asks-asha-bhonsle_118275.html
10. 'Asha Bhosle's "Sur Kshetra" to go on air, thanks to Raj Thackeray', Agencies, 7 September 2012, http://archive.indianexpress.com/news/asha-bhosles--sur-kshetra--to-go-on-air-thanks-to-raj-thackeray/998749/
11. Interview with author on 9 February 2019.
12. Interview with author on 10 March 2019.
13. Interview with author on 25 January 2019.
14. Interview with author on 25 January 2019.
15. Interview with author on 23 January 2019.
16. Interview with author on 21 January 2019.
17. Raj Thackeray admires development of Singapore, 26 February 2010, https://www.youtube.com/watch?v=NnVPREXpNIw&t=45s, accessed on 16 February 2019.
18. Interview with author on 9 February 2019.
19. 'MNS would support Narendra Modi as PM: Raj Thackeray', PTI, 19 September 2011, https://www.ndtv.com/india-news/mns-would-support-narendra-modi-as-pm-raj-thackeray-468050)
20. Interview with author on 13 January 2019.

21. Interview with author on 21 January 2019.
22. Sandhya Nair, 'Don't give your land for bullet train: Raj Thackeray to farmers', 1 May 2018, https://timesofindia.indiatimes.com/city/mumbai/dont-give-your-land-for-bullet-train-raj-thackeray-to-farmers/articleshow/63991073.cms
23. 'I told Advani not to sack Modi after Godhra riots: Thackeray', Rediff.com, 25 February 2009, https://www.rediff.com/news/2009/feb/25i-told-advani-not-to-sack-modi-after-guj-riots.htm
24. 'Sushma Swaraj is Bal Thackeray's only choice for PM from BJP', PTI, 9 September 2012, https://www.indiatoday.in/bal-thackeray/story/sushma-swaraj-is-bal-thackeray-only-choice-for-pm-115555-2012-09-09
25. Interview with author on 13 January 2019.
26. Interview with author on 30 January 2019.
27. Pradip Kumar Maitra, 'Gadkari describes *Saamna* editorial as "unfortunate"', *Hindustan Times*, 6 March 2014, https://www.hindustantimes.com/india/gadkari-describes-saamna-editorial-as-unfortunate/story-i6Yd6Ksw1TlVA5ucvOzV5I.html
28. Interview with author on 7 January 2019.
29. Interview with author on 7 January 2019.
30. Interview with author on 4 January 2019.
31. Conversation with journalists in 2014.
32. Conversation with journalists in 2014.
33. Interview with author on 16 January 2019.
34. Interview with author on 16 January 2019.
35. Interview with author on 9 February 2019.
36. Interview with author in January 2019.
37. Interview with author on 27 December 2018.
38. Interview with author in December 2018.
39. Interview with author on 29 December 2018.
40. Interview with author on 20 December 2018.
41. *Loksatta* interview with Raj Thackeray, https://www.youtube.com/watch?v=Xq9WW3R_MPY, accessed on 8 February 2019.
42. 'India will have to use nukes if Pak does not mend its ways, says Uddhav Thackeray', *India Today*, https://www.indiatoday.in/india/story/modi-nuclear-bomb-pakistan-nawaz-swearing-in-uddhav-thackeray-shiv-sena-194370-2014-05-26

43. Interview with author on 30 January 2019.
44. Interview with author on 30 January 2019.
45. '"What is this sari and shawl diplomacy?" Shiv Sena opposes talks with Pakistan', PTI, 22 July 2014, https://www.deccanchronicle.com/140722/nation-current-affairs/article/%E2%80%98what-sari-and-shawl-diplomacy%E2%80%99-shiv-sena-opposes-talks
46. 'Narendra Modi upset with Shiv Sena over Sanjay Raut's sari-shawl jibe', *DNA*, 26 July 2014, https://www.dnaindia.com/mumbai/report-narendra-modi-upset-with-shiv-sena-over-sanjay-raut-s-sari-shawl-jibe-20053380.
47. Interview with author on 13 January 2019.
48. Dhaval Kulkarni, 'Shiv Sena mouthpiece *Saamna* warns Mumbai's Gujaratis not to neglect Maharashtra', *DNA*, 2 May 2014, https://www.dnaindia.com/mumbai/report-shiv-sena-mouthpiece-saamna-warns-mumbai-s-gujaratis-not-to-neglect-maharashtra-1984162) and author's notes.
49. Ibid., and author's notes.
50. Dhaval Kulkarni, 'Shiv Sena & BJP need each other, willy-nilly', *DNA*, 31 October 2015, https://www.dnaindia.com/mumbai/report-shiv-sena-bjp-need-each-other-willy-nilly-2140763
51. Multiple conversations with BJP leaders.
52. Conversation with reporters before 2014 state assembly elections.
53. 'Maharashtra polls: BJP-Sena seat-sharing tangle continues', IndiaToday.in, 21 September 2014, https://www.indiatoday.in/assembly-elections-2015/maharashtra/story/bjp-shiv-sena-maharashtra-polls-uddhav-thackeray-seat-sharing-293607-2014-09-21
54. Multiple conversations with BJP leaders; 'BJP angry over Uddhav deputing son for talks', TNN, *Times of India*, 21 September 2014, https://timesofindia.indiatimes.com/india/BJP-angry-over-Uddhav-deputing-son-for-talks/articleshow/43037911.cms
55. 'Maharashtra elections: BJP ends 25-year-old alliance with Shiv Sena as seat sharing talks fail', News 18, 25 September 2014, https://www.news18.com/news/politics/senavsbjp-716371.html); Maharashtra assembly polls 2014: NCP ends alliance with Congress, PTI, 25 September 2014, https://economictimes.indiatimes.com/news/politics-and-nation/maharashtra-assembly-polls-2014-ncp-ends-alliance-with-congress/articleshow/43448370.cms); author's notes.

56. Author's interview with senior BJP leader on 14 January 2019.
57. Interview with author in January 2019.
58. Interview with author in January 2019.
59. 'Raj Thackeray about plans for negotiation with Shiv Sena falling through', Loksatta Live, https://www.youtube.com/watch?v=02KOo2_NSJI&t=9s, accessed on 11 February 2019
60. Author's interview with senior Shiv Sena leader on 13 January 2019.
61. Venkat Ananth, 'The Raj factor', *Mint*, 7 October 2014, https://www.livemint.com/Politics/XwvS1nnQ99Rv1OphNzFYmK/The-Raj-factor.html); 'Raj Thackeray unveils Maharashtra Navnirman Sena's "blueprint" to develop state', PTI, 26 September 2014, https://www.financialexpress.com/archive/raj-thackeray-unveils-maharashtra-navnirman-senas-blueprint-to-develop-state/1292994/) and http://mnsblueprint.org/pdf/Blueprint_booklet_English_Online.pdf
62. 'Team Modi's Campaign is like Afzal Khan's Army, says Uddhav Thackeray', NDTV, https://www.ndtv.com/assembly/team-modis-campaign-is-like-afzal-khans-army-says-uddhav-thackeray-675637
63. 'Even Modi's father couldn't have won without Sena's support, says *Saamana* article, Uddhav distances himself', India TV news desk, 14 October 2014, https://www.indiatvnews.com/politics/national/saamana-article-even-modi-father-couldnt-have-won-without-sena-20934.html) and; 'Modi accused of opportunism, *Saamna* writes Modi's father could not have secured a majority', Aaj Tak, 14 October 2014, https://aajtak.intoday.in/story/saamna-claims-narendra-modi-opportunist-writes-modis-father-did-not-give-it-an-absolute-majority-1-783744.html
64. Interview with author on 30 January 2019.
65. Election Commission of India, https://eci.gov.in/files/file/3726-maharashtra-2014/
66. Author's conversation with a former cabinet minister on 28 January 2019.
67. Author's interview on 19 April 2019, with a senior journalist close to the Thackeray family, who has covered the Shiv Sena for over three decades.
68. Interview with author on 27 January 2019.

69. Interview with author on 27 January 2019.
70. Interview with author on 9 February 2019.
71. Interview with author on 24 January 2019.
72. 'During his last days, Bal Thackeray survived on soup sent from my home', *Indian Express*, https://indianexpress.com/article/india/india-others/during-his-last-days-bal-thackeray-survived-on-soup-sent-from-my-home/
73. Interview with author on 25 January 2019.
74. Multiple interviews.
75. Interview with author on 25 January 2019.
76. Interview with author on 18 April 2019
77. Author interview with a senior Yuva Sena leader on 22 January 2019.
78. Interview with author on 3 January 2019.
79. Interview with author on 4 January 2019
80. '2 dead, 54 hurt in Mumbai protest over Assam violence', Express News Service, 17 August 2012, http://archive.indianexpress.com/news/2-dead-54-hurt-in-mumbai-protest-over-assam-violence/987126/0
81. 'Mumbai violence: Woman cops molested by rioters', Little Yadav, *DNA*, 12 August 2012, https://www.dnaindia.com/mumbai/report-mumbai-violence-woman-cops-molested-by-rioters-1726932
82. Interview with author on 1 May 2019.
83. Gaurav Sabnis, 'Full text: What Raj Thackeray said at Azad Maidan', Firstpost.com, 22 August 2012, https://www.firstpost.com/politics/full-text-what-raj-thackeray-said-at-azad-maidan-425690.html) and Raj Thackeray speech at Azad Maidan, https://www.youtube.com/watch?v=NE-xnH_IXrM, accessed on 29 June, 2019
84. NCP offers outside support to BJP, PTI, 19 October 2014, https://indianexpress.com/article/india/politics/ncp-offers-outside-support-to-bjp/
85. Kumar Ketkar, 'After the split, Shiv Sena's message to BJP: Tiger zinda hai!', *Indian Express*, 24 January 2018, https://indianexpress.com/article/opinion/after-the-split-shiv-senas-message-to-bjp-tiger-zinda-hai-5036958/
86. Ketki Angre, 'NCP is "Naturally Corrupt Party", says PM; Sharad Pawar Hits Back', 13 October 2014, https://www.ndtv.com/

assembly/ncp-is-naturally-corrupt-party-says-pm-sharad-pawar-hits-back-678450
87. Interview with author on 11 January 2019.
88. Interview with author in January.
89. 'Fadnavis sworn in Maharashtra CM, Uddhav attends ceremony', PTI, 31 October 2014, https://timesofindia.indiatimes.com/india/Fadnavis-sworn-in-Maharashtra-CM-Uddhav-attends-ceremony/articleshow/44995214.cms
90. Makarand Gadgil, 'Fadnavis govt wins trust vote amid Congress, Shiv Sena protests', 12 November 2014, https://www.livemint.com/Politics/ja9qOFnUDuxySMNgY3qvyO/Devendra-Fadnavisled-BJP-govt-wins-trust-vote-in-Maharashtr.html
91. Dharmendra Jore and Surendra Gangan, 'Maharashtra double play: BJP wins trust through voice vote, does not get seen with NCP', *Hindustan Times*, 13 November 2014, https://www.hindustantimes.com/india/maharashtra-double-play-bjp-wins-trust-through-voice-vote-does-not-get-seen-with-ncp/story-ag1RMdJ1klFne5FVfyvjhN.html
92. Interviews with several Shiv Sena legislators and functionaries since 2014.
93. Author's interview with BJP minister on 13 January 2019.
94. Conversations with Shiv Sena leaders between 2014 and 2019.
95. http://www.mahasamruddhimahamarg.com/project-statistics
96. 'Name Samruddhi Expressway After Bal Thackeray, says Shiv Sena', PTI, https://www.ndtv.com/mumbai-news/name-samruddhi-expressway-after-bal-thackeray-says-shiv-sena-1946845
97. Interview with author.
98. 'BMC Polls: BJP MP Kirit Somaiya threatens to expose shell companies of Uddhav Thackeray', *DNA* correspondent, 9 February 2017, https://www.dnaindia.com/india/report-bmc-polls-bjp-mp-kirit-somaiya-threatens-to-expose-shell-companies-of-uddhav-thackeray-2318142); 'After BJP's Kirit Somaiya targets "Bandra Sahib" over "corruption", Shiv Sena "unearths" SRA scam', *DNA* web team, 15 May 2016, https://www.dnaindia.com/india/report-after-kirit-somaiya-targets-bandra-sahib-over-corruption-shiv-sena-unearths-sra-scam-2212581
99. Ketaki Ghoge, 'Mumbai civic polls: Shiv Sena leaders involved with shell firms, says BJP MP Kirit Somaiya', *Hindustan Times*, 14

February 2017, https://www.hindustantimes.com/mumbai-news/mumbai-civic-polls-shiv-sena-leaders-involved-with-shell-firms-says-bjp-mp-kirit-somaiya/story-YIXkaBEKhbxN9gqgP2hhbL.html

100. Shruti Ganapatye, 'MNS tries to woo Shiv Sena for BMC elections alliance', *Asian Age*, 30 January 2017, http://www.asianage.com/metros/mumbai/300117/mns-tries-to-woo-shiv-sena-for-bmc-elections-alliance.html
101. Raj Thackeray at party foundation rally in 2017, ABP Majha, 9 March 2017, https://www.youtube.com/watch?v=zzHejaFISV0
102. Interview with author on 2 May 2019.
103. Interview with author on 28 January 2019.
104. 'MNS left with just 1 BMC corporator after Shiv Sena poaches 6', *HT* correspondent, 14 October 2017, https://www.hindustantimes.com/mumbai-news/bjp-shiv-sena-tussle-in-mumbai-intensifies-somaiya-tells-sec-major-party-is-buying-corporators/story-0NfSkK6fJXNnu1W8wDXyVN.html
105. 'Raj Thackeray attacks Shiv Sena after six of seven corporators defect', https://www.youtube.com/watch?v=KznQtbkxGs8, accessed on 11 February 2019.
106. 'Raj Thackeray: Dawood may come back to India', *DNA*, 22 September 2017, https://www.dnaindia.com/mumbai/report-raj-thackeray-dawood-may-come-back-to-india-2547476
107. Kamlesh Damodar Sutar, 'Government with Owaisi to stage riots on Ram mandir issue: Raj Thackeray', *India Today*, 4 December 2018, https://www.indiatoday.in/india/story/government-with-owaisi-to-stage-riots-on-ram-mandir-issue-raj-thackeray-1401842-2018-12-04
108. 'Raj saheb baher ya, Shiv Sainikianchi ghoshnabaji' (Raj saheb come out: Shiv Sainiks), *Maharashtra Times*, 1 October 2017, https://maharashtratimes.indiatimes.com/maharashtra/mumbai-news/shiv-sena-worker-meets-mns-chief-raj-thackeray-in-dadar/articleshow/60900721.cms
109. Manasi Phadke, 'Shiv Sena threatens to pull out of Maharashtra government again', *Hindustan Times*, 19 September 2017, https://www.hindustantimes.com/mumbai-news/shiv-sena-threatens-to-pull-out-of-maharashta-government-again/story-3sIBXgwJspDA8WxewFByUP.html

110. Interview with author on 13 January 2019.
111. Interview with author on 11 March 2019.
112. Sanjay Raut, 'Shiv Sena "Big Brother" will shake Delhi throne', IANS, 28 January 2019, https://www.mid-day.com/articles/sanjay-raut-shiv-sena-big-brother-will-shake-delhi-throne/20311176
113. 'Shiv Sena chief Uddhav Thackeray targets BJP over Rafale deal, recent assembly poll results', PTI, 24 December 2018, https://timesofindia.indiatimes.com/india/shiv-sena-chief-targets-bjp-over-rafale-deal-recent-assembly-poll-results/articleshow/67232535.cms
114. 'After Rahul Gandhi, Now Uddhav Thackeray Says "Chowkidar Chor Hai" To Attack PM Modi', Outlook Web Bureau, 24 December 2018, https://www.outlookindia.com/website/story/india-news-after-rahul-gandhi-now-\uddhav-thackeray-says-chowkidar-chor-hai/322306
115. Interview with author in May 2019.
116. Interview with author on 15 June 2019.
117. Dhaval Kulkarni, 'Daggers out: Shiv Sena blames BJP for loss in Aurangabad and Amravati', *DNA*, 27 May 2019, https://www.dnaindia.com/mumbai/report-daggers-out-shiv-sena-blames-bjp-for-loss-in-aurangabad-and-amravati-2754061

Chapter 10: The Snake That Ate Its Own Tail

1. Conversation with author on 2 January 2019.
2. Vaibhav Purandare, *The Sena Story*, Business Publications Inc, Mumbai, 1999, pp. 231–32.
3. Gerard Heuze, 'Cultural Populism: The Appeal of the Shiv Sena', *Bombay: Metaphor for Modern India*, Sujata Patel and Alice Thorner (eds), Oxford University Press, Bombay, 1995, p. 216.
4. Ibid., p. 217.
5. Jayant Lele, 'Saffronisation of Shiv Sena: Political Economy of City, State and Nation', *EPW*, 24 June 1995.
6. Ibid.
7. Gerard Heuze, 'Shiv Sena and "National" Hinduism', Part-I, *EPW*, 3 October 1992.
8. Gerard Heuze, 'Shiv Sena and "National" Hinduism', Part-II, *EPW*, 10 October 1992.

9. Interview with author on 3 January 2019 and 8 February 2019.
10. Interview with author on 3 January 2019 and 8 February 2019.
11. Interview with author on 3 January 2019.
12. Interview with author on 7 February 2019.
13. Hemali Chhapia and Vinamrata Borwankar, 'Enrolment in BMC schools falls, maximum in Marathi medium', 23 January 2017, https://timesofindia.indiatimes.com/city/mumbai/enrolment-in-bmc-schools-falls-maximum-in-marathi-medium/articleshow/56724302.cms
14. Multiple interviews, notes and conversations during reporting career.
15. Interview with author on 27 January 2019.
16. Interview with author on 27 January 2019.
17. Gerard Heuze, 'Cultural Populism: The Appeal of the Shiv Sena', *Bombay: Metaphor for Modern India*, Sujata Patel and Alice Thorner (eds), Oxford University Press, Bombay, 1995, p. 225.
18. A.G. Noorani, 'Has Shiv Sena a future?', *Frontline*, 1–14 March 2003, https://frontline.thehindu.com/static/html/fl2005/stories/20030314000307600.htm
19. Sushant Pathak and Jamshed Adil Khan, 'India Today investigation finds how MNS resorts to vandalism, threats for money', *India Today*, 27 October 2016, https://www.indiatoday.in/india/story/maharashtra-navnirman-sena-raj-thackeray-extortion-mumbai-goonda-raj-protests-vandalism-bmc-348884-2016-10-27
20. Sudha Gogate, *The Emergence of Regionalism in Mumbai: History of the Shiv Sena*, Popular Prakashan Pvt. Ltd, Mumbai, 2014, p. ix.
21. Neera Adarkar, 'The Lost Century: How the textile workers of Mumbai got short shift', *Mumbai Reader* 07, Urban Design Research Institute, Mumbai, 2008, p. 137.
22. Interview with author on 4 January 2019.
23. Anupama Katakam, 'Vanishing mill lands', *Frontline*, 10–23 September 2005, https://frontline.thehindu.com/static/html/fl2219/stories/20050923002304300.htm
24. Anupama Katakam, 'All for the builder', *Frontline*, 25 March–7 April 2006, https://frontline.thehindu.com/static/html/fl2306/stories/20060407003003800.htm
25. Interview with author on 4 January 2019.

26. Gangadhar Chitnis, *Manzil Ajun Durach*! (The Destination is Still Far Away), Secretary, Comrade Govind Pansare Amrut Mahotsav Samiti, Kolhapur, 2010, pp. 393–94.
27. Ibid., pp. 391–95.
28. Interview with author on 30 January 2019.
29. Interview with author on 7 February 2019.
30. Interview with author on 7 February 2019.
31. Interview with author on 16 April 2019.
32. Laxman Singh and Sanjana Bhalerao, 'BMC budgets for Rs 30,692.59 cr, 12.6 per cent jump in outlay', *Indian Express*, 5 February 2019, https://indianexpress.com/article/cities/mumbai/bmc-budgets-for-rs-30692-59-crore-jump-in-outlay-5569353/
33. 'Goa CM presents Rs 455.10 Cr revenue surplus budget', UNI, 30 January 2019, http://www.uniindia.com/goa-cm-presents-rs-455-10-cr-revenue-surplus-budget/west/news/1483529.html
34. Chaitanya Marpakwar, 'Rajasthan's mini Mumbai', *Mumbai Mirror*, 25 February 2018, https://mumbaimirror.indiatimes.com/mumbai/cover-story/rajasthans-mini-mumbai/articleshow/63061636.cms
35. Interview with author on 3 May 2019.
36. Interview with author on 3 January 2019.
37. Gyan Prakash, *Mumbai Fables*, HarperCollins Publishers India, Noida, 2011, p. 250.
38. Kumar Ketkar, 'Bal Thackeray's Fractured Legacy', *Forbes India*, 27 November 2012, http://www.forbesindia.com/article/special/bal-thackerays-fractured-legacy/34151/1
39. Interview with author on 10 February 2019.
40. Interview with author on 10 February 2019.
41. Interview with author on 6 February 2019.
42. Gerard Heuze, 'Cultural Populism: The Appeal of the Shiv Sena', *Bombay: Metaphor for Modern India*, Sujata Patel and Alice Thorner (eds), Oxford University Press, Bombay, 1995, p. 233.
43. Nagari Nivara Parishad website, http://www.nivara.org/pag1.htm
44. Interview with author on 23 January 2019.
45. Interview with author on 23 January 2019.
46. Interview with Rakshit Sonawane on 6 and 10 February 2019.
47. Interview with author on 28 January 2019.

48. Raj Thacketay on Maratha quotas, https://www.youtube.com/watch?v=BN14kgxbFjM, accessed on 21 June 2019
49. Vidya, 'Bombay High Court upholds Maratha quota, says cut it from 16% to 12%', *India Today*, 27 June 2019, https://www.indiatoday.in/india/story/bombay-high-court-upholds-maratha-reservation-bill-quota-1557213-2019-06-27
50. Interview with author on 1 December 2018.
51. Interview with author on 1 December 2018.
52. Interview with author on 27 January 2019.
53. Interview with author on 20 December 2018.

Afterword: The Men behind the Image

1. Interview with author in November 2018.
2. Interview with author in November 2018.
3. Interview with author on 18 January 2018 and multiple interviews with author in the past.
4. Shrikant Thackeray, *Jasa Ghadla Tasa*, Chinar Publishers, Pune, 2002, p. 114.
5. Interview with author in November 2018.
6. Interview with author on 25 January 2019.
7. Multiple interviews with author.
8. Interview with author on 8 January 2019.
9. Multiple interviews with author.
10. Sandeep Ashar, 'BMC elections 2017: The creative firms behind the high-pitched poll campaign', *Indian Express*, 15 February 2017, https://indianexpress.com/article/india/bmc-elections-2017-the-creative-firms-behind-the-high-pitched-poll-campaign-4525445/
11. Milind Gunaji (writer), Uddhav Thackeray (photos), *Havai Mulukhgiri* (Aerial Tours), Riya Publications, Kolhapur, 2018, p. 10.
12. Ibid.
13. Ibid., p. 42.
14. Interview with author on 20 December 2018.
15. Interview with author on 4 January 2019.
16. Interview with author on 20 December 2018.
17. Interview with author in December 2018.
18. Interview with author on 20 December 2018.

19. Interview with author on 20 December 2018.
20. Author's interview with one of his friends in November 2018.
21. Author's interview with senior journalist on 13 March 2019.
22. Milind Gunaji (writer), Uddhav Thackeray (photos), *Havai Mulukhgiri* (Aerial Tours), Riya Publications, Kolhapur, 2018, p. 74.
23. Interview with author in December 2018.
24. Interview with author in December 2018.
25. Interview with author in December 2018.
26. Varun Singh, 'Raj Thackeray's wife to build 17-floor Dadar complex', *DNA*, 29 June 2017, https://www.dnaindia.com/india/report-raj-thackeray-s-wife-to-build-17-floor-dadar-complex-2486891
27. Interview with author in November 2018.
28. Author's interview with a former Shiv Sena leader in January 2019.
29. Milind Gunaji (writer), Uddhav Thackeray (photos), *Havai Mulukhgiri* (Aerial Tours), Riya Publications, Kolhapur, 2018, p. 80.
30. Interview with author in December 2018
31. Interview with author in December 2018.
32. 'MNS chief Raj Thackeray's son Amit gets engaged to fashion designer Mitali Borude', Eeshanpriya M.S., *Hindustan Times*, https://www.hindustantimes.com/mumbai-news/raj-thackeray-s-son-amit-to-get-engaged-to-mumbai-based-fashion-designer-today/story-bMQJzIlPhfgh49z8VqPI4N.html
33. 'Raj ki baat', Zee Marathi, Diwali issue, 2018.
34. Author's interview on 3 May 2019, with a senior journalist close to Raj Thackeray.
35. 'Raj ki baat', Zee Marathi, Diwali issue, 2018.
36. Ibid.
37. Ibid.
38. Ibid.